Capitalizing on Knowledge

From e-business to k-business

David J. Skyrme

OXFORD   AUCKLAND   BOSTON   JOHANNESBURG   MELBOURNE   NEW DELHI

Butterworth-Heinemann
Linacre House, Jordan Hill, Oxford OX2 8DP
225 Wildwood Avenue, Woburn, MA 01801-2041
A division of Reed Educational and Professional Publishing Ltd

℞ A member of the Reed Elsevier plc group

First published 2001

British Library Cataloguing in Publication Data
A catalogue record for this book is available from the British Library

ISBN 0 7506 5011 7

Typeset by Academic & Technical Typesetting, Bristol
Printed and bound in Great Britain by Biddles Ltd, *www.biddles.co.uk*

FOR EVERY TITLE THAT WE PUBLISH, BUTTERWORTH-HEINEMANN
WILL PAY FOR BTCV TO PLANT AND CARE FOR A TREE.

Contents

List of case studies

The following organizations are featured in the text as case studies. There are, in addition, many other short examples throughout the main text. Refer also to the companies featured in the knowledge nuggets (opposite).

List of knowledge nuggets

These short knowledge nuggets appear in boxed panels and give examples of practice, survey results or illustrate other key points.

Preface

Organizations are in the midst of two significant transformations. The first is the positioning of knowledge centre stage as a valuable resource and a driver of wealth creation. The second is the impact of the Internet, leading to the evolution of businesses into e-businesses. Until recently these developments were considered in isolation. But there are connections, and these are becoming increasingly apparent. Knowledge is an asset that can be re-packaged into knowledge-based products and services. The Internet provides an effective vehicle for marketing and delivering knowledge. Combine the two strands and you have the basic ingredients for a k-business – an online knowledge business that capitalizes on an organization's knowledge and exploits the Internet as a means of marketing and delivering it.

Capitalizing on knowledge

The first focus of many knowledge initiatives in organizations is one of identifying and sharing existing knowledge more widely: 'if only we knew what we know'. Better management of this knowledge is used to improve business processes, increase productivity, reduce new product development times and achieve many other benefits. Beyond these initial benefits, organizations then turn to ways in which knowledge management can be used to improve their external performance.

While many companies, particularly pharmaceutical firms and management consultancies, have an established track record in generating revenues from their knowledge, many others give scant attention to identifying their knowledge assets and assessing their marketability. One company that has gone further than most is Skandia. Since 1994 it has routinely measured and reported its intellectual capital, which includes knowledge assets. An organization does not have to embark on such a measurement system to capitalize on its knowledge, but it is missing an opportunity if it does not explicitly address external knowledge exploitation as part of its business strategy. Much internally generated knowledge is applicable externally and can be converted into viable knowledge-based products and services. This process of commercializing knowledge is the first major theme of this book.

As in many other types of business, the Internet offers many advantages for a knowledge business. It reduces transaction costs, extends market reach and allows round-the-clock trading. For products and services which are digitized, immediate electronic delivery can also take place. Most organizations are becoming e-businesses to a greater or lesser extent. An e-business is one where the majority of activities are carried out online, most using the Internet and Internet-related technology. The Internet is a hotbed of innovation. Many new e-business models are continually being introduced. Some, like business-to-business marketing and auctions, have parallels in traditional commerce. For these, the Internet significantly extends functionality and market scope. Other innovations, like business-to-business exchanges, online communities, electronic marketplaces and dynamic pricing, are impractical or not cost-effective using traditional media. The impact of the Internet and how to harness it effectively is the second major theme of this book.

By combining the potential of the Internet with an explicit approach to commercializing its knowledge, virtually every organization can create k-business opportunities. It may sell its knowledge directly as in business-to-consumer or business-to-business marketing. On the other hand, new kinds of knowledge trading facilities are emerging, such as knowledge markets, online advice networks, knowledge auctions and other similar initiatives. Not all are successful. A pioneering knowledge market, iqport.com, abandoned full commercialization after its market trial. As other dot.com companies have learned to their cost, the road to Internet riches is not always paved with gold. This book goes beyond the dot.com marketing hype and takes a critical look at how the Internet can be used as a vehicle for creating and sustaining a successful k-business.

About this book

While there is a strong Internet and e-commerce strand throughout this book, this is not its primary emphasis. Many other books address these topics in detail. Few, if any, give much coverage to the online trading of knowledge. Similarly, the number of books on knowledge management continues to grow exponentially. Most of these address the management of knowledge within organizations, rather than its external exploitation. The combination of these two themes – online trading and knowledge commercialization – is the unique positioning of this book.

Anyone who has knowledge to exploit will benefit from reading this book. You don't need to belong to a large organization with a knowledge initiative to have know-how and ideas that are commercially exploitable. In fact, the trend towards global market niches will often favour individuals who have some unique experience or knowledge that is useful to others, but who are not constrained by the bureaucratic product creation processes found in many organizations. On the other hand, if you are reading this book from an organizational perspective, then it will encourage you to look at different ways of capitalizing on your organizational knowledge.

This book is primarily for practitioners. With much of an organization's inherent value being in its knowledge, every professional, manager or consultant will find useful ideas and guidance on how to package and exploit it. That said, those most directly involved with developing new business opportunities should benefit most. This includes, but is not restricted to, business development and marketing managers, product and service managers, knowledge specialists and IT professionals. To help you build a thriving knowledge business you will find practical guidelines and examples of what other organizations have done. There are 14 case studies and more than 40 knowledge nuggets – small boxed panels containing pertinent examples of organizational practice, survey results or best practice guidance. I have also introduced models and frameworks that have proved useful in my own work. They are the result of my personal experience and thinking, rather than that of rigorous academic research. In my busy life as a consultant I do not have time to apply academic rigour, nor to carry out extensive literature searches. I need practical tools that deliver results. Furthermore, in this period of fast change, I feel it preferable to get the ideas out quickly into the open where they can be tried and tested in practical situations. I therefore apologize to academics and students who are looking in vain for the validated underlying theories. Nevertheless, I believe that you too will benefit from reading this book, since there are many questions that remain unanswered and would merit additional study.

While the organizational emphasis is clearly towards commercial businesses, many of the concepts and lessons are equally applicable to non-profit and public sector organizations. Any individual, team or organization who provides information and knowledge to others, can benefit by packaging some of it and making it available online. It does not matter if your primary aim is not to generate revenues. If you are to deliver a cost-effective service you will still need to identify the knowledge that your 'customers' need, package it effectively, and make it easily accessible online.

How this book is organized

The first two chapters cover the two main foundations of a k-business – knowledge and e-business. Chapter 1 charts the recent course of knowledge management and revisits the way in which value is generated through knowledge. A distinction is made between object-based and people-based knowledge. The chapter also demonstrates how knowledge management teams can act as exemplars in exploiting their own knowledge. Chapter 2 considers the rapidly changing developments in e-commerce and the evolution of e-businesses. These are set within the framework of a multi-layered Internet market model. The various approaches and methods that are used in e-businesses are then reviewed for their applicability where knowledge is the product.

Chapter 3 examines in more detail the evolution of Internet markets and business models. It considers various roles in a knowledge value system that might serve as the focus for a k-business. Also discussed are the different ways in which revenue may be generated. Chapter 4 is devoted to evaluation of knowledge markets. After introducing some key concepts, most of the rest of the chapter is spent in addressing the question: what makes a successful knowledge market? Particular attention is given to some early pioneers and learning from their contrasting experiences.

The focus of Chapter 5 is the packaging and productizing of knowledge. It shows how different methods may be more effective for different types or combinations of knowledge asset. Many of the most effective knowledge products and services are hybrids involving a mix of object-based and people-based knowledge. An important concept introduced in this chapter is that of the product wrapper, which describes and promotes the underlying package. The chapter concludes by addressing the challenge of how to create a balanced portfolio of knowledge products and services.

The next two chapters look at marketing, both from a perspective of marketing intangibles and of using the Internet as the main marketing medium. Chapter 6 explores how the Internet changes the conventional precepts of marketing – the 3Cs (customer, competitors, company) and the 4Ps (product, price, promotion, place). Chapter 7 introduces a new set of Ps relevant to the new medium – the 10Ps of Internet marketing. These are positioning, packaging, portals, pathways, pages, personalization, progression, payments, processes and performance.

The concepts from the previous four chapters are drawn together in Chapter 8, which looks at the practicalities of developing an online knowledge business. It is organized according to a set of seven success factors for a k-business. These include product development, operational excellence, technical infrastructure and delivering a good customer experience.

The final chapter of the book, Chapter 9, looks ahead at some directions in the wider context of the online knowledge economy. It highlights some of the technological, economic and regulatory factors that pose challenges to organizations and governments alike. Many of these challenges are posed in the form of dilemmas – choices of strategy or policy that are not easy to resolve.

Books tend to be passive conveyors of knowledge. They are the result of packaging knowledge (a topic discussed in Chapter 5) but as a result lose much of the richness that would come from active knowledge exchange. One way of getting a better learning experience from a book is to react to it as you read it. At the very least, you should make good use of coloured highlighters. Also write ideas, notes, examples and memory joggers in the margins. To stimulate active learning, I have posed a set of 'points to ponder' at the end of each chapter. Use them to think about the opportunities for capitalizing on knowledge, both your organization's and your own. Discuss your thinking and findings with colleagues. That way you will gain much more knowledge and understanding than I can convey through the medium of the printed word. Also to help you in a practical way are appendices of templates, checklists and working tools to help you create a k-business for your organization or yourself.

Keeping pace with change

A problem with any book that covers fast-changing fields like the Internet and e-commerce is that it is in danger of becoming obsolete even before it is published. E-businesses change names frequently as they merge, restructure or simply disappear. Products change names as new versions are introduced. Technology continues to advance, making some of today's predictions and waves of enthusiasm appear ridiculous in hindsight. New solutions appear with new nomenclature. The vocabulary of the Internet evolves fast.

I have attempted to overcome these problems in several ways. First, the primary emphasis of the book is about key concepts, guiding principles and practical guidelines. Many of these are fundamental and should change only slowly. Readers should therefore concentrate on the broad principles, while recognizing that some of the fine detail will change. Indeed, for topics that you deem highly relevant, you could well benefit from updating your knowledge from more recent sources and seeking specific examples from the Internet. Second, where developments or trends are still embryonic, I have suggested alternative scenarios, since the actual outcome may well depend on a finely balanced set of influences. Third, in those areas where change is most likely – such as website locations, statistics, illustrative examples and product names – a thorough check was made in October 2000, the latest practicable time to make changes prior to publishing. Another problem arises with company or programme names in that they also frequently change over the course of the period of a case study. I have generally used the name relevant at the time or that best reflects its origins, such as Teltech rather than Sopheon, or Ernst & Young rather than Cap Gemini Ernst & Young.

The final solution to addressing the updating problem is to use the medium that is widely discussed throughout this book – the Internet. A website for the book will keep readers informed of main developments. This will be hosted at:

http://www.skyrme.com/kcomm/index.htm

In addition, I invite you to contact me via email (david@skyrme.com) to provide updates, give me your feedback, suggest other examples, and offer any other comments. These will be shared with other readers through the website.

Acknowledgements

Many people, too numerous to mention individually, have contributed ideas and examples from which this book has developed. Articles and news stories, casual conversations at meetings and a myriad of Internet Web pages have all added to my understanding and knowledge of the subjects covered. For this free flow of knowledge from those unknown benefactors whose names I failed to record in the flow of the moment, I give my heartfelt thanks.

There are, however, a few people who have made a significant contribution to the final shape and content of this book, although perhaps they might not have realized it. I would particularly like to thank Catherine Coxon, events organizer at Aslib, who commissioned from me a series of e-commerce, marketing and Internet workshops. This stimulus gave me the excuse and opportunity to bring my research in these topics up to date and to organize my knowledge about them into a coherent framework.

I also thank participants in these courses for their critical questioning and contributions that have further enriched my writing.

Many other individuals are to be thanked for their contributions, and are duly recognized where their work is cited. Two of this group deserve special mention. Tony Brewer was one of the first people I became aware of who actively promoted the term commercializing knowledge. His research study on the topic in 1998 did much to confirm my confidence that this was a subject worth pursuing (*Commercializing Knowledge* was the original working title for this book). Another person who has stimulated my thinking in new directions is Bryan Davis of the Kaieteur Institute of Knowledge Management who has kept me informed on his investigations into knowledge markets. In addition, many individuals in companies large and small replied to my requests for clarification and information, and where needed gave permission to reproduce content, such as quotations and website images.

I would also like to thank the staff at Butterworth–Heinemann who have steered this book from hazy concept to final publication, especially Kathryn Grant for her interest in this title and her ongoing support, and to Assistant Editor Nicki Kear.

Finally, I would like to thank the many readers of my articles, Web pages and other publications, for expressing their interest in my writing, and who through their questions and feedback have encouraged me to capitalize on my own knowledge.

David J. Skyrme
Highclere
England
October 2000

Chapter 1

Knowledge inside-out

The value of what you know can only be seen in what you do.

(Klas Mellander, Chief Designer, Celemi)

In just a few years knowledge management has gone from consultants' hype to an established management strategy. Many people are now talking about a 'second generation' of knowledge management. Views of what this is vary widely. Some consider that it is an emphasis on organizational learning rather than managing knowledge in databases and over intranets. Others consider that it is a focus on innovation through better conversion of new knowledge rather than better deployment and use of existing knowledge. Whatever your own perspective on the next generation, there is little doubt that most organizations are a long way from fully institutionalizing knowledge management or exploiting their knowledge. The central premise of this book is that an important area of under-exploitation is that of converting an organization's internal knowledge assets into externally marketed knowledge-based products and services, in other words a knowledge business. To do this organizations must turn their knowledge inside-out.

This chapter summarizes developments in knowledge management, a prerequisite for building a knowledge business. It starts by reviewing its recent evolution and main characteristics. Examples are given of organizational benefits and the knowledge strategy levers by which these are achieved. Although multi-faceted and broad in scope, knowledge management is epitomized by several increasingly used practices. These include sharing best practices, developing expertise directories, using intranets to improve access to knowledge repositories, and nurturing communities of practice. Another defining characteristic of knowledge management is the perspective of knowledge as a valuable organizational asset. The concept of value is therefore explored from two perspectives – the intrinsic value of knowledge as well as value added through its use. Ways of increasing value are introduced. One that will be reiterated throughout the book is that of relevance and customization to users' needs.

The next part of the chapter deals with the interface between an organization's knowledge management programme and its external environment. This is explored from two perspectives: the outside-in and the inside-out. The first refers to harnessing customer knowledge, and the second to capitalizing on an organization's knowledge externally. This leads to the concluding part of the chapter, the consideration of the core elements of a k-business.

The evolving knowledge agenda

All indications are that knowledge management is still in its early growth phase. Its emergence as a formal management activity started in 1995, with a high profile international conference, and the publication of the ground-breaking book by Nonaka and Takeuchi.[1]

Since 1997, when many senior managers viewed knowledge management as a passing fad, it has gradually been adopted as a mainstream activity by many organizations. From its early acceptance in pharmaceutical firms, oil multi-nationals, high technology companies and management consultancies, it is now prevalent in most large corporations and many public sector bodies. Why this burgeoning interest? Part is due to the growing recognition of the value of intangible assets. Many knowledge intensive companies, such as biotechnology and software companies, have a stock market value 5–10 times higher than that of their physical assets. Another is that many organizations,

> **Intangible value**
>
> The balance sheet of Glaxo Wellcome, the world's largest pharmaceutical company, showed that it had $10 billion in assets at the end of 1999. Yet its value as expressed by its market capitalization was over $50 billion. Much of the difference is accounted for by its knowledge assets – its patents, its R&D pipeline of new drugs, and its leading scientific know-how.

having gone through periods of restructuring and downsizing, have realized only when it is too late the extent to which they have lost knowledge held in people's heads. A further factor is that technology, and especially the Internet, makes it easier to connect people to share knowledge and also to disseminate information quickly and cheaply. By accessing and reusing knowledge more effectively, pioneers of knowledge management have applied it to achieve significant benefits, ranging from faster product development to better customer service (see Table 1.1).[2]

Table 1.1 Benefits of knowledge management with some typical examples

Benefit	Example
Faster access to knowledge	Through its knowledge centres, American Management Systems estimates that its consultants now find the information they need eight times faster than if they did it themselves
Better knowledge sharing	By concentrating on improving the flow of knowledge from its field engineers, Xerox generates 5000 useful tips per month. In France it has achieved a 5–10 per cent savings in service costs
Cost savings	Chevron credits knowledge sharing as an important contributor to saving $200 million a year in energy costs
Cost avoidance	Sharing best practice between its semiconductor fabrication plants has enabled Texas Instruments to save investing in a new plant (over $500 million)
Increased profitability	Integrating customer knowledge at the Middle Market Banking Group of Chase Manhattan Bank has resulted in better relationships and more profitable customers
Less down-time for maintenance and refurbishment	Better sharing of lessons learned by BP reduced a refinery shut down time by 9 days, resulting in a cost savings of $9.6 million
Shorter time-to-market	Better sharing of product and customer knowledge allowed Hewlett–Packard to bring the DeskJet to market months earlier than similar printer models
Improved customer relationships	Capturing the 'best work' of the previous 30 years has helped Burston Marsteller achieve a leading position in public relations. Its 'perception management' knowledge base has helped it gain new clients
Faster revenue growth	By developing new measures of intellectual capital and goaling its managers on increasing its value, Skandia has grown its revenues much faster than the insurance industry average
New business opportunities	Through collaborative knowledge sharing with universities, DuPont gained unexpected knowledge that has resulted in the development of a completely new range of polymers

The net result of these developments is that at the end of 1999 over a third of large companies had a formal knowledge management programme in place while a similar proportion were in the throes of planning one. Analysis of recent surveys indicates that knowledge management is delivering business benefits but faces a number of ongoing challenges (see below).

Knowledge management in organizations: state of play (1999–2000)

- 80 per cent of all companies have some knowledge management (KM) projects.
- 40 per cent of organizations have a formal KM programme in place; an additional 30 per cent were planning to create one.
- The main benefits perceived are better decision-making, faster response to key business issues and better customer service.
- Knowledge management is viewed as a significant contributor to competitive advantage, marketing, improving customer focus, innovation, revenue growth and profit.
- The largest funding source for KM projects is a central corporate budget, followed by the MIS function, then marketing.
- Key technologies that support knowledge management are Internet/ intranet, data warehousing and mining, document management systems.
- Key activities within a KM programme are (in order of frequency):
  - □ creating a knowledge strategy
  - □ KM training and awareness
  - □ implementing an ERP (Enterprise Resource Planning) system
  - □ sharing of best practice
  - □ benchmarking KM status
  - □ establishing formal KM networks
  - □ rewarding people for knowledge sharing
  - □ developing communities of practice
  - □ creating knowledge centres.
- 25 per cent of organizations have a Chief Knowledge Officer, although half of these do not have a dedicated budget or staff.
- Main difficulties and challenges (in order of frequency):
  - □ no time to share knowledge
  - □ information overload
  - □ not using technology to share knowledge effectively
  - □ reinventing the wheel
  - □ difficulty of capturing tacit knowledge.

Sources: Annual Knowledge Management Survey 1999, KPMG (2000); *Beyond Knowledge Management: New Ways to Work and Learn*, The Conference Board (May 2000)

Despite its growing adoption, there are still a large number of organizations that have not systematically developed their knowledge agenda. Even those organizations that are recognized as leaders in knowledge management believe they have much to do before knowledge management is organization-wide and an integral part of daily business activities. KPMG's analysis for its 1999 knowledge management survey indicated that 43 per cent of the 423 organizations polled were only at the first stage (knowledge chaotic) of its five-stage model of knowledge maturity, with only 10 per cent at the two most advanced stages (knowledge managed and knowledge-centric).[3]

Two thrusts and seven levers

What knowledge strategies are organizations using to maximize the organizational benefits? In my book *Knowledge Networking* I identified two main thrusts and seven strategic levers.[4] The first thrust is that of making better use of the knowledge that already exists within the firm. Ways of doing this include the sharing of best practices, developing databases of solutions to problems, drawing out lessons learned from completed projects, and systematically recording details of customer engagements. This thrust is often paraphrased as: 'if only we knew what we know'. Too frequently people in one part of an organization 'reinvent the wheel' or fail to solve customers' problems because the knowledge they need is elsewhere in the company but not known or accessible to them. The second thrust is that of innovation – the creation of new knowledge and its conversion into new processes, products or services. Here the focus is on more effective ways of nurturing creativity, better matching of unmet customer needs with potential solutions, and improving knowledge flows in the innovation process.

> **Can NASA put a man on the moon?**
>
> No longer, according to Geoffrey Petch. The blueprints for the Saturn rocket have been lost and much of the knowledge of the 400 000 engineers that made the first moon landing possible lies in documents that are devoid of meaning without the contextual and personal knowledge of those who generated them. NASA now has a programme of 'knowledge archaeology' to excavate and add meaning to the repositories of information, in order to prepare for a future manned landing on Mars.
>
> Source: 'The cost of lost knowledge', Geoffrey Petch, *Knowledge Management*, Freedom Technology Media Group, October 1998

Analysis of successful knowledge initiatives indicates seven commonly used strategic levers:

* *Customer knowledge* – developing deep knowledge through customer relationships, and using it to enhance customer success through improved products and services.

- *Knowledge in products and services* – embedding knowledge in products and sur-rounding them with knowledge-intensive services.
- *Knowledge in people* – developing human competencies and nurturing an innova-tive culture where learning is valued and knowledge is shared.
- *Knowledge in processes* – embedding knowledge into business processes, and giving access to expertise at critical points.
- *Organizational memory* – recording existing experience for future use, both in the form of explicit knowledge repositories and developing pointers to expertise.
- *Knowledge in relationships* – improving knowledge flows across boundaries: with suppliers, customers, employees etc.
- *Knowledge assets* – measuring intellectual capital and managing its development and exploitation.

The core levers are knowledge in people, processes and products. Most successful knowledge initiatives require a focus on just two or three of the seven levers.

Multiple perspectives

Knowledge management means different things to different people. There are examples of knowledge management activities associated with organizational learning, business transformation, intangible asset management, innovation and information management initiatives. Indeed, several such initiatives have subsequently been renamed as knowledge management initiatives. In a similar vein, many software products that started life as document management systems, groupware, intelligent agents and intranet portals have been relabelled as knowledge management solutions. Knowledge management has evolved to be a convenient umbrella term and focus for many different methods, practices and tools. While this diversity has added richness to the field, it has also spawned confusion and led to detractors. It is therefore not surprising that virtually any description of knowledge management is prefaced with the author's own definition of the term, for which mine is:

> *the explicit and systematic management of vital knowledge and its associated processes of creating, gathering, organizing, diffusion, use and exploitation in pursuit of organizational objectives.*

This sidesteps the definition of knowledge itself, which is another area where confusion reigns. The question: 'what is knowledge?' is addressed more fully in *Knowledge Networking*.[5] Management writers have described it in various terms such as 'a fluid mix of framed experience, values, contextual information and expert insight',[6] 'experience or information that can be communicated or shared'[7] or more simply as 'a capacity to act.[8] More significant than the definition is the common practice of distinguishing two main types of knowledge – explicit and tacit.[9] Each requires managing in different ways. Explicit knowledge is that which is codified, such as in documents and databases. Tacit knowledge, such as knowing how to ride a bicycle, is in people's heads, experiential and is not easy to express in an explicit form. This distinction has led to two complementary perspectives of knowledge management (Figure 1.1):

> **'We know more than we can tell'**
>
> The concept of tacit knowledge was explored in detail by scientist turned philosopher Michael Polyani. He noted how we can recognize a person's face out of many thousands, yet cannot say in words how we recognize it. He described any attempt at formalizing all such knowledge as 'self defeating'. In modern knowledge management the concept of tacit knowledge was brought to the fore by Ikujiro Nonaka and Hirotaka Takeuchi in their book *The Knowledge Creating Company* (Oxford University Press, 1995).
>
> *Source: Tacit Knowledge*, Michael Polyani, reprinted as chapter 7 in *Knowledge in Organizations* (ed. Laurence Prusak, Butterworth–Heinemann, 1997)

1 *Managing knowledge as objects.* The emphasis is on managing explicit knowledge or information. Common practices from this perspective are conducting information audits, populating intranets, creating best practice databases, classifying content and creating knowledge maps.
2 *Nurturing knowledge networking.* Since tacit knowledge is in people's heads, the emphasis here is on managing knowledge workers and the environment in which they work. Creating 'communities of practice',[10] designing knowledge

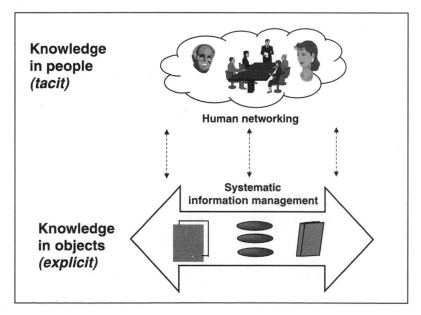

Figure 1.1 Two complementary perspectives of knowledge management

sharing workspaces, encouraging learning and innovation, practising skilful dialogue and storytelling, are core practices that encourage tacit knowledge development and sharing.

A problem with many knowledge initiatives is that they place too strong a bias on the first perspective. Intranets are put in place, yet professionals do not submit their knowledge into its databases. The MIS department introduces a customer relationship management system, yet users find it cumbersome to use and receive inadequate training. A KM project is viewed as an IT project, rather than one that involves people, processes and content. This is misguided, since the majority of knowledge in an organization (most people reckon some 70 per cent) is its tacit knowledge. Just because tacit knowledge is difficult to grasp does not mean that it should receive only scant attention. A good knowledge management initiative will therefore blend these two perspectives into a coherent programme with supporting organizational practices. A good example of such a programme is that at Siemens (see below).

Knowledge networking at Siemens

Siemens is a company that takes knowledge management seriously. With 440 000 employees in 190 countries across the world, sharing knowledge is a major challenge. Siemens Business Services faced such a challenge in 1997. Like many other Siemens' divisions, knowledge management started as a bottom-up activity. Enthusiastic employees had created over 100 intranets with little coordination between them. To overcome these knowledge silos, SBS defined a global KM strategy and created a core knowledge management team in 1998.

Anne Jubert, European information manager of Siemens–Nixdorf stresses that knowledge management is primarily a people issue, where 'real working knowledge lies in relationships' and that 'communities of practice are the critical building blocks of a knowledge-based company'. Taking full advantage of intranet technology, her part of Siemens created the NewsBoard system to give employees seamless access to a wide range of internal and external knowledge – best practices, customer partner databases, expertise directories, project databases, industry news and so on. NewsBoard users are categorized into three levels – general users, communities of practice and expert.

Communities of practice (CoPs) are widespread in Siemens. In semi-conductor manufacturing, for example, CoPs in special topics such as etching or lithography may have 100–150 members who participate in sharing and learning, with 10–20 of them being world-class experts. The worldwide sales force in information and communications networks is another community. It uses a system called ShareNet to share solutions knowledge globally.[11] At a press conference in October 2000, Siemens' CEO Dr Heinrich v. Pierer described the case of their regional company in Malaysia who had an opportunity to bid for an optical fibre ASDL solution for the Multimedia Super Corridor linking Kuala Lumpur and its new airport. The local company lacked the knowledge to place a bid, but through posting their problem on ShareNet found colleagues in Denmark who had supplied a similar network to Tele Danmark. Other users of ShareNet provided valuable tips and suggested strategies. As a result, Siemens received an order for the pilot project.

It goes without saying that one of the communities is a KM community, where experience and lessons from over 150 KM projects throughout Siemens is shared. Knowledge management in Siemens is overseen by a corporate KM board and there is a central core of expertise in the corporate KM office. As well as sharing best KM practice, the central role is one of leadership, promotion, coordination and support. It evaluates and deploys KM tools, develops a road map for the future and orchestrates future watch teams for the knowledge economy. Its overall perspective is one of knowledge management as a socio-technical system where KM processes blend the best of people and the best of technology. E-business is transforming Siemens and knowledge management is viewed as one of its four core building blocks, in which electronic networking and human networking complement each other in the Siemens' e-community.[12]

As the Siemens case and similar examples illustrates, an effective knowledge management programme is holistic in nature. An analysis of many successful programmes shows that the recurring critical success factors are as follows:[13]

- *Clear and explicit links to organizational strategy and objectives.* The contribution of knowledge towards achieving business objectives is clearly articulated. Knowledge is explicitly considered when developing business strategies and operational plans.
- *A compelling vision and architecture.* This is often a simple visual framework that is easily understood and communicated. It portrays the role of knowledge in an organization's success and depicts the key activities and responsibilities for its management.
- *Knowledge leadership.* There are knowledge leaders throughout the organization. Top management is supportive of, or even actively promotes, the knowledge agenda. There are individuals, such as a Chief Knowledge Officer (CKO), who have specific responsibilities for enhancing corporate strategy through better application and management of knowledge. There are knowledge champions throughout the business.
- *A well-developed information and communications infrastructure – the 'hard' infrastructure.* At the physical level, there must be reliable and responsive access to the

corporate network, from any work location. Knowledge sharing is then facilitated through organization-wide deployment of collaborative technology, such as an intranet and facilities for managing online communities. In addition, some groups will need more specific computer-based knowledge tools such as decision support systems and case-based reasoning.

- *A knowledge creating and sharing culture – the 'soft' infrastructure.* (This is sometimes referred to as the 'harder' infrastructure reflecting the more difficult problem of handling people-related factors.) This is an environment that encourages knowledge sharing, experimentation and innovation. Rewards and sanctions help to break down any 'not invented here' or 'knowledge is power' attitudes, as does working environment, personal behaviours and management style.
- *Emphasis on continuous learning.* Time is allowed, even encouraged, for individuals and teams to step back from frenetic day-to-day activity for review and reflection. Successes and failures are analysed. Discussions take place on how organizational effectiveness and performance can be improved. Lessons learned are recorded and categorized for future use. Mistakes are not necessarily penalized, but viewed as learning opportunities.
- *Systematic information and knowledge processes.* Information and knowledge are managed as vital resources, for example through having knowledge centres as focal points. There are standards and procedures covering the format and quality of documents, submission to databases and other content. There are clear policies covering the life cycle of records, knowledge ownership, validation, valuation and protection. Senior managers regularly review knowledge assets, policies and programmes.

Plentiful practices

As knowledge management has gained momentum, it has gathered under its label a wide range of existing management practices as well as some unique ones of its own. Table 1.2 shows a representative sample of these from over a hundred that have been reported as key elements of knowledge management programmes. They are grouped according to the main phases of a knowledge management cycle, although it must be borne in mind that many practices span several phases.

Such practices are an essential part of the toolkit of a knowledge management team. Some may become established as widespread practice in the organization, such as BP's use of After Action Reviews. Some may be more formally embedded into an organization's core processes or business practices. In some organizations, for example, project plans are not approved until there is evidence that knowledge from existing best practices and related project histories have been incorporated into the plan. Other practices may be used more selectively and may require the help

Table 1.2 Representative knowledge management practices

Phase of knowledge cycle	Practice	Description
Creating	Creativity techniques	Numerous techniques to stimulate thinking by individuals and groups, e.g. brainstorming, word association, concept mapping, morphological analysis
	Simulation	Using computer-based models to discover interdependencies between business processes and causal relationships between different factors and resulting outcomes
	Structured dialogue	Structuring and capturing the flow of conversation in meetings, so that issues are addressed systematically; inputs are gathered in parallel and grouped, e.g. using Post-It™ notes or a computer-based decision support system
Identifying	Knowledge inventory (information audit)	Identifying core knowledge, its sources, users and uses; also recording other attributes such as format, location, accuracy, access rights and review date. The information, which is usually gathered via questionnaires and interviews, focuses on the knowledge that is needed to make important decisions and carry out core business activities
	Content analysis	The systematic analysis of the content of documents, interviews, meetings etc. to identify common themes, trends or discrepancies
	Text mining, concept analysis	A computer technique that aids the process of content analysis. It distils the key concepts from large text documents. Sometimes the interrelationships between concepts in different documents are also graphically displayed (concept mapping). Such outputs are a useful contribution to knowledge mapping (see organizing)

Table 1.2 Continued

Phase of knowledge cycle	Practice	Description
	Expertise profiling	Identifying and recording information on people's skills and knowledge, usually in the form of a 'Yellow Pages'™ database, so called because they are organized by people's skills and not by department or name. Although types of expertise codified into agreed categories helps in searching for experts or making comparisons, much of the value of expertise profiling comes from allowing users to enter information using their own words
Gathering	Knowledge elicitation	A formal process with its origins in the development of expert systems. Experts are interviewed using structured templates to elicit knowledge about their decision and thinking processes, and hence derive 'rules' that are embedded in a system. More common but less formal are semi-structured interviews by researchers or communicators, to elicit knowledge for entry into knowledge repositories for re-use
	Search/retrieval	Much knowledge is gathered through the use of search engines over the Internet. Such a process can be automated by using intelligent agents that deliver new information that matches a user's pre-defined profile. By monitoring which items are used, the user's profile can be continually updated
Organizing	Thesaurus management	Developing a controlled vocabulary for indexing documents and assigning keywords. It involves the creation of schema or taxonomy (classification scheme) for information and knowledge. With today's search engines, the need for this is sometimes questioned. But when they return thousands of hits for a simple query the need is more apparent. A good thesaurus helps to bring

Table 1.2 Continued

Phase of knowledge cycle	Practice	Description
		together information that might otherwise be classified separately, because of the use of different terminology for what is essentially the same concept
	Knowledge mapping	A broad term used to describe several practices. One type of mapping is the visual representation of core knowledge as schematic blocks showing interrelationships, for example the relationship of knowledge elements to business processes. A map may be a knowledge schema, depicted as a hierarchical tree. The term is sometimes used to describe a knowledge inventory – a database of where different knowledge resides
Sharing	Best practices	The best practices in a specific business activity are identified, codified and widely shared. Although the existence and nature of a best practice may be recorded in a best practices database, most of the benefits arise from tacit knowledge sharing, involving site visits or secondments. Some organizations have an Office of Best Practice specifically to search out, codify and disseminate best practice
	Share fairs, knowledge sharing events	Events designed to bring creators and users of knowledge together, usually in an exhibition-like setting. A typical example is a research division having booths at a sales conference. Such events are used as an efficient way to make personal connections and knowledge exchange that might not otherwise take place
	Communities of practice (CoPs)	Informal knowledge networks that span departmental and organizational boundaries and draw together people with a shared interest. Knowledge is developed and exchanged on a functional specialization, industry practice or other common business issue

Table 1.2 Continued

Phase of knowledge cycle	Practice	Description
Sharing	Cross-functional teams	These bring together people with different perspectives, knowledge and experience. Although mostly found in project teams, many organizations are making a point of bringing together a rich mix of knowledge into many different types of work group. Skandia's 'future teams' specifically include individuals from three age generations – the 20s, 30s and 40+s – to give a broader perspective than might otherwise be the case
	Work space design	The past few years have seen a growing recognition that the design of office workspace plays a crucial influence on the ease with which knowledge is shared. Modern designs create a variety of workspaces that offer 'caves' and 'commons', i.e. private work areas for concentrated thinking and shared areas for conversation and meetings. Informal areas, such as knowledge cafés, create opportunities for serendipitous connections and conversations[14]
Learning	After Action Reviews (AARs)	An approach first developed by the US Army to extract learning after every operational assignment. A structured process is used with key participants to understand what went right, what went wrong, what has been learnt, and how similar operations can be performed better in future
	Decision diaries	A logbook of activity, but where the background to a given decision is also recorded – the assumptions, alternatives, why a particular decision was selected and what additional knowledge may have helped to improve the decision or reduce risk. The entries are periodically reviewed to derive lessons that are more general

Table 1.2 Continued

Phase of knowledge cycle	Practice	Description
	Project histories	Using elements of the previous two techniques, these are more formal records of the results of projects. The day-to-day records are refined into summaries, lessons learnt and recommendations for similar projects in the future
	Storytelling	People tend to recall knowledge better when it is received in the form of an anecdote or story. Over many eons, storytelling was the primary way of transferring knowledge between generations. Now, it has been revived as a tool for knowledge transfer and learning within organizations[15]
	Learning network	Similar to a community of practice, this is another kind of network where the primary focus is personal development and organizational learning
Applying	Decision support systems	Almost every task of a knowledge worker involves the retrieval and application of knowledge. This knowledge can be embedded in computer software that guides users through a structured approach to decision making. This class of system includes group decision support systems (GDSS), workflow systems and case-based reasoning (CBR)
	Process management	The creation and application of business processes provides a systematic approach to the use of knowledge to carry out routine business tasks
Exploiting	Intellectual asset management	The knowledge assets of an organization are identified (e.g. by conducting a knowledge inventory) and their exploitation potential assessed from two perspectives – for internal use or external sale. Exploitation is systematically pursued through a variety of means, e.g. through creation of knowledge products or the licensing of intellectual property

Table 1.2 Continued

Phase of knowledge cycle	Practice	Description
Protecting	Intellectual property rights (IPR) management	Additional protection for valuable knowledge is gained by converting it to a form protectable by law. This includes designs, patents, copyrights and trademarks. Active IPR management involves the registering of this intellectual property and rigorously pursuing redress against violators of the owner's rights
Evaluating	KM assessment	Reviewing the extent and quality to which different KM practices are applied throughout the organization. Usually carried out using a set of diagnostic questions
	KM benchmarking	The comparison of KM practices across organizations. This may be done relatively informally through visits and knowledge sharing, or more formally as part of a structured programme of evaluation by external independent evaluators
	Intellectual capital (IC) accounting	'What gets measured gets managed' goes the adage. Therefore, a growing number of organizations, inspired by Skandia's example, are identifying the different components of intellectual capital – human capital, structural capital and customer capital – and developing indicators to track their growth and development

of a few organization-wide specialists or external consultants. For any knowledge professional, what is more important than the know-how for each practice is knowing when and where to use it for best results.

Corresponding software tools support many of these practices. For example, facilities for building expertise directories and knowledge thesauruses are found in knowledge management software suites. The functionality and versatility of knowledge software tools are expanding rapidly and beyond the scope of this book.[17] Technology plays an important part in almost every knowledge initiative, but problems of implementation are widespread. An IDC report predicts that by 2003,

Fortune 500 companies can expect to lose $31.5 billion in revenues through poor knowledge management systems.[18] Even so, most knowledge managers agree that technology is not their major challenge. Typical of their views is the following comment: '10 per cent of my challenges are technological; 20 per cent are concerned with content and processes; 70 per cent are people-related'. The social side of knowledge management is therefore very prominent in most knowledge initiatives. Changing corporate culture, introducing knowledge development into personal development plans, rewarding and recognizing knowledge contributions are all part of a typical knowledge management programme. But whatever the programme mechanics, its strategic goal must be focused on creating value through knowledge.

Value through knowledge

Much of the value of a company is in its intangibles. These include assets such as brands, customer relationships, patents, trademarks and, of course, knowledge. Yet, while most businesses have accountants, financial analysts and auditors identifying and accounting for their physical assets, few have attempted to systematically measure their intangible assets. These 'unreported' assets represent the intellectual capital of a firm. The growing discrepancy between book value and market value has stimulated several pioneering organizations to embark on programmes of intellectual capital measurement. Notable among these pioneers is Skandia, which since 1994 has published intellectual capital supplements to its six-monthly financial reports. A growing number of organizations have followed suit and in 1998 the Danish Ministry of Trade and Industry embarked on a pilot project with 19 organizations to produce intellectual capital reports and to develop some workable guidelines.[19]

An interesting finding from KPMG's 1999 knowledge management survey is that although over 70 per cent of respondents expected knowledge management to reduce

> **Intangible assets – a visible difference**
>
> Celemi, a Swedish developer of learning tools, has published Celemi Monitor – its annual intangible asset accounts – since 1996. It reports measures in three main categories – customers, people and organization, the latter two constituting what it calls its knowledge capital. One people indicator that it reports on is the 'rookie ratio', the percentage of employees that have been in the company for less than one year. The measurement process has given the organization a deeper understanding of the factors that drive its future success. Colour coding of measures maintains visibility of intangible asset performance against Celemi's strategic goals.
>
> *Website:* http://www.celemi.se

costs and improve profit, only 28 per cent expected it to increase shareholder value. In other words, they could not see the direct relationship between knowledge management and intellectual capital growth. Two common problems may help explain this. First, most companies do not have in place methods to measure their intellectual capital, as do Skandia and Celemi. Second, the causal links between knowledge management activities and the resultant business benefits are often complex and difficult to unravel. Let's now consider these two challenges.

Measuring intellectual capital

There are now several methods of measuring intellectual capital (IC), most inspired by the work of Swedish knowledge management pioneer Karl Erik Sveiby. His Intangible Assets Monitor (IAM) considers three categories of intangible assets – customers (external structure), organization (internal structure) and competence. Each is further subdivided into efficiency, stability and growth/renewal indicators. A good measurement system will have a balance of indicators in all nine categories. Similar IC measurement systems include the Skandia Navigator, Intellectual Capital Services' IC Index™ and Philip M'Pherson's Inclusive Valuation Methodology (IVM™).[20] The starting point of every method is the identification of intellectual assets and their grouping into categories. One popular subdivision (similar to Sveiby's competence, internal and external structure) is:

1   *Human Capital* – that in the minds of individuals: knowledge, competences, experience, know-how etc.
2   *Structural Capital* – 'that which is left after employees go home for the night': processes, information systems, databases etc.
3   *Customer Capital* – customer relationships, loyalty, brands etc.

One variant of this categorization separates out intellectual property as a fourth group. This includes trademarks, patents, designs, copyrights and licences. Within each category a set of indicators is developed that tie in with organizational objectives and can be used to assess progress. Edvinsson and Malone, for example, list 90 measures used in the Skandia Navigator grouped into five categories – financial, customer, process, renewal and development, human. It is quite a challenge to develop indicators that are at the same time both meaningful and measurable. A further difficulty, when comparing IC accounting with financial accounting is that the different elements are not additive. There is no common measurement unit like dollars, and frequently different combinations of assets are worth more than the sum of the parts. These and other complications arising from the unique characteristics of knowledge mean that IC accounting has a long way to go before becoming widely accepted by the accounting profession.

Undeterred by these difficulties, companies that do use intellectual capital approaches find that it gives them better understanding of the underlying drivers of market value, the interactions between different types of asset and sensitivities to risk. Using IC measures as a core part of a performance measurement and appraisal system focuses management attention on the protection and enhancement of these vital assets.

Intrinsic value

Even with IC measurement systems in place, determining the value of knowledge is difficult to determine in absolute terms. This is primarily because the value of knowledge is so context and time dependent.[21] Knowing how to repair a leaking pipe that is damaging your new carpets just a few hours before you go away on holiday is worth a lot to you. Stock market dealers pay hefty sums for real-time stock price information, which some 15 minutes later is available free on the Internet. How much you are prepared to pay for such market knowledge depends on a number of factors, not least of which is how much extra value you can generate by having this information ahead of others. The price that you are prepared to pay will be different in different circumstances. Other people may be prepared to pay much more or much less for the same knowledge at the same time. Value, as the adage says, is in the eyes of the beholder.

Such variations in the perception of value for the same knowledge create an interesting pricing challenge for any knowledge supplier. They must learn as much as possible about the needs and value perceptions of specific groups of customers in different circumstances. They must understand how their customers add value in their own businesses using the knowledge supplied. Irrespective of the value attributes in specific cases, there are some generic ways of increasing the intrinsic value of knowledge, especially explicit knowledge (Table 1.3). Typically, these will save the consumer time or money, increase their earnings, create new opportunities or minimize risk.

Utility value

Beyond its intrinsic value, knowledge has utility value that becomes more evident as it is shared and used. Knowledge can help to solve problems faster, improve the efficiency of business processes, develop better products and so on. The tools, techniques and infrastructure of knowledge

Table 1.3 Ten ways to add value to knowledge

Timely	Up to date knowledge generally commands higher prices, so time-to-market of perishable knowledge is crucial
Meta-knowledge	Knowledge about knowledge – directories, indexes, summaries, abstracts etc. One of the most visited (and valuable) Internet sites is Yahoo! that provides meta-knowledge in the form of structured directory listings
Validated and assessed	Content is accurate, reliable, credible and validated, e.g. it may be reviewed and rated by an independent assessor
Accessible and usable	The right knowledge is easy to find. There are pointers, tables of contents and indexes that guide users quickly to the relevant items
Customized	Only that knowledge directly relevant to the user is provided. It is filtered and formatted ready for use
Contextualized	Examples of applications and guidelines for effective use are provided. Users are given opportunities to dialogue to help them internalize the knowledge for their specific application
Connected	There are links to related documents and sources
Know-who	Connections and contact details are also provided to experts who can add further knowledge and insight
Refined	The knowledge is continually summarized and improved through use
Marketed	Marketing helps to create demand. This increases knowledge of use that feeds back into higher quality and additional knowledge

management are used to maximize this utility value and deliver organizational benefits such as those illustrated in Table 1.1 (page 3). One of the most problematic aspects of knowledge management is demonstrating a direct relationship between KM activities and the resultant bottom-line benefits. A tool that is helpful in identifying these links is the knowledge management benefits tree, an example of which is shown in Figure 1.2.

The most direct benefits of knowledge management are those closely related to information and knowledge processing, shown in the left hand column of the figure. Generally, these are the most visible or quantifiable. At Arthur Andersen, an internal survey has quantified the time saved by consultants using KnowledgeSpace®, its intranet-based knowledge

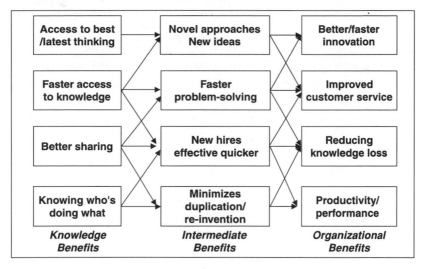

Figure 1.2 A knowledge management benefits tree

repository. On average consultants saved 6.7 hours in creating reports and 6.5 hours in developing work plans and approaches.[22] In turn, better access to knowledge leads to further benefits that can be expressed in terms of efficiency or effectiveness. A common example is that the sharing of best practices helps to improve the performance of less efficient groups towards that of the best. Eventually the intermediate benefits flow through into wider organizational benefits that impact the bottom line or contribute to key goals, such as better customer service.

Identifying and quantifying these causal links requires detailed analysis of the way that information and knowledge is diffused and applied around an organization. Each business process needs to be examined from the perspective of knowledge flows – knowledge inputs, outputs and outcomes. Much of this information can be gathered during an information audit. While not a trivial exercise when done thoroughly, even a cursory exercise will start to highlight common connections and build up an outline tree. The tree will contain many value creating paths. A typical path that can be traced through Figure 1.2 is that of giving new hires easy access to accumulated

Where KM projects deliver business benefits

A survey by Teltech of 93 KM projects showed that their main business objectives were as follows:

- revenue generation: 45 per cent
- cost savings: 35 per cent
- enhancing customer service: 10 per cent
- improving quality: 6 per cent
- refining internal processes: 4 per cent

42 per cent of the high impact projects did not initially use the term knowledge management.

Source: 'Making KM pay off', Carol Hildebrand, *CIO* (15 February 1999)

organizational knowledge. By having it on tap, they can become proficient more quickly, which in turn can help them deliver better service to customers. Benefit trees can quickly provide insights into where knowledge adds value to an organization's processes, products and services.

As the illustrative benefit tree implies, benefits accrue from faster diffusion of knowledge to those who need it. It also comes from combining different sources of knowledge and from a mix of tacit and explicit knowledge. Tacit knowledge underpins many of the generic value factors depicted in Table 1.3. Humans add value through filtering, interpretation, and determining how to use knowledge in a given context. But, as has already been said, tacit knowledge is often difficult to access. If, however, some of it can be codified into explicit knowledge, such as a best practices database, it can be readily shared over an intranet. Many knowledge initiatives therefore invest time and effort into harvesting some of the knowledge that is in people's heads. This investment is only worthwhile where the knowledge has high potential value. This value will be higher where the knowledge is unique, is likely to be reused many times, where it is difficult to access it from the person who has it, and where the organization may suffer severely if it is lost. Much tacit knowledge, by its very nature, is in any case difficult to articulate and codify. A judgement that every knowledge worker and manager faces is what personally held knowledge should and can be codified.

Codification and value

Knowledge in every domain evolves in similar ways. Nonaka and Takeuchi use the concept of a knowledge spiral to describe how an individual's tacit knowledge becomes more codified and diffused as it progresses through the spiral from the individual to the organizational level. Similarly, Boisot describes ways in which knowledge traces different pathways through his model of I-space.[23] This has three dimensions: codification, abstraction and diffusion. A typical evolution path goes from uncodified personal knowledge, to codified proprietary knowledge, then to diffused textbook knowledge, and ultimately to common sense (diffused yet uncodified). In practice, as knowledge evolves, it is continually converted from tacit to explicit and vice versa, as well as being disaggregated and recombined in different ways. But overall, the corpus of codified knowledge grows and is more widely shared.

As a new body of knowledge evolves over time, its value changes as it becomes codified. A typical value-time plot is shown in Figure 1.3. In the early stages, many ideas have little commercial value, even if they

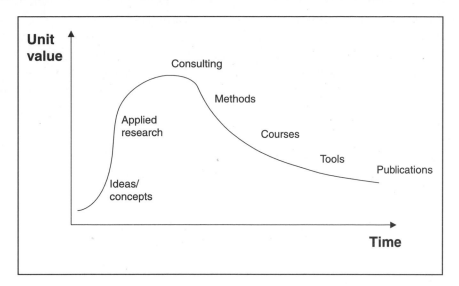

Figure 1.3 Codification and decay of knowledge value over time

are partially codified as in an academic paper or a memo. As these ideas are refined and applied, knowledge about their applicability and use-fulness is gained. It is here that many fall by the wayside, while those that are retained may need considerable investment and effort to turn them into commercial products. By this stage, the people involved have gained considerable knowledge, which it is difficult for emulators to copy. The diffusion of their knowledge is constrained by their availability and willingness to share. They face a difficult balancing act in apportioning their time to communicating what they already know versus continuing its codification and ongoing development.

As demand for this body of knowledge increases, organizations seek ways to exploit it more widely. Other individuals may be exposed to it and trained to deliver it, perhaps as a consultancy service. Increased familiarity through use leads to a degree of delivery standardization based on what works well. This is an opportune time to codify some of it into methods and training courses. Eventually a major chunk of this knowledge is made widely available in various formats, such as publications.

Increasing codification leads to commodification over time. Lack of scarcity leads to expectations of lower prices, even though its value to buyers may still be high. It is not uncommon for suppliers to try to restrict this price erosion. Knowledge owners may try to limit unauthorized diffusion through non-disclosure contracts with buyers and employees. Highly valuable knowledge, such as the formula of Coca-Cola, may be jealously guarded by restricting it to a chosen few. An unfortunate reality for those who try to limit diffusion is the propensity of knowledge to leak. Even where leaks do not occur, the chance of similar knowledge being created or discovered by others working in the same field is very high. Therefore, an optimum strategy is to plan a timely progression down the commodification curve, while at the same time continuing to innovate by generating new knowledge to start another traverse of the curve. At any point, a supplier's potential revenues are the unit price multiplied by the market demand. Lower prices generally stimulate demand. As has been shown in the case of software, a $10 000 product may only sell a few thousand copies. Repackage the same software into a $100 shrink-wrap product, and it may easily sell over a million copies and generate much higher profits.

Judging the right price for knowledge products and services is a major challenge for any knowledge business. Particularly difficult to gauge is the value of experience. There are many apocryphal (and true) stories along the lines of a problem solving expert (ranging from a plumber to a lawyer) who spends a short time on a job yet charges much more than would be expected from the time spent. A typical anecdote is that of a chemical engineer who for a few hours' work charged his client $10 000 to diagnose and fix a problem. When challenged on his invoice, the engineer replied: 'I only charged you $250 for my time, but $9750 for knowing where to look and which part to replace based on my lifetime of experience.' If downtime on continuous operations in a process plant costs $1 million a day in lost production, and an expert has unique knowledge that will get it back on stream within hours rather than days, then $10 000 represents excellent value for money. For similar reasons, a growing number of knowledge businesses, such as consultancies, are moving towards some form of value pricing that recognizes the value of their knowledge assets in terms of the benefits that they deliver to customers. Pricing and codification strategies are considered in more detail in Chapters 3 and 5.

The value of combination

Aggregated knowledge is often worth more than the sum of the parts. It takes time and money to collect it from multiple sources. Consumers benefit from a one-stop-shop. Apart from saving them time, expertly collated and edited information will eliminate overlaps while highlighting contrasts. The richness and depth in one place will aid understanding and offer new insights.

A particularly powerful combination is that of tacit and explicit knowledge. While codified generic knowledge may have relatively low value, the addition of human judgement and experience can considerably enhance value. A geological map and seismic data have considerably higher value when combined with the knowledge of a petroleum geologist who has a successful track record of finding oil. One without the other has limited value; together they are a powerful combination.

Beyond knowledge management

Although knowledge management has been widely adopted, few organizations have made it a universal practice or fully integrated it into their main business processes and management decisions. Most organizations have unfinished knowledge agendas. Some functions, such as R&D and marketing are further ahead with its use than others. It is also accepted culturally in some countries more than others. It has yet to make a significant impact in areas such as corporate audit and accounting, outsourcing, risk management, merger and acquisition planning. As such, it still has several years before it is part of everyday organizational activity. When that happens, it may simply be an integral part of every manager's job, rather than a separate initiative. The name knowledge management may even be subsumed into something new.

As it evolves, knowledge management will spawn specialist branches, such as knowledge mapping and intellectual capital measurement. There will also be flavours that integrate more closely with existing activities such as R&D, marketing and customer relationship management (CRM). Ever improving technologies and software solutions will stimulate more innovative methods and new opportunities to harness knowledge. Knowledge will be more portable and packaged, allowing workers to access knowledge wherever they are. Artificial intelligence will allow computers to act as symbiotic partners with knowledge workers, adapting their actions to user behaviour by predicting their knowledge needs and searching and retrieving it in advance. In many situations, knowledge management will be seamless and invisible, its processes being embedded into computerized processes. There are many ways in which knowledge management may evolve.

Stepping back from the detail, a more general trend is already evident. This is a shift from a predominantly inward looking perspective to an external one (Figure 1.4). Most knowledge initiatives start with a focus of reusing existing knowledge to improve internal processes. Then attention switches to knowledge and innovation, in order to create better products and services. (These are the two thrusts mentioned earlier.) The next logical move is to extend the scope of knowledge

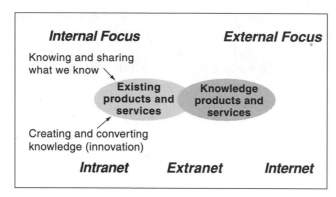

Figure 1.4   The shift of knowledge management from an internal to external focus

management beyond the enterprise. As organizations start to recognize their internal knowledge as a valuable asset, then why not exploit it externally?

A similar change of emphasis is seen in the use of an intranet as an enabler of knowledge sharing. Installing or improving an intranet is an early activity in most knowledge initiatives (between a third and a half according to surveys). Its primary aim is to simplify knowledge sharing within the organization. As its useful content builds up, it is often realized that parts of it are of interest to customers. As they demand more information than is readily available on an organization's Internet website, it makes sense to convert parts of the intranet into an extranet. In this, customers are given selective access to intranet content, databases, information and applications relevant to their dealings with the organization. This new external orientation means that more information and knowledge flows across the boundary between an organization and its marketplace in both directions – from the outside-in and the inside-out.

Outside-in

In almost every survey, customer knowledge comes out top as an organization's most important knowledge. Knowing more about your customers, their needs and what makes them successful is vital knowledge. They can provide revealing insights into how your products and services are used, and how they can be improved.

Good customer knowledge management involves setting up systems to capture, analyse, disseminate and apply the knowledge gained from every interaction between your organization and its customers. Salespeople can enhance the customer experience by having ready access to details of purchases, recent meetings and conversations. Service representatives need access to the customer's product details, their usage, service records and solutions problems. Marketing departments need analysis of customer knowledge to learn which customers are the most profitable or what new products to develop. At Pillsbury, for example, analysis of customer comments about Toaster Strudel, a frozen breakfast pastry, uncovered an unmet need for a chocolate flavoured variety, which was subsequently introduced.[24] A good customer relationship management system will aggregate information for specific customers from multiple systems – ordering, logistics, finance, support lines etc. (see Chase Manhattan case study).

Customer relationship management at Chase Manhattan

At Chase Manhattan Bank, customer relationship managers in its Middle Market Banking Group did not have ready access to information they needed when visiting their customers. The information was often inadequate or fragmented. They were spending as much as a third of their time at their desk when they should have been with their customers. This was one trigger in 1993 for the development of Chase Manhattan's RMS (Relationship Management System). Other needs were to see the complete set of relationships with a single customer and to learn how different customer relationships contribute to profitability. RMS was developed to integrate information from multiple sources and reduce the time relationship manager's previously spent hunting for information.

The way that the system was conceived and developed illustrates several examples of good KM practice. The working patterns of the six top performing relationship managers were analysed and used to guide how information was gathered and presented. A multi-disciplinary advisory board determined the functionality required in the system. Experts from different parts of the bank were called on to give their expertise when needed. Risk managers, for example, contributed knowledge about global exposure. The IT systems team was co-located with a business team to facilitate knowledge sharing during development. The system has discussion databases which provide a forum for ongoing knowledge sharing and one of several channels, both formal and informal, that are used to provide feedback. Suggestions for improvements are evaluated by subject matter experts and approved by the RM advisory board. As a result of this fast learning process, the system progressed through six release versions in its first two years. These examples illustrate the explicit attention given to identifying existing expertise, eliciting and refining knowledge, and ensuring good knowledge flows not just during the development phase, but also in an ongoing way.

The resultant system gives each relationship manager a complete picture of the relationship between the bank and a specific customer.

Discussion databases allow representatives to share problems and get help from others who have been in similar situations. It also provides a way of sharing best practice. Analysis tools help marketing managers prioritize investments, devise new products and tailor offers and promotions to specific groups of customers.

As a result of RMS, Chase Manhattan report several benefits. It estimates that it contributed 10–20 per cent of its incremental revenues and 40 per cent of its cost reductions, amounting to around $28 m in its first five years of operation. Relationship managers increased their call rates on clients by 33 per cent. The information used by all staff is now consistent. Marketing managers report that RMS helps them make better marketing decisions. Finally, the relationship knowledge stays within Chase Manhattan after relationship managers leave the bank.

Sources: 'Relationship Management at Chase Manhattan', Lotus Consulting & Waite and Co., *Knowledge Management Review* (May/June 1998); 'Chase Manhattan builds powerful relationships', Mary G. Gotschall, *Knowledge Inc.* (November 1998)

The Internet adds a whole new dimension to the capture and usage of customer information. Some can be collected automatically. Knowledge about a user's interests can be gauged to some extent by analysing which pages they visit on a website. A snapshot of this information, known as a 'cookie', can be stored on the user's PC.[25] This information allows the Web server to customize pages next time that user views the same website. More sophisticated software and services analyse Web users' surfing patterns and attempt to link visitor data to customer and personal databases. The topic of gathering and integrating Internet and offline customer knowledge is covered more fully in Chapter 6.

There are many other ways of encouraging inward knowledge flows over the Internet. Making good use of email is the obvious one. Less frequently used, but very effective, is a customer-driven community that uses an email discussion group or Web-based forum. These can provide valuable customer and market knowledge at a fraction of the cost of conventional research (see K-Community in Chapter 3).

Outside or inside knowledge?

In the common practice of benchmarking, an organization seeks to compare its own activities against the best practices externally. In 1996, BASF initiated a benchmarking programme to find how other organizations measure and improve customer satisfaction. It quickly became apparent that with 75 diverse businesses, best practice knowledge already existed within BASF itself. A 90-page report was produced. Its key findings and contact details of internal experts were posted on the company's intranet.

Source: 'An inside job', Paul Roberts, *Exec*, pp. 37–39 (Unisys, May 1999)

Inside-out

Many activities within an organization generate knowledge that has value in the external marketplace. Some of this knowledge is embedded in products or services, such as knowledge of the properties of chemicals in a washing powder. Frequently, much of the knowledge that goes into designing a product is subsequently not used or not visible to the consumer. These are where there are opportunities for exploitation. As an example, an engineering company's vast experience in the installation and application of its products may be profitably packaged and marketed as training courses and advisory services. Another source of exploitation is knowledge that is generated as a by-product of normal business trans-actions. An equipment leasing company, for example, will gain extensive knowledge on user preferences, equipment reliability and the relative performance of repairers. This can be collated and sold back to the manufacturers.

Knowledge management provides a basis for identifying and exploiting such knowledge. A knowledge initiative may already have developed mechanisms for collecting, organizing and applying this knowledge internally. It takes only a few further steps to reorient these activities to an external revenue generating focus (Table 1.4).

There are a growing number of examples of this happening, especially among knowledge intensive companies. Ernst & Young introduced Ernie®, a subscription based online advisory service (http://www. ernie.ey.com). Email enquiries are routed to the relevant internal experts for advice. Arthur Andersen has extended some of its internal Global Best Practices® to paying clients (http://www.globalbestpractices.com). Lawyers Linklaters has exploited its knowledge, documents and docu-ment management expertise in creating a customized service on regulatory

Table 1.4 Opportunities for revenue generation from KM activities

Internal activities		External knowledge 'products'
Sharing best practices	→	Best practice databases
Expertise directories	→	Consultancy teams
Intellectual assets	→	IPR; licences, patents etc.
Intranets	→	Extranets
Domain know-how	→	Expert systems (consultancy)
Communities (internal)	→	Communities (external)
Customer knowledge	→	Customer profiles, databases
Knowledge centres	→	Advisory services

issues. Its 'Virtual Lawyer' is an interactive advisory database of international securities and derivative regulation. Enron has created a number of businesses based on its internal expertise in trading energy. These include credit risk management solutions, weather risk management and a number of online transactions services and exchanges such as EnronOnline (trading in energy and related commodities) and WaterDesk (for water industry suppliers and buyers).

In several cases, knowledge management teams have themselves packaged their expertise for external use. The software templates and process behind BP's Connect, an intranet expertise directory, is now used by a number of other organizations. BG Technology now markets the software and methods behind its intranet as MAiNS (Managed Intranet Solution). Ford repackaged and now licenses a 62-step methodology that it originally developed for its internal sharing of best practices.

Frequently the transition from an internal activity to external revenue generation occurs because of the high interest shown by outsiders. This is another reason for having in place systems that collate knowledge picked up from the outside. Customers, suppliers or business partners hear about practices and tools that deliver business benefits to the firms who developed them. When most of these internal activities are started, direct external exploitation is rarely a consideration. Yet they often generate valuable practical knowledge of value to others. Explicit consideration of its external exploitability could generate additional revenues from the sale of knowledge products and services. It is important to consider whether making such knowledge more widely available may do your organization more harm than good. It may fall into the hands of competitors, or the investment to package it as a product or service may divert effort from its internal exploitation. On the other hand, there are many situations where deliberate exploitation has actually generated more profits than when used internally. Two classic examples are the cases of Pilkington and American Airlines. Pilkington licensed its float glass process to competitors, thus

---

A knowledge knowledge business

BP has long been recognized as a leader in Knowledge Management. Following a merger and reorganization in 1999, four core members of its internal Group KM Team left and set up their own KM consultancy; Knowledge Transformation International (www.ktransform.com). Ktransform offers KM training and consultancy; deploys a set of tools and techniques based around the themes of 'Learn before, learn during and learn after' an activity; provides tools and techniques for the creation and re-use of Knowledge Assets; and establishes critical knowledge roles and communities for its multi-national clients.

A virtual company, with no central office, Ktransform's consultants work from their homes and client offices and use virtual tools extensively to coordinate their project work. Knowledge is the core of their business in more ways than one.

generating far more revenues and profits than simply keeping it to itself. By making its SABRE reservation system available to other airlines and travel agents, American Airlines has in some years generated more profit from this line of business than in flying aircraft. Capitalizing on internal knowledge by commercializing some of it through the creation of external knowledge products and services should be a core activity of any forward-looking business.

Commercializing knowledge

Commercializing knowledge is not new. There are many service industries where knowledge is a core element of the product and service they offer – health-care, consulting engineering services, pharmaceuticals, to mention a few. There are several industries where information and knowledge is their *raison d'être* – education, training, scientific publishing, management consultancy etc. There is much that any organization can learn from the ways in which companies in these industries turn their basic material knowledge – into commercially viable products and services.

In a study done for Wentworth Research, Tony Brewer identifies three main ways of commercializing knowledge:[26]

1 *Knowledge enriched products and services.* Knowledge is used to add value to the basic offering; for example, telecommunications companies advise their customers on how to configure and make best use of the equipment and services they offer.

2 *Advisory services.* The know-how of people is used to solve customers' problems; for example, consultancies customize their know-how and offer specific advice.

3 *Publishing.* Knowledge is converted into information packages and sold in various formats; for example, market research companies package their information and knowledge into online databases and reports tailored to accommodate the different needs of their clients.

> **Zurich exploits its knowledge of risk**
>
> As a major industrial insurer, Zurich has developed an extensive business intelligence system over many years. In order to save costs and enhance customer service, its US subsidiary launched RiskIntelligence, an extranet service for its corporate clients to track and analyse their own claims. Following its success, the concept has been extended to a worldwide Global Financial Intelligence Service. Using a personalized risk intelligence 'cockpit', subscribers can use a knowledge navigator to review risk knowledge in various categories. They have flight maps and risk simulators, can receive risk alerts, view news and book online courses at the Risk Engineering Virtual University. There are also industry and risk-specific discussion groups.
>
> *Website:* http://www.risk-engineering.com

Many knowledge businesses blend more than one approach. Management consultancies offer advisory services that they enrich by giving their consultants access to their knowledge bases. Educators and trainers supplement published course material with expert guidance. Publishers of market research also advise clients on how to exploit emerging market opportunities. Every business can package and repackage its knowledge into a variety of knowledge products and services to serve different customer needs. This important topic of productizing knowledge is the focus of Chapter 5.

K-business

Creating knowledge products and services is only one aspect of creating a profitable knowledge business. All businesses need to reinvent themselves as the Internet and electronic commerce change many traditional ground rules. The way that products are marketed is being fundamentally altered. The Internet also opens up a new channel of distribution for knowledge-based products. No longer is e-commerce just another way of conducting a sales transaction. It is part of a larger change in the way that businesses operate. Combine all these strands, and the result is what we refer to in this book as a k-business – a business that markets and sells knowledge over the Internet (Figure 1.5).

Some developments that are shaping the nature of the emergent field of k-business include:

- Electronic communities, many of which have a trading element, such as Geocities (http://www.geocities.com).
- Online events, either synchronous (such as via a Webcast) or asynchronous, such as in a Web conference; the *Knowledge Ecology Fair* is a good example

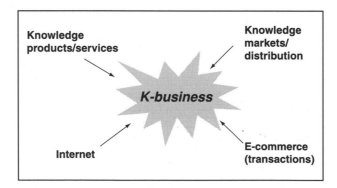

Figure 1.5   The core elements of a k-business

of such an online event that took place over a 3-week period in 1999 (http://www.Co-I-I.com).

- Information providers offering 'knowledge' on a pay-per-view or subscription basis, such as Dialog, FT Profile or NewsEdge.
- Access to specific expertise via the Web and email through so called 'answer-nets'. Teltech.com has a network of experts and many databases. As clients call in with problems, a knowledge analyst can help find experts who can solve their problem.
- Markets in intangible products, such as financial futures, patent licences, copy-rights etc. The Alba Centre in Scotland provides an online infrastructure for trading blocks of virtual intellectual property, specifically designs of functional elements for integrated circuits.
- Online knowledge markets and exchanges, which bring together buyers and sell-ers of knowledge. Etrask provides an online matchmaking between buyers and sellers of advisory services in Europe. Knexa is an online trading and auction website for knowledge.
- Virtual organizations that on a project-by-project basis bring together the expertise needed to serve specific customers. SciNet Bioproducts specializes in the development of bioactive proteins. It creates project teams by drawing together the appropriate experts from its network of highly qualified scientists, engineers, economists and lawyers in the biotech triangle of Northern Germany (Braunschweig–Hannover–Göttingen).

Few of these initiatives would be commercially viable without exploiting the Internet to create, market or deliver knowledge products. Even so, as will become apparent after reading Chapters 2 and 3, commercial success is far from guaranteed. As a supplier, you must find the often elusive online busi-ness formula model that will lead to a profitable future. K-businesses are relatively new. The ground rules for success are not always obvious. Even where they become apparent, the pace of change and rate of knowledge diffusion mean that a k-business will need to remain innovative. Not only is knowledge its core product, but it is the lifeblood of its innovation process. It needs good knowledge management to exploit its knowledge both externally and internally. As well as productizing knowledge and moving it inside-out, knowledge must also flow outside-in. A k-business and knowl-edge management are inseparable.

Summary

A focus on knowledge is helping many organizations improve their performance. Significant bottom line cost savings, faster time to market for new products and improved customer service are some of the benefits that are regularly reported as a result of knowledge management. It helps organizations gain a better understanding of knowledge, its flows and its business impact. The knowledge movement is still relatively new and even the most advanced organizational KM initiatives still have much to do before KM is fully institutionalized. In most organizations the challenges of developing appropriate cultures, introducing new technologies and of measuring the value of knowledge are far from resolved.

Even as organizations gain benefits by applying knowledge management internally, there is potentially more scope by shifting to an external focus. The tools and techniques of knowledge managers help them gain better knowledge about their customers and their unmet needs. It also helps them identify knowledge that has value outside the organization. Many opportunities can be created by capitalizing on an organization's knowledge by converting some of it into knowledge products and services.

The Internet is significantly changing the nature of the business environment. It is spawning new ways of sharing and developing knowledge, new ways of interacting with suppliers and customers, and new ways of trading using e-commerce. Almost every business will need to become an e-business to survive and prosper. The next chapter describes how e-business is another essential foundation for creating a thriving k-business.

Points to ponder

1   How far is your organization along the KM maturity curve? Complete the *K-business Readiness Assessment* in Appendix A.
2   Which practices listed in Table 1.2 do you use? Which do you do well? Which could you improve?
3   Which of the seven strategic knowledge levers are the most significant for your organization?
4   Assess the impact of poor access to knowledge in your department.
5   Have you conducted a knowledge inventory in your department? If not, why not?
6   Identify three sets of knowledge in your organization which is currently not codified but could be much more useful if it was. Consider the cost and the benefits of codification, and what form of codification would be most appropriate.
7   List ten key knowledge assets in your organization that could be good potential for external exploitation.
8   Review the quality of customer knowledge in your organization? How accessible and useful is it?
9   Consider the various external knowledge sources you use in your job. Categorize them according to whether they are bought as knowledge products from a knowledge business or from other sources. List the benefits of each approach.
10 Do a search of the Internet using the terms 'knowledge', 'knowledge services' and 'knowledge business' combined with your industry or field of expertise. Do the results suggest any opportunities or threats?

Notes

1 *Knowledge: The Strategic Imperative*, symposium sponsored by Arthur Andersen and the American Productivity and Quality Center, Houston (September 1995).

2 These examples are taken from a database of cases that has been created by the author synthesizing information from a wide range of sources including case studies from *The Journal of Knowledge Management, Knowledge Management* (Ark Publishing), *Knowledge Management* (Freedom Technology Media Group), *Knowledge Management* (Learned Information), *Knowledge Inc!, Knowledge Review* and several conference proceedings, including 'Most Admired Knowledge Enterprises 1999', Business Intelligence, London (May 1999) and *Knowledge Summit '99*, Business Intelligence, London (November 1999).

3 *Annual Knowledge Management Survey 1999*, KPMG (March 2000).

4 *Knowledge Networking: Creating the Collaborative Enterprise*, David J. Skyrme, pp. 49–59 (Butterworth–Heinemann, 1999).

5 *Knowledge Networking*, ch. 2.

6 *Working Knowledge: How Organizations Manage What They Know*, Thomas H. Davenport and Laurence Prusak (Harvard Business School Press, 1998).

7 *The Knowledge Evolution: Expanding Organizational Intelligence*, Verna Alle (Butterworth–Heinemann, 1997).

8 *The New Organizational Wealth: Managing and Measuring Knowledge-based Assets*, Karl Erik Sveiby (Berrett-Koehler, 1997).

9 The distinction was first clearly articulated for knowledge managers in *The Knowledge-Creating Company*, Ikujiro Nonaka and Hirotaka Takeuchi (Oxford University Press, 1995). The concept of tacit knowledge was described in *The Tacit Dimension*, Michael Polyani (Routledge & Kegan Paul, 1966). An introductory extract from this work can be found in Chapter 7 of *Knowledge in Organizations*, ed. Laurence Prusak (Butterworth–Heinemann, 1997).

10 'Communities of practice' is a term coined by Etienne Wenger as a result of studies in apprenticeship conducted in the early 1990s. For in-depth material read *Communities of Practice*, Etienne Wenger (Cambridge University Press, 1999). For an introduction read 'Communities of practice: the structure of knowledge stewarding', chapter 10 in *Knowledge Horizons*, ed. Charles Despres and Daniele Chauvel (Butterworth–Heinemann, 2000).

11 ShareNet has now been spun off into a separate company – Agilience, in which Siemens retains a minority stake. (*Source: Time*, 13 November 2000).

12 Sources include: 'The Internet connection', Anne Jubert, *Knowledge Management* (Ark Publishing, September 1998); 'Developing knowledge management for successful implementation', Josef Hofer-Alfeis, *Most Admired Knowledge Enterprises 1999*, Business Intelligence Conference, London (19 May 1999); 'Siemens – the e-driven company', Heinrich v. Pierer, Press Conference (10 October 2000). Siemens defines the other elements of an e-business as e-procurement, internal value creation and e-commerce.

13 These success factors were first identified as a result of the research reported in *Creating the Knowledge-based Business*, David J. Skyrme and Debra M. Amidon (Business Intelligence, 1997).

14 Several knowledge managers I know describe how the smoking room fulfils the role of a place for informal conversation where knowledge is exchanged across organizational boundaries. They strive to create the non-smokers' version of such a place, but which has a similar motivating factor that will encourage people to spend time there.

15 David Snowden of IBM Global Services has used this technique in consulting situations for several years. See for example 'Three metaphors, two stories and a picture – how to build common understanding in Knowledge Management programmes', *Knowledge Management Review* (March/April 1999). The use of storytelling in The World Bank's knowledge management programme is told in *The Springboard: How Storytelling Ignites Action in Knowledge-Era Organizations*, Stephen Denning (Butterworth–Heinemann, 2000).

16 One of the better known is the KMAT™ (Knowledge Management Assessment Tool) jointly developed by Arthur Andersen and the American Productivity and Quality Center (APQC). A similar tool is described in chapter 7 of *Knowledge Networking: Creating the Collaborative Enterprise*, David Skyrme (Butterworth–Heinemann, 1999) or can be viewed at http://www.skyrme.com/tools/know10.htm.

17 An introduction to the range of knowledge software available is given in 'Technology: the knowledge enhancer', chapter 3 of *Knowledge Networking: Creating the Collaborative Enterprise* (Butterworth–Heinemann, 1999); also the updates to this chapter at http://www.skyrme.com/knet/ch3.htm. To keep fully abreast of such developments, readers will need to subscribe to one of the subscription services provides by IT research companies, such as Gartner, Giga, Forrester or Delphi Group.

18 Cited in 'Out of the labs and into profit', Richard Poynder, *Knowledge Management* (Learned Information, December 1999/January 2000).

19 'Developing Intellectual Capital Accounts: Experiences from 19 Companies', Danish Agency for Trade and Industry (August 1999). Online version at http://www.efs.dk/publikationer/rapporter/ud-videneng/.

20 *Intellectual Capital: The New Wealth of Organizations*, Thomas A. Stewart, Doubleday/Nicholas Brealy (1997) – gives a general overview, not specifically focused on measurement, though does contain an indicative example of a 'knowledge accounting' balance sheet. *The New Organizational Wealth: Managing and Measuring Intangible Assets*, Karl Erik Sveiby (Berrett–Koehler, 1997) – describes the Intangible Assets Monitor. *Intellectual Capital: Realizing Your Company's True Value by Finding Its Hidden Brainpower*, Leif Edvinsson and Michael S. Malone (HarperBusiness, 1997) – discusses the development of intellectual capital measurement at Skandia, and gives detailed itemization of measures used in The Skandia Navigator. *Intellectual Capital: Navigating in the New Business Landscape*, Johan Roos, Göran Roos, Leif Edvinsson and Nicola Dragonetti (Macmillan, 1997) – describes the Intellectual Capital Index.

21 This is also true to a degree in other goods and services, especially perishables, such as flowers and airline seats. Coca Cola have even floated the idea of having variable prices at their vending machines, charging more when the temperature rises and people are prepared to pay more. Following negative reaction to this value pricing idea, it was abandoned, at least for the moment.

22 Arthur Andersen, internal survey, cited in 'Creating customer value and loyalty through knowledge', Terry Finerty, Arthur Andersen, *Most Admired Knowledge Enterprises 1999*, Business Intelligence Conference, London (May 1999).

23 The knowledge spiral is described in *The Knowledge-Creating Company*, Ikujiro Nonaka and Hirotaka Takeuchi, pp.70–73 (Oxford University Press, 1995). I-space and the diffusion of knowledge is the main topic of *Knowledge Assets: Securing Competitive Advantage in the Knowledge Economy*, Max H. Boisot (Oxford University Press, 1999).

24 'A digital doughboy', Roger O. Crockett, *Business Week e.biz*, pp. 47–49 (3 April 2000).

25 Many users were initially unaware of this intrusion into their personal computer. Wide publicity has increased awareness and some users prefer to disable 'cookies' by changing preferences in their browser. Any connection to the Internet raises the possibility of depositing or extracting information from a user's computer files. One popular email programme extracts information on usage and sends it back to the software provider. In this case, the user is alerted and has to explicitly give permission. In other cases, no such warnings are given, and data are transmitted back automatically. The growing use of these so called ET programmes (a name inspired by a telephone company's advertising campaign where the Extra Terrestial from the film 'calls home') has led to a vigorous debate on personal privacy and the rights of Internet users. This debate continues.

26 'Commercializing Knowledge', Tony Brewer, *Knowledge Summit '99*, Business Intelligence Conference, London (November 1999). The work was done for a research report of the same title commissioned by Wentworth Research.

Chapter 2

E-business: a platform for knowledge

The successful companies will be those that are forward looking and understand the true dramatic impact of the Internet. This is the industrial revolution of the new millennium.

(Ed Zander, President and Chief Operating Officer,
Sun Microsystems)

Most large organizations are in the throes of embracing the Internet as a core element of business strategy. At the same time, hundreds of Internet start-up companies are attracting attention for their innovative business approaches. Once the stock market favourites, many of these dot.com firms have fallen out of favour with investors. Some have already ceased trading and many more are expected to do so. Which of the many hopefuls have the right capabilities and business models to succeed over the long haul? What impacts will developments in the Internet and e-business have on every organization? How should knowledge-based businesses exploit the opportunities that are emerging in this fast-changing environment? These are the themes examined in this chapter.

First, the evolution of e-business is analysed, from its origins in private virtual networks to its ubiquitous and open nature on the Internet today. The advantages of e-business are then assessed, with special consideration given to those for a knowledge business. Next, a five-layer model of the Internet is introduced. This is used as a basis for analysing trends and likely future developments. Innovation is occurring in all layers, and especially the enabling and application layers that deliver services to end-users.

For knowledge-based products and services, these innovations have far reaching effects, many of which we do not yet fully understand. Some of the effects are predicted by the way that the Internet distorts the volume and price curves. Others are surmised by the success or otherwise of early efforts to create knowledge markets, a subject covered more fully in Chapter 4.

No chapter on e-business is complete without a discussion of the dot.com phenomenon, the rise and fall of many once promising Internet start-up companies. An analysis of what separates winners from losers is offered. The lessons are relevant to any organization that uses the Internet to reach its marketplace. In today's networked knowledge economy, this is virtually every organization. Agility to adapt to the dynamics of the Internet is identified as a key factor in the ongoing survival and success of a knowledge-based enterprise.

From EDI to Internet commerce

Fundamentally, electronic commerce means carrying out transactions over electronic networks. In the early 1990s, electronic commerce was synonymous with EDI (Electronic Data Interchange). Transactions were carried over private networks or commercially available VANS (value-added network services) using proprietary software. Transaction details were exchanged using common information formats.

Quite separately, the Internet was emerging from its academic and research origins to become more widely used by businesses. E-commerce suppliers were initially very dismissive of the Internet, criticizing its lack of functionality and security. A sea change took place around 1995–6, when EDI suppliers realized that the Internet was unstoppable, and therefore adapted their software to work over the Internet. The Internet offers several advantages over EDI. It is more universally accessible. It uses open (non-proprietary) standards. The software to use it is relatively cheap, or even free. A key advantage is that transactions can be more spontaneous, without the need for any prior trading relationship between buyer and seller. A potential buyer can browse the net, select products, choose a supplier and place an order, all within minutes.

To use EDI, on the other hand, buyers and sellers need to have set up common systems and procedures beforehand. EDI therefore comes into its own for repetitive purchases within an established customer–supplier relationship.

Today the majority of e-commerce is Internet commerce (Figure 2.1). A typical e-commerce website has an online catalogue, a shopping basket

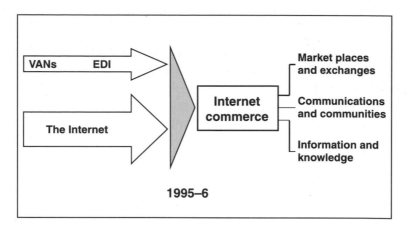

Figure 2.1   The evolution of electronic commerce

and order form, and a secure online payment processing system. By using XML (eXtensible Markup Language) a Web page can now incorporate structured data elements, such as product code and invoice address, an inherent feature of EDI. Internet commerce is embracing the best of both worlds – formal structures of EDI and the ad-hoc informality that is the heritage of the Internet.

The power of Internet commerce is that it offers much more than the mere handling of online transactions. First, it offers a wealth of information and knowledge that can help buyers assess their requirements, identify suitable products and suppliers, and get online after-sales support. Multimedia, in the form of images, audio and video clips, can further enrich the buying experience. Second, the Internet is an effective communications medium, where all kinds of one-to-one, one-to-many and many-to-many communications are possible. Online communities, which act as focal points for discussion on specific topics, are extremely popular. Thirdly, because of global connectivity, the Internet opens up worldwide electronic marketplaces, which are a hotbed of innovation in new ways of trading. The most prominent of these at the time of writing are business-to-business exchanges. These bring together buyers and suppliers to share information on wants and offers, and to negotiate deals.

Because of developments in the Internet, the uptake of e-commerce has been rapid. Analysts estimate an overall market growing from less than $100 billion in 1998 to more that $5000 billion in 2003. Of this, more than 90 per cent is expected to be for business-to-business commerce (B2B) with the remainder business-to-consumer commerce (B2C). To put these numbers into perspective, perhaps 7 per cent of world trade will be online in 2003, growing to an estimated 30 per cent by 2010.[1] For business-to-business transactions, the proportion is higher, with some companies such as Cisco and Dell already doing the majority of their sales online. The change in the business landscape will be significant. According to one survey of European chief executives, e-commerce headed the list of strategic investment priorities, while 69 per cent of them expected it to completely or significantly reshape their business.[2]

The e-advantage

The advantages of e-commerce over conventional trading are significant. Benefits for suppliers include:[3]

- *24-hour, 365-day opening.* Fully automated e-commerce means that customers can access information and place orders at any time convenient to them. Digitized products, such as publications or music, can be instantaneously delivered.
- *Lower transaction costs.* A commonly cited example is that of a bank transaction. What costs $1.50 face-to-face costs 50 cents over the phone, and less than 10 cents online.
- *Efficiency gains.* The scope and scalability of the Internet brings economies of scale. Once an e-commerce site is up and running, the incremental costs of handling more users are relatively small.
- *Extended market reach.* Suppliers can reach more buyers. They can enter new geographies without investing in a local sales presence.
- *Improved customer service.* Online customers can serve themselves and solve problems in a timely fashion. This adds convenience as well as increasing customer satisfaction.

These can be converted into comparable benefits for buyers, who in addition gain advantages of:

- *Lower procurement costs.* Prices of physical products sold via the Internet are typically 10 per cent lower than when bought through conventional channels, and can be as high as 40 per cent (for electronic components).[4] It is also easier to shop around and compare prices. British Telecom estimates that online buying will reduce its direct costs of purchases by 11 per cent and its transaction costs by 90 per cent.
- *Streamlined processes.* Information can be quickly accessed by interrogating online databases. Forms and paperwork can be quickly and automatically routed to many people simultaneously. IBM has streamlined its procedure for recruiting temporary staff through the use of online requisition forms that are sent to several agencies. Suitable résumés are returned within hours, saving time and money – an estimated $3 million a year.[5]
- *Avoiding salespeople.* Many professionals do not like dealing with salespeople but would prefer to make buying decisions in their own time armed with pertinent information. The online Electronic Design Center of component distributor

Marshall provides designers with product data sheets and simulation software, allowing them to make informed decisions.

There are of course downsides to e-commerce. The largest is the loss of physical contact, which prevents scrutiny of products and lack of face-to-face interaction. There have been other barriers to acceptance. The main ones are concerns about security and confidentiality of transactions, the authenticity of suppliers, trust in their ability to deliver and the legal enforceability of contracts. Through careful planning, and wider industry and government initiatives, most barriers are surmountable and detract little from e-commerce's significant advantages.

Cisco – a comprehensive e-business

Cisco started a wholesale move of its business systems to the Internet in 1995. Today much of its business is conducted online. By 1999, nearly 80 per cent of its orders, some $30 million a day, were taken over the Web. The online Internetworking Product Center helps customers properly configure their orders. As a result, errors have fallen from the previous rate of 20 per cent to less than 2 per cent. Eighty per cent of customer problems are now solved online. Over half of Cisco's orders to subcontractors are placed online. Overall it is estimated that the company has saved $3 billion over three years through its use of Internet commerce.

Sources: 'Meet Cisco's Mr Internet', *Business Week e.biz,* (13 September 1999) and http://www.cisco.com

---

The e-business

The e-business is the culmination of a series of stages through which most organizations go in developing their Internet presence. Figure 2.2 shows a typical sequence.

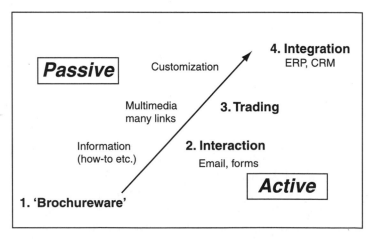

Figure 2.2   Internet evolution in a typical enterprise

1   *'Brochureware'*. Many organizations start their Internet presence with a website that simply transfers some marketing material, such as a few brochures, into the new medium. The results are usually disappointing.
2   *Interaction*. Web pages allow some two-way information flow with the organization, usually through email hotlinks for enquiries and online order forms. Completion of the order does not take place online but may be done by telephoning credit card details or by printing out the form and faxing it with an authorized signature or posting it with payment. At this stage, more helpful information and multimedia enhance the appeal of the Web pages.
3   *Trading*. Full e-commerce facilities are provided, with orders and credit card payments being processed online. Authorization of the credit card transaction usually takes place within seconds through online links to a payment services provider and the buyer's card issuer. Web pages are enhanced through better links to related products and services or to non-competing specialist portals.
4   *Integration*. The website is fully integrated with the organization's core computer systems including customer management, order fulfilment and finance systems. Web pages are customized; they can be generated 'on-the-fly' from databases; information flows seamlessly between the various supporting systems.

In mid-2000 most organizations were still at the second or third stage. A survey of large European companies conducted by KPMG in 1999 showed that only 12 per cent integrated online purchases into back office systems. Many small and medium-sized businesses are even further behind. Less than a half of those in the US had a website at the end of 1999, according to Yankee Group survey, while in Europe UFB Locabail put the figure at 32 per cent.[6] Most organizations need to accelerate their progress along the e-business path in order to use the advantages of the Internet for capitalizing on their knowledge.

The techniques of knowledge management will help this progression run more smoothly. Each phase requires input of knowledge, perhaps much of it initially from outside. Technical, e-business, market and competitive knowledge need to be acquired and regularly updated. Sources and gaps in your expertise will need identifying and filling. The accumulated knowledge needs to be managed and accessible. Each step of the progression should be treated as a learning exercise with your repository of knowledge being refined and updated in the light of experience.

Knowledge on the Internet

The Internet provides five essential functions that an online knowledge business can profitably exploit:

- *Connections*. Widespread access to a common medium creates many pathways to connect people to information and people to people. The extended reach of the Internet, such as through mobile telephones, means that knowledge is accessible almost everywhere.
- *Communications*. People can converse with each other through email, voice or video conferencing, either on a one-to-one or group basis. Information can be shared in many ways. It can be 'pushed' as email attachments or 'pulled' from shared Web pages. It can be communicated in many formats including Word documents, images, video clips and presentations.
- *Content*. The Internet is a vast repository of explicit knowledge. For creators, new knowledge can be published and made widely available as soon as it is produced.
- *Communities*. Either Web-based or in the form of email discussion lists, communities are meeting places for people who share a common interest. Participants can collaborate in knowledge sharing and development – give and receive advice, solve problems, coordinate tasks, generate new ideas and validate knowledge.
- *Commerce*. The Internet adds an effective channel for marketing knowledge-based products and services. E-commerce adds facilities for ordering and payment.

Two of these functions, content and communities, are the focal points for creating an Internet-based knowledge business. Knowledge content can be packaged and sold in many ways – from individual data items to comprehensive reports; from offline courses to online consultations. The interactive nature of the Internet means that more users are likely to receive content in small information blocks as they search and browse. Communities provide opportunities to sense the pulse of the market and act as a hub for knowledge exchange or trading. Many knowledge-intensive sites use a combination of content and community. Drkoop.com is an example in the field of medical knowledge.[7]

Drkoop.com: online medical knowledge

Drkoop.com bears the name of a former US Surgeon-General, C. Everett Koop. With two other founders who had experience in developing medical systems, their Internet health website was conceived in 1998 and formally launched in early 1999.

The site is impressive for its amount of content. There are sections on diseases, family health, preventative health, alternative health and health news. Resources include details on drugs and their effects, a medical encyclopaedia, health related links and how to find a doctor near you (for those in the USA). One of the main sections is called Conditions and Concerns. This has over 90 categories and lists diseases as varied as arthritis, cancer, heart disease and migraine. Each condition has a short description, a library of articles covering causes, diagnosis, treatment, research and so on, and the latest news on curing the condition. There are also links to other websites that specialize in the particular conditions and are given Drkoop star ratings.

Other content is embedded in a helpful set of tools, including a diabetes risk calculator, a bladder control calculator and a caregiver's readiness indicator. In a typical tool, users respond yes or no to a set of 10 questions, after which guidance is offered. The Health and Wellness section includes the Preventionnaire™, a questionnaire on your medical history and lifestyle. After processing your answers, it advises on ways of reducing your risk of illness and suggests what routine tests you should take. Quite frequently the advice given by the tools is 'visit a physician', but you can do so armed with your questionnaire responses. All content is accompanied by a warning that it should not be used to make a diagnosis or determine a course of treatment, since these should only be done by a qualified doctor.

Drkoop.com host two kinds of communities. These are message boards and chat rooms. The former allows people to post and respond to messages at any time. The latter provide synchronous communication at specified times. Each major condition has one or more message boards, and there are 50 chat support groups that meet on a weekly basis. Many of these are more general covering topics such as women's health, communities on ageing, parenting and children's health.

Drkoop.com provides an extensive range of medical knowledge free for consumers. Unfortunately, like many other dot.com ventures, Drkoop has struggled to fully capitalize on its knowledge. It generates its revenues mostly from advertising but made a loss of $65 million on just $7 million of revenues for the first six months of 2000. It received a new injection of funds and was restructured in August 2000, which may save it from collapse. Even if Drkoop fails, health is one area where there is high knowledge demand, and any gap will undoubtedly be filled by other health sites like NetDoctor, WebMD and HealthGate.

The Internet effect

Commercializing knowledge usually requires making a trade-off between value and volume. Knowledge has higher value when it is customized to the context and human experts are involved. An expert, for example, charges clients much more for consultancy than for the book that he or she has written. When delivering their knowledge personally, they have selected from their vast store of expertise that which is most relevant to the specific situation. Unfortunately, consultants cannot be cloned and

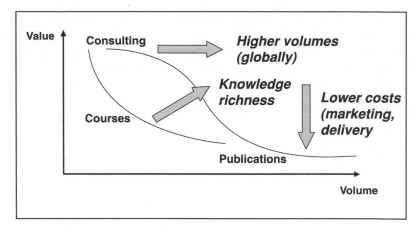

Figure 2.3   How the Internet alters the conventional value-volume curve

distributed as widely as their book! What the Internet can do is alter the shape of the typical knowledge volume-value graph (Figure 2.3).

At the high value end, consultants can be much more efficient, drawing on existing knowledge more readily, such as their firm's intranet knowledge repositories. They can work with their clients virtually, reducing the time spent for travel and meetings. Some of their tacit knowledge can be packaged and sold over the Web. These practices contribute to their ability to supply their expertise in higher volume. At the other end of the spectrum, low Internet production and delivery costs mean that prices for publications can be significantly reduced, thus stimulating higher volumes. In all parts of the spectrum value can be increased by enriching knowledge through the addition of features such as online communities, offering email or video links to knowledge creators, and interactive tools. Evans and Wurster have described the Internet effect as adding both richness and reach – richness through features such as customization and interactivity; reach through access to a much larger market.[8]

The k-advantage

We saw earlier the general advantages of Internet commerce for all businesses (the e-advantage). As well as the benefits of richness and reach just described, a knowledge business can gain additional benefits:

* *Direct access to end-users.* Creators can bypass intermediaries to communicate directly with customer and end-users. This gives them more direct access to customer knowledge and improves knowledge flows. However, intermediaries still have an important role to play, either as a delivery channel or as an aggregator (see page 76).

- *Closer customer relationships.* Individual customer knowledge can be automatically captured from online interactions, making it cost-effective to develop one-to-one marketing relationships.
- *Customization.* Offers can be customized to individuals, based on knowledge of their preferences, past purchases and online usage. Information products can be customized by assembling the relevant information components for the specific needs of each customer.
- *Better products and faster time to market.* A wider range of customer inputs can be gathered online, and new ideas incorporated into products. Open Source products are a good example of this.

> **Open Source – the advantage of collective knowledge**
>
> The Open Source software movement actively harnesses the knowledge of software users. Users are encouraged to develop and improve software whose source code is freely available on the Internet. Many people may contribute to the development of a single product, such as the Linux operating system. This cooperative effort results in faster bug fixes and more reliable software for the community at large. Many of the Internet's essential building blocks, such as DNS (domain name service) and the Apache Web server, were developed through the Open Source approach.
>
> *Website:* http://www.opensource.org

To gain the knowledge advantage, an organization must systematically gather and manage the knowledge that flows over the Internet to and from its customers, suppliers and other partners. More will be said about harnessing this knowledge in Chapter 6.

Internet innovations

Every e-business depends on a set of reliable Internet-based products and services. Figure 2.4 shows a five-layer Internet model, which groups these

Figure 2.4 Internet five-layer model

essential e-business foundations into a series of layers, each one building on the capabilities of the one below. Generally, products and services in the lower two layers tend to be volume commodities with minimal differentiation, while those at higher layers are much more context- and organization-specific. The high demand for Internet products and services is generating a constant influx of new products and services at every level. The main developments are now considered, giving special attention to those that have the most potential for a k-business.

Infrastructure

There is ongoing investment in the telecommunications backbone to cope with the growth of Internet traffic, which doubles roughly every 100 days. This rapid growth is due to a combination of several factors – new users, new applications and greater use of multimedia. The quality and reliability of the infrastructure has improved significantly, while reasonable cost access to the Internet has made it affordable in most countries of the world. A significant change has been the shift from what were once proprietary online services, such as CompuServe and MSN (Microsoft Network), to direct Internet access. This is provided by Internet Service Providers (ISPs) who give end-users their connections into the Internet infrastructure. Although there has been some consolidation among them, many local providers continue to thrive through provision of supporting e-commerce software and services. One development in Europe has been the creation of several hundred ISPs offering free Internet access (other than telephone and line costs). In the UK, within a year of its launch in 1998, Freeserve surpassed AOL's top spot with over 1.5 million subscribers. Its revenues come from a combination of a share of line usage costs, advertising and commissions on e-commerce transactions. As demand for bandwidth increases several alternatives to the ubiquitous modem connection are becoming popular. In addition to ISDN and cable, many home-based subscribers can now access their ISP through DSL (Digital Subscriber Line), which gives an always-on connection at speeds up to 8 Mbps.[9]

Another more significant change is the growth of wireless infrastructure, fuelled by adoption of mobile phones. Until now bandwidth for data has been relatively limited, typically 9600 bits per second. This situation will change dramatically as third generation (3G) networks are rolled out across the world from 2001 to 2003. They will offer bandwidths of 2 Mbps (Megabits per second) or more. Demand for 3G operating licences by network operators is high, since it gives them the ability to offer a range of information-intensive and customized services to subscribers.[10] An idea of the kinds of service that will be available is indicated by NTT DoCoMo's i-mode service, introduced in Japan in February 1999, and attracting over 10 million subscribers by mid-2000. With permanent Internet access, users access email, surf 15 000 i-mode websites, swap digital photographs, and carry out e-commerce transactions from their mobile handsets. In the office too, wireless technology such as Bluetooth will permit cable-free connections between PC, phone, peripherals and other devices.

Such developments herald the arrival of new mobile commerce (m-commerce) opportunities based on geographic knowledge. The cellular network 'knows' your location to within a few hundred metres, or even more precisely if your communications device is integrated with a geographical positioning system (GPS). By integrating knowledge of your preferences, location and immediate needs a service provider can give you directions, highlight attractions in the locality, book you into a local restaurant and order your first course before you even arrive. This is but one example of knowledge-enriched m-commerce.

Overall, developments in fibre optics, routing hardware, and intelligent network software will allow infrastructure bandwidth and reliability to keep abreast of user demands. There are problems of congestion in certain locations, and an innovative service by Akamai has over 2000 servers where it hosts most popular pages from its customer's websites. Perhaps the biggest threat to the infrastructure is that caused by malicious activity. A concerted 'denial of service' attack on high profile websites in April 2000 swamped parts of the infrastructure and the target servers with unwanted traffic. Such attacks have alerted service providers and users alike of the need for continual vigilance to maintain the integrity of the basic building blocks on which all other layers depend.

> **Internet telephony**
>
> A growing proportion of telephone traffic is digitized and sent over networks using Internet technology and protocols. New Internet-based networks are being built from scratch. Qwest created a 2.4 Gigabit 25 000 mile network in North America, while Global Crossing has almost completed a global network of 162 500 kilometres. Analysts estimate that new technology is reducing bandwidth costs by 50 per cent annually. The cost of a transatlantic telephone call, now less than 10 cents a minute with some operators, will fall even further.

Software and access

Today the PC remains the dominant way of accessing the Web. A few years ago, there were high expectations that television set-top boxes would become a popular means of access. This failed to materialize, partly because of limited functionality, but also because the domestic and social setting of a TV is not always conducive to interacting with the Internet. Although access by TV is likely to increase as digital television becomes more established, personal devices that connect via wireless networks are likely to provide the predominant means of Internet access. Any number of devices will be used, ranging from Internet phones, palm-held organizers, pocket PCs, wearable PCs and WAP-enabled mobile phones.[11] The nature of some of these devices, with their small screens and keypads, creates usability problems and means that providers of services will need to rethink the way in which they present information. Particularly useful for knowledge workers will be a new generation of PDAs (personal data assistants), that combine the communications function of a mobile phone with the information handling capabilities of a small PC (see Figure 2.5). Also, expect significant developments in voice-activated software and services using speech recognition technology.

For the PC user, the browser, such as Internet Explorer, remains the main software through which Web pages are accessed. The current HTML standard (version 4) gives the provider of information more control

Figure 2.5 The Nokia 9110 – an example of the new generation of hand-held devices combining voice and information functions

than previous versions of how a Web page will appear on the user's screen. Alternatively, documents can be put on the Web in the commonly used PDF (Portable Data Format), which when viewed with Adobe's Acrobat reader allows users to see them precisely as they were created, with images and diagrams interspersed with text. A number of common 'software' plug-ins for browsers gives the user multimedia, animation and other capabilities. Desktop conferencing software provides virtual communications, in which documents or Web pages can be viewed in one display window, while other windows show the faces of the participants. Capabilities continue to improve with better compression techniques, new hardware, improved software and increased Internet bandwidth. The result of such interactive multimedia is that knowledge exchange over the Net is further enriched.

An area of growing importance is that of intelligent agents. One variety of intelligent agent is the shopping agent or 'smart bot', that will search the net and compare prices, mySimon.com being a good example (see page 57). For less structured information, Kenjin from Autonomy is an example of an agent that analyses documents for key concepts. As a user works on a document or reads an email, it prompts them about related documents it has found on their computer, their local intranet and the wider Web. It will also let users join a community of other people who are accessing similar material. Intelligent agents can act as personal assistants that collect and organize knowledge for users, based on their interests and computer usage patterns. We can expect many more such 'know bots' in future.

As e-commerce matures, common business processes are codified into pre-packaged software products that need minimal user effort to install. What was once custom-built software is now straight 'out-of-the-box'. Examples include catalogue and shopping systems (e.g. Actinic), supply chain inventory management (e.g. i2), software to create business exchanges (CommerceOne), intranet portals (e.g. Plumtree) and so on. Such developments allow e-businesses to concentrate on developing content and presentation, rather than new software.

> **Peer-to-peer file sharing**
>
> Upstart Napster created a stir amongst music copyright holders with their innovative file sharing application launched in September 1999. After downloading a small piece of free software users can search Napster servers for details of music files held on other users' computers and then copy them. In less than a year, Napster had 20 million users. At any one time some 5000 user libraries and 20 000 different titles are accessible. More recent file sharing software like Gnutella and Freenet do not use a central server, but allow direct peer-to-peer links. Whether or not pending lawsuits force such companies out of business, what they have shown is that there are novel ways of sharing information over the Internet without using the Web.
>
> *Source:* 'The hot idea of the year', Amy Kover, *Fortune*, 26 June 2000

Enabling services

The next layer of the model includes a set of enabling services for e-commerce. Some of the earliest, and still the most popular, are online directories and search engines. Yahoo!, started in 1995, now attracts over 150 million hits on its pages every day.[12] These services have converged and evolved into what are now known as portals, which offer users a wide range of information and services. As well as clicking through information hierarchies, users can do free text searches. Most high volume portals also have news, weather and regional variants, e.g. Lycos Asia, Yahoo! Seattle. Several, like Excite, host message boards and chat room facilities. Yahoo! has expanded into auctions and shopping.

For users that still yearn after a simple search engine, newcomer Google.com comes to the rescue. It is nothing but a search engine, and a good one at that. It claims to have the largest index, with 1.25 billion Web pages indexed at October 2000.[13] Results are weighted according to the link structure of the Web, giving priority to pages that have the most incoming links from related pages. Northern Light is a favourite among information searchers and librarians, in that you can search by field, such as author, and its index includes material from non-Web material such as publications and online databases (Figure 2.6).

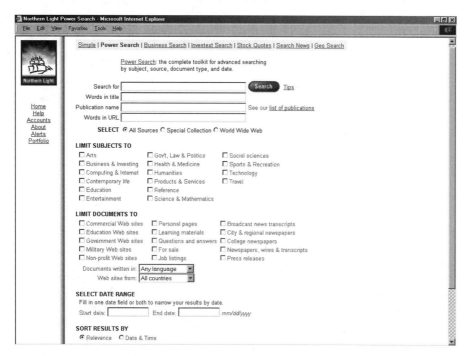

Figure 2.6 The multi-field search screen of Northern Light

Web advertising is another service in this layer. The once popular banner ads, that place adverts very visibly across the top of a reader's Web page, are waning in popularity as 'click through' rates decline to half a per cent or less. With appropriate software, the ads can be targeted. When you use popular search engines, the ads you see are related to the search terms you typed in. There are services such as LinkShare, Be Free and Smart-Age that create affinity groups and place your banner advertisements on the most relevant pages.

Online payment services are another class of enabling services that has grown rapidly. Traditional banks were originally reluctant to support payments over the Web. The vacuum has been filled by several start-ups, such as WorldPay and NetBanx, who act as intermediaries between websites and card issuers. They deal with a range of card brands and multiple currencies. To complete an online transaction, the payment and buyer's credit or debit card details are encrypted and sent along directly to the payment service. After processing, the seller's website is notified whether the payment transaction was successful or not, and continues order processing accordingly. The buyer's card details bypass the seller's site and so remain confidential. All these information exchanges take only seconds to complete, and provide prompt and guaranteed payment to the supplier.

15 landmarks in the history of the Internet

1. Freeserve launched a free Internet access in the UK (22 September 1998).
2. Mosaic was the first widely distributed Web browser (1993). Its developers went on to create Netscape, which was downloaded by six million people within two months of its launch.
3. Microsoft Internet Explorer 2.0 (1995) was given away free.
4. The dot.com stampede: in 1998–9 everyone wanted to jump onto the Internet commerce bandwagon.
5. Amazon.com (1995) popularized e-shopping.
6. The development of MP3 which compresses CD-quality audio by a factor of 12 (1998).
7. Proprietary online service providers such as CompuServe and MSN eclipsed by ISPs (1997–9).
8. From geek to chic. From around 1997 the Internet is no longer viewed as something just for technical enthusiasts.
9. Frames (which divide the screen into separate scrollable areas) come and go out of fashion (1996–7).
10. Google, an extremely fast search engine, goes live (September 1999).
11. The net goes mobile with WAP phones (late 1999).
12. The iMac was launched making connecting to the net easy for the technical neophytes (August 1998).
13. FTP (File Transfer Protocol) wanes against HTTP (Hypertext Transfer Protocol). Unlike the early days, the majority of Web files are now downloaded using HTTP (though FTP remains the common way of uploading files to Web servers).
14. Hotmail introduces free Web-based email – a boon for backpackers and travellers to keep in touch by going to the nearest Web browser or Internet café (Summer 1996).
15. UK domain name prices drop to £5 for resellers (September 1999).

Source: Steve Hill and Richard Dinnick, *Internet Magazine*, July 2000

As e-commerce gains popularity, there is a growing need to ensure buyer trust and confidence. One requirement is for buyer and seller to ascertain the authenticity of the other party. This can be achieved using encrypted digital signatures. These signatures need two digital 'keys' to decode and validate. A third party trusted by both buyer and seller holds one key, while the other is transmitted as part of the online trans-action. In the UK, the Royal Mail was one of the first organizations to set itself up as a trusted third party. Another way of boosting consumer con-fidence in the supplier is through various accreditation schemes such as TRUSTe and TrustUK. These give suppliers seals of approval for meeting certain minimum online trading standards. Just how much these will be used remains to be seen.

A k-business will find many of the services on offer an attractive alterna-tive to implementing them in-house. They will certainly need some form of payment processing mechanism, and will benefit from ensuring highly placed entries in search engines (for which there are various placement services). Just how much they need advertising and a range of other inno-vative marketing services depends on their chosen marketing strategy, a topic we return to in Chapters 6 and 7.

Applications and markets

This layer is where some of the most innovative activities on the entire Internet are currently taking place. Different ways of trading are evolving, some of which are transplants of methods used in conventional commerce, while others take full advantage of the Internet's special characteristics. Auctions, for example, can attract many more viewers and buyers than could be accommodated in an auction room. An overview of some of the more popular and innovative models is shown in Table 2.1, together with some leading exemplars.

Auctions
The online auction model has gained prominence though the success of eBay. At any one time it lists around four million auctions in over 4000 categories. By offering guarantees against fraud to buyers and sellers, and having over 50 local sites, eBay has made it relatively easily to auction tangible items online. Auction sites can also be used as sales outlets for standard products, where the auction is ongoing and the price can be fixed or dynamically adjusted according to the strength of demand.

The use of auctions for knowledge products is currently limited. Infor-mation products, such as publications, lend themselves most easily to the auction model. Auctions have also been used to sell the services of

Table 2.1 Types of e-commerce

Model	Typical features	Exemplars
B2B	Direct selling from an organization's website, often with customer specific areas for tracking orders and viewing tailored offers	Dell, Cisco, Federal Express, Marshall Industries
B2C	Direct selling to consumers. Books, CDs, travel and gifts are among the most popular items sold	Amazon.com, Travelocity, Lastminute.com, eToys
Auctions	Auctions organized by category of goods and last for a specified period of time. Bidders may see suppliers' satisfaction ratings as given by previous buyers	eBay, QXL (Europe)
Reverse auctions	Buyers state their needs and the price they seek. Alternatively, suppliers reduce price until buyers are found (Dutch auction)	Most auction sites offer some form of reverse auction. Pioneers of online reverse auctions are Priceline.com (Name Your Own Price®) and Freemarkets.com for B2B
Comparison shopping	Sites that compare prices across a number of shopping sites. They make their money from advertising or affiliate fees	mySimon (2000 US sites), Kelkoo (25 000 mostly in Europe)
Buying groups (demand aggregation)	Use group buying power to achieve discounts. Higher discounts are achieved when more buyers sign up within the specified buying period	LetsBuyIt.com, Mobshop marketplace
Vertical portals (vortals)	Shopping areas offering goods from many suppliers aimed at buyers in a given vertical market or industry. Many also run auctions. Most B2B portals are now exchanges	SciQuest.com, PlasticsNet.com

Table 2.1 Continued

Model	Typical features	Exemplars
Horizontal portals	Shopping areas for products that are used in all industries, especially office supplies	Works.com (US), Modus.com (Europe)
Exchanges	Market hubs where needs and offers can be matched. Additional features may include pre-qualification of buyers, community space and private auction areas	Chemdex (now Ventro) was the pioneer of the concept. VerticalNet hosts 57 such exchanges. See Table 2.3

knowledgeable individuals. Sellers portray their competencies and offer their services in discrete units of time. By offering their skills to a large market, they hope to achieve a high price for their services. One offer on eBay, that had to be hurriedly withdrawn, was the services of a disgruntled investment team at a merchant bank. For many knowledge services it is difficult to convey succinctly the specific nature of what is on offer. In addition, many aspects of selling knowledge rely on intangible attributes, such as personal relationships, credibility and relevant experience. This use of online auctions for selling knowledge is addressed more fully in Chapter 4.

Buyer power
The capability of the net to connect buyers is opening up ways for them to exert their combined buying power. Websites like the MobShop network and LetsBuyIt.com aggregate purchases to gain volume discounts from suppliers. A buying cycle for a particular product is specified, typically a few days to a week, and buyers invited us to express their interest. The current number of buyers and the next discount point are regularly updated.

Another emergent model is that of the buyer setting the price they are prepared to pay. Websites like Priceline.com make buyer's offers visible to potential suppliers. This is particularly useful for perishable commodities, such as hotel rooms or airline seats. Another way in which buyers are gaining power is through better knowledge of the market place. Many sites do comparative shopping. In the UK, BookBrain will search 14 popular book sites for your chosen title and show a listing of resultant searches by price. Intelligent agents, in the form of shopping 'bots', take this a stage further. They search multiple websites to find the best prices on specific items. MySimon.com list prices from 2000 sellers in 14 categories. Mercata combines these two concepts. Consumers say what they are prepared to pay, while Mercata negotiates for a group discount. Once a price has been agreed with the supplier, potential purchasers who bid higher than this price, receive the goods at the lower group rate, while those who bid below it are rejected.

Another example of consumer power is that of consumer ratings. Consumers are invited to rate a product on several attributes and make individual comments. At Amazon.com, for example, website visitors can read reviews of books by other readers.

> **Deja.com – empowering consumers through knowledge**
>
> Deja.com 'empowers consumer decision-making through the exchange of user-generated information, knowledge and opinions'. This website features over 17 000 products in 650 categories. Consumers rate products against several features, such as effectiveness and ease-of-use, on a scale of 1 to 5. For a given group of products, say naturopathy products in the alternative health section, the site lists the top-rated products, shows individual comments, and provides links to related communities. Since its launch, over one million individual consumer ratings have been posted.
>
> *Website:* http://www.deja.com

As with auctions, well-defined commodity items are best suited to these kinds of approaches. Since knowledge products and services are usually more differentiated, comparing alternative offers is like comparing apples and oranges. Knowledge suppliers, in general, should not compete on price but on value-added benefits that command premium prices. Nevertheless, such developments in the consumer marketplace indicate that knowledge suppliers can expect their potential buyers to be better informed about competitive offerings and how they compare.

Business-to-business exchanges (B2X)

Electronic markets, such as those described above, are far from perfect. Most have only a limited selection of products, and few participating buyers and sellers. Most are also aimed at consumers and are open to all-comers. By focusing on narrow specific market places, business-to-business exchanges hope to overcome these difficulties.

Chemdex, now renamed Ventro, was the pioneer of business-to-business exchanges. Conceived during a team project by students at Harvard Business School, a B2X like Ventro brings together buyers and sellers in a controlled environment. Its essential characteristic is the posting of needs and offers, against which other market participants can bid or make alternative proposals. These exchanges also have many portal-like features in that they provide relevant information about developments in the specific market place, such as news and analysis. Many also have discussion groups or communities. Other frequently found features are

Table 2.2 Benefits of business-to-business exchanges

Supplier benefits	Buyer benefits
Greater access to marketplace	One-stop shop
Global reach	Ability to find best fit for needs
Lower selling overheads	Lower prices for bought-in goods
Smoothing of production schedules	Better supply chain management
Better inventory management	Enforcing corporate purchasing policy
Access to pre-qualified buyers	Reduced costs of purchasing

the pre-qualification of participants, the ability to create closed groups or private exchanges, anonymous bidding, provision of e-commerce services and management information. Through offering useful information and a place to share knowledge they hope to create an attractive trading hub for market participants. Table 2.2 shows the potential benefits of such exchanges to buyer and seller.

Despite being a relatively new concept (Chemdex was launched in 1997), some 600 industry-specific exchanges had been announced by mid-2000, although the majority had not launched or started volume trading.[14] Table 2.3 shows a list of some typical exchanges across a range of industries. As well as individual exchanges, some companies are providing software and services for a group of exchanges. VerticalNet, for example, hosts 57 exchanges in markets as diverse as textiles, dental supplies and photonics. Such is the enthusiasm for exchanges, that some analysts believe that half to three-quarters of B2B commerce will take place through such exchanges by 2005. Is this a realistic expectation? Large corporations, who have spent significant investment in developing their supply chains and deepening their supplier relationships, might not want to participate in exchanges alongside their competitors, as well as giving commission to the exchange operator. Nestlé, Wal-Mart and Unilever are among those that have shown little interest in joining an exchange (mid-2000). On the other hand, some exchanges were created by consortia of the largest buyers in their sector, seeking to buy competitively from thousands of their suppliers.

The success of these exchanges depends on attracting a critical mass of buyers and sellers. Frequently, several exchanges woo the same buyers and sellers. How many exchanges can each industry support? Perhaps only two or three in the long-term. Because of uncertainties in how market dynamics will play out, and the current surfeit of unproven exchanges, many are unlikely to survive in their present form. Obviously, if an exchange manages to enable a worthwhile trading relationship that

Table 2.3 Examples of business-to-business exchanges

Exchange	Industry	Founders/key participants	Special characteristics
CheMatch	Chemicals	Independent. Corporate investors include Bayer, DuPont, Millennium Chemicals, Reed Elsevier, Computer Sciences Corporation and GE	A spot market for petrochemicals, plastics and fuel additives. Anonymous trading. Pre-screening of participants. Real-time auctions
Metalsite	Metals	Founded by Weirton Steel, LTV Steel and Steel Dynamics, but operates independently	QuoteFinder – an RFP generator to make it easy for buyers to specify requirements. Prices, statistics and news
NECX.com	Electronics	20 000 industry participants	Access to 10 billion parts. Auctions. Personal buy and sell portfolios. Chat with traders. Now one of VerticalNet's 57 marketplaces
E2open.com	Computing, electronics and telecommunications	Founders include Hitachi, IBM, Nortel and Toshiba	Design Win Collaboration – a secure environment for cross-company teams to collaborate
Covisint	Automobile components	Joint venture of General Motors, Ford and DaimlerChrysler, later joined by Renault/Nissan	A merger of two earlier exchanges which will allow auto-makers to seek bids from 30 000 suppliers
GlobalNetXchange	Retail	Sears Roebuck, Carrefour and 50 000 suppliers	Access to catalogues, auctions and closed environments for supply chains

Table 2.3 Continued

Exchange	Industry	Founders/key participants	Special characteristics
Band-X	Telecommunications bandwidth	1500 buyers and sellers, many of who resell bandwidth on to consumers	Because of variations in specifications etc., Band-X limits itself to introducing buyers and sellers who post offers and wants
PaperX	European paper products	A start-up funded by venture capitalists	Catalogues, online forum. Trading takes place directly between exchange participants. PaperX does not act as an intermediary or run auctions
Catex	Catastrophic risk	170 organizations and 2000 members including intermediaries, reinsurers, insurance carriers, and corporate risk managers	Swaps catastrophic risk exposure in areas such as aviation, health, marine, energy, political risk and weather. Private networks. Market transparency through showing main details of all postings and completed transactions
Farms.com	Cattle, hogs and poultry	An independent software company started in Chapel Hill, NC in 1995	Content, communities and commerce. Online real-time auctions. Agricultural careers and jobs

previously did not exist, such as between small businesses, then it does fulfil a useful role. There will always be a need to match buyers and sellers, and to supplement established buyer–seller arrangements as requirements change.

As with other electronic markets, business-to-business exchanges work best for commodity items where there are established customers, a choice of suppliers, and well defined and understood product descriptions. For a commodity like telecommunications bandwidth, there is no standard package of bandwidth or commonly agreed set of technical terms and contract conditions. Band-X, an exchange that deals with surplus bandwidth, therefore merely acts as a broker between buyer and seller who then proceed to negotiate between themselves. This market-making capability may well be the model that early knowledge exchanges will need to follow.

User services

The top layer of the model comprises a number of ancillary services. Some, like Web design and systems development, are needed during the construction of an e-commerce site. Others, like analysis and surveys, are for the benefit of the wider supplier and user community. Dot.com start-ups will need access to venture capital and other business services. As in the other layers, the range of services grows rapidly and attracts many new entrants. Web design companies were virtually unheard five years ago, yet today Razorfish has over 1800 employees. Typical of other services are those of Viant, who provide e-commerce consultancy. All these services are truly knowledge-based. Descriptions of them are outside the scope of this book, although generic principles behind their marketing and delivery are covered in other chapters.

Context and environment

During the past few years the usage and demographic profile of Internet users has changed significantly. While the US boasts over 40 per cent of households with Internet connections, the figure is less than 10 per cent in Eastern Europe. Once with a strong bias towards younger and more affluent men, the profile is now closer to that of the population at large. In the US, the fastest growing group of users are aged 55 or over. There has also been significant growth in non-English speaking countries and especially Asia, where 233 million users are expected to be online by 2003.[15] When work-based and public access points such as libraries are considered, there are not many potential purchasers that are beyond reach.

The pace of Internet development is much faster than the ability of legislators around the world to catch up. As a result there are inconsistent approaches to taxation, contract law, intellectual property rights, and privacy laws to name but a few. We return to these issues in Chapter 9.

Dot.com winners and losers

Although the future may be rosy for electronic commerce as a whole, it is not so for many individual dot.com companies. Several analysts predict that three-quarters of dot.com start-ups will not survive long-term.

One early high profile failure was boo.com, an online supplier of fashion goods.[16] Quite simply, its cash ran out, and its financial backers would fund it no longer. Analysts blame a combination of factors for its demise. It was over-ambitious technically, exploiting 3-D imagery and other wizardry. However, users had to have the latest browsers, the right plug-ins and high-speed Internet connections for best performance. Even worse, Apple Mac users could not access the site at all. Boo.com is also reported to have spent lavishly on marketing and unnecessary frills. Many more dot.coms will suffer its fate.[17] Analysts are even querying the staying power of Internet commerce pioneers such as Amazon.com and CDNow. Achieving high market share is one thing. Converting it into a profitable business is another. Who are likely to be the winners and losers in Internet commerce, and why?

The losers

The obvious losers have been investors and venture capitalists who ploughed money into ventures that have already failed or may soon do so. Others are professionals and managers who enjoyed solid, though perhaps unexciting, careers in blue-chip companies, but which they deserted for the lure and buzz of a dot.com start-up. Many now find themselves jobless but wiser. Perhaps the knowledge they have gained will allow them to create a successful dot.com in the future. Suppliers, employers and some consumers have also lost out. Other losers will be traditional companies that do not adapt quickly enough to the net. The online success of Amazon.com, for example, has acted as a wake-up call to traditional booksellers like Barnes & Noble and W.H.Smith. The latter made up for lost time by buying The Internet Bookshop (http://www.bookshop.co.uk).

The causes of failure?

The general youthfulness of the management teams of many dot.com companies means that they lack the depth of solid business experience of their elders. On the other hand, they don't necessarily want a head of finance who was formerly a Chief Financial Officer of a large multinational. While some corporate CFOs can adapt to such a career shift, others cannot. Another lesson evident to those who have built up large and successful businesses is that you don't treat yourself and your friends to riches and junkets that the new business cannot afford. Companies like HP and Yahoo! started very modestly in low-cost premises. In contrast, those dot.coms that host lavish launch parties, have prestigious premises, and pay high basic salaries (rather than emphasizing stock options) need to be investigated closely to see if such expenditure really is needed for 'marketing' as claimed.

To be fair, most dot.com founders are committed to making their venture succeed and put a tremendous amount of energy and enthusiasm into it. Even so, as any student of innovation will tell you, only a small fraction of new business ideas translate into commercial success. This is why venture capitalists have been willing to pour money into a string of dot.com ventures, on the basis that they only need one success like Yahoo! to compensate for all their write-offs. This suggests that a dot.com developed around a single idea needs to expand its portfolio with proven ideas and business models in order to minimize risk. How2.com, for example, found that its original idea of consumer 'how-to' guides was too broad and has recently reinvented itself as www.parago.com, an application service provider focusing on customer management systems. It retains only a few niche product-care guides from its original portfolio. Another long-term survival strategy is to partner with a complementary supplier or more established company. Thus Infoseek, one of the Internet's earliest search engines, is now part of Disney Corporation's Go.com.

Some of the main reasons why Internet commerce ventures fail are:

*   *Customer ignorance.* One analyst reckons that even if boo.com had managed its cash flow better, got its technology right first time, that it still might not have succeeded. Observation of young consumers buying fashion goods – Boo's target market – suggests that they like trying clothes on in front of friends, and that they relish the physical and social experience. Do they really want to buy these goods in the privacy and isolation of their homes? In other words, did boo.com have sufficient in-depth knowledge of its potential market and customers? In the B2B marketplace, many websites are irritating and slow, and professionals cannot quickly find the information that they need. With such an experience, many will not visit again.

- *Marketing myopia.* Although first mover advantage is important in many markets, too many dot.coms put undue faith in the belief that advertising will get them market share fast. Certainly, it has helped companies like Amazon.com, but the best advertising is often free. One of the founders of clicklocum.com (a service to provide locums to doctor's practices and pharmacists) wrote how venture capitalists laughed him and his colleagues out of the door, since its well-researched business plan did not have an advertising budget of at least £10 million. Despite this, their company became a market leader in its niche through carefully targetted promotions that cost a fraction of advertising.[18] Do you recall ever seeing advertisements for M3.com or Napster.com? I don't. But there's probably no music-loving student anywhere that has not heard about these websites.
- *Big number fantasies.* 'Reach over 100 million customers' claim advertisements enticing small businesses to have a presence on the Web. This overlooks the fact that there are probably over 10 million suppliers also vying for their attention, and that only a small proportion of them will even be slightly interested in your products and services. Likely losers seek mass markets with shoestring levels of investment and without the pull, reputation and service of established brands. In contrast, the net is a great marketplace for specialist suppliers selling into niche markets on a global scale.
- *Inappropriate business models.* These are not necessarily unproven, since there are some innovative yet unproven models that will become the tomorrow's winners. Inappropriate may be relying on a subscription model when pay-per-view is what customers want. It may mean relying on high advertising revenues when the general price per click-through is declining rapidly. E-businesses must understand what their customers value and will pay for. A model appropriate for Yahoo! or CBS Sportsline is likely to be totally inappropriate for a business-to-business equipment supplier.
- *Selling at a loss.* Although this may sound rather trite, it is one thing to be showing an accounting loss due to high startup costs. It is quite another when your gross margin on the variable costs of sales is negative.[19] The premise behind such a model is that low prices gain market share, and that over time a strong market position and economies of scale will permit a healthy profit margin. This of course assumes that the high margin does not attract other market entrants, and that the cost of entry is high – dubious assumptions in the fast-changing Internet marketplace.
- *Incoherent systems and processes.* Unlike established businesses, one of the potential advantages of start-up ventures is that business processes and systems can be developed from scratch. This means customer facing systems can be designed to integrate well with back office systems including order processing, finance and order fulfilment. Yet several dot.coms do not think through the total system and issues of scalability and integration upfront.

The winners

The main winners are the dot.coms who aren't dot.coms! IBM, for example, sold \$15 billion worth of e-commerce related goods and services in 1999 and is very profitable! Many software and service providers in the dot.com supply chain are also very profitable. Among these are HP, Sun, Dell and Cisco. Other winners are established companies who have created dot.com ventures, but while funding them have let them operate autonomously so that they remain innovative and entrepreneurial. Two very good examples in the UK are Freeserve (a spin-off from retailer Dixons, and now the country's largest Internet Service Provider) and Egg.com (an online bank off-shoot of Prudential insurance).[20]

Of the new dot.coms, several features are apparent in those that have a large presence in their chosen markets (that does not necessarily mean they are profitable, but number of unique visitors is an important interim metric):

- *Compelling content.* They provide information that is unique or is aggregated and formatted in a way that is easy to use. They become a first port of call for those interested in researching or updating on a specific topic. That's how Yahoo! got started and how more recent specialist sites like soccernet.com attract audiences.
- *Interest and flair.* It is often remarked that the most interesting tourist and sports club sites are not the official one, but those set up by individuals or fan clubs. Turning them from a hobby into a commercial proposition is the challenge that they face. Formula 1 racing fans will find www.f1grandprixracing.com interesting, with its circuit details, 3-D car models, news and technical details. It was built by someone who gave up his job – dedicated his time and £30 000 – but in its second month of operation was already attracting 86 000 hits a month.[21]
- *Know their customers' needs and interests.* They gain customer knowledge and use it to personalize pages and tailor promotional offers. Amazon.com is renowned for doing this well, as well as providing reliable service (which is why it has a loyal customer following and gains sales even when newer competitors are cheaper).
- *Exploit the special characteristics of the Internet.* eBay is profitable since it offers virtual auctions without itself having to handle the goods. Other winners exploit the global market reach of the Internet, to address overseas markets without associated market entry costs. Business-to-business exchanges may well offer unique facilities that help SMEs market their products. Analysts expect Vertical-Net (mentioned earlier) to break even within about a year, from revenues generated by transaction commissions, advertising and e-commerce services.
- *Have reliable and responsive technology.* The days of gimmicky frames and glitzy graphics are receding in favour of content-rich sites that work well and fast, and with transaction and payment systems that are straightforward and

robust. The most popular sites make sure that they provide mirror sites around the world to ensure good response. Sausage.com is one company that has built a thriving Web-based software business that way.

- *Have a lean and mean business model.* Many of the success stories started with small teams, they outsource specialized activities (e.g. many of the financial outgoings for fl grandprixracing.com mentioned above were for graphics, press pictures and e-commerce development of its online shop). As they grow, they stay lean and mean. It is possible to run a successful worldwide online business with only a handful of key people.

Many of these characteristics represent commercial common sense, interlaced with a dose of entrepreneurial spirit and enthusiasm. With the right blend of each, there is no reason why there should not be many more winners. Unfortunately misplaced investor enthusiasm during 1999 outweighed Internet commerce reality. Hopefully this rose-tinted phase has passed as organizations get down to serious and sustainable e-business. As in the real world, there are mass markets and niche markets. All the indications are that dot.com start-ups that address niche markets are likely to show earlier profits than those who address mass markets, where they have to fight tooth and nail for market share alongside established companies with deep pockets.

Internet stock valuations

One of the consequences of the 1999 dot.com frenzy was the seemingly unrealistic valuation of Internet companies. Priceline.com was valued more than Delta, US Air and United Airlines combined. eToys was worth as much as Toys 'R' Us even though its revenues were equivalent to that of two retail stores (Toys 'R' Us has nearly 1500) and made a loss in 1998.[22] AOL was worth 1.4 times that of Times–Warner (with whom it later merged). Amazon.com was worth four times that of traditional bookseller Barnes & Noble with only a quarter of the revenues and large losses. Even in mid-2000, after the severe setback in Internet stock prices, Amazon.com still had a market valuation of $18 billion, against revenues of $1.6 billion and losses of $720 million. Even profitable Yahoo! ($101 million pre-tax profit in 1999) was capitalized at $73 billion on revenues of $588.6 million and a projected price earnings ratio of 620; the technology sector norm is 50. An analysis by Regent Associates of 402 Internet stocks of showed total revenues of $28 billion, losses of $4 billion, yet a combined valuation of $996 billion.[23] Do such valuations make sense?

The normal basis for valuing companies is on projected future earnings and cash flow. On this basis even optimistic analysts believe that Amazon.com will need to grow by 70 per cent per annum for over five years and achieve gross margins on product sales of 20 per cent or more (its gross margin in 1999 was negative).[24] Even today's successful companies like Microsoft, Dell and Cisco achieved only 60 per cent growth in their best five years of revenue growth.

Another school of thought is that Internet stocks should be valued in a totally different way, since much of their value is in their intellectual capital and knowledge. For example, Amazon.com holds some business method patents, including that for 1-Click[SM] ordering. It is also true that several Internet start-ups have been bought by larger organizations at substantial premiums. This gives credence to the view that intangible assets, such as an established customer base and e-commerce know-how, have intrinsic market value. It may take several years before we really understand how to select and value Internet companies properly.

The agility gap

The path to e-commerce is not straightforward. Research by Gartner Group suggested that three quarters of e-commerce projects will fail due to poor planning and unrealistic expectations of technology.[25] Organizations face several challenges:

- Inertia – whereas the benefits of e-commerce in general are evident, many established businesses feel that whole-hearted embracing of e-commerce will threaten existing profitable lines of business.
- Legacy systems – many existing business processes and information are spread across a disparate variety of older computer systems.
- Addressing users' needs and concerns – for several years, security of transactions was a major concern; more recently, users are concerned about their personal privacy.

Christmas 1999, sometimes dubbed the first e-Xmas, really tested many organizations' systems and the wider infrastructure to the limits. A survey by Andersen Consulting cited these percentages of respondents reporting problems:

- out of stock: 64 per cent
- not delivered on time: 40 per cent
- connection problems: 36 per cent
- no confirmation of delivery status: 28 per cent
- limited selection: 27 per cent
- website too difficult to navigate: 26 per cent
- not enough information to make a purchase: 25 per cent.

These responses illustrate that e-commerce can fall down because of its dependence on the wider organizational system. If a site attracts too many buyers, the site itself may fail. Within hours of launching a new online banking service in June 2000, Abbey National, one of Britain's largest banks, found its site could not cope and for a couple of days many people could not log on. Even if people can handle the online processes, is the rest of the supply chain closely integrated such that the rest of the customer experience is satisfactory? Failure to respond to email enquiries is a common criticism. A survey by Elan Marketing of financial organizations, found that over 60 per cent did not respond within 5 days, and over 20 per cent of these, not at all.

Other responses indicate that the flow of information to and from customers is lacking. A good e-business is one where the total customer experience has been thought through and effectively implemented. In retail, the market dominance by start-up dot.com companies is fast eroding as traditional companies fight back.[26] They already have in place fulfilment and customer support systems.

The common thread through all of the above difficulties is lack of agility. Organizations need to respond much more quickly to changes – in customer expectations, buying patterns, and in the overall way in which business is conducted. Working on the Internet magnifies any imperfections in an organization's infrastructure several-fold. The Internet world talks of an Internet year being equivalent to three months of real time. This means that product development and introducing new business models happens four times faster than it did before. No longer do companies have the luxury of planning their e-business strategy or analysing it in depth. They have to get something up and running within 100 days, learn rapidly what works well and what doesn't, and adapt fast. Agility is the key. And better knowledge management, using techniques such as project reviews, lessons learned databases, helps you be more agile. This is another example of the interplay between knowledge management and e-business.

Summary

The Internet is changing the way that every business operates. While the main attraction of e-commerce has been to reduce transaction costs and increase the market reach for tangible products, the use of the Internet to market and deliver knowledge offers potentially greater opportunities. K-businesses exploit the Internet to distort the normal trade-offs between richness and reach to increase volume and value in their favour.

The Internet is a hotbed of innovation which k-business can exploit to their advantage. In our five-layer model, we identified faster connections, more bandwidth and mobility as key developments in the infrastructure layer. In access and software, new devices and multimedia are enriching the Internet experience for the average user. The enabling layer is one that has matured rapidly in the past few years, delivering many of the basic services needed for e-commerce in a straightforward 'out-of-the-box' manner. The most dynamic changes are taking place in applications and new ways of trading. While auctions and portals are growing in popularity, the business model that most companies are now scrutinizing closely is that of business-to-business exchanges. Many of these, like other dot.com start-up companies, are unlikely to survive for long. Our analysis of dot.com winners identified the need for good business experience laced with a dose of entrepreneurial enthusiasm. All e-businesses, and that includes traditional organizations adjusting to the realities of the Internet, need agility to cope with the dynamics of the Internet commerce environment. Most will have to reinvent their e-businesses every 100 days. Old business models will have to be abandoned in place of new ones, many of which have yet to be proven. The next chapter looks at some of the choices of model.

Points to ponder

1   What measurable benefits has your own organization's Internet presence delivered? What scope is there to achieve more?
2   How far up the e-commerce maturity ladder (Figure 2.2) has your organization progressed? What is stopping it from moving ahead faster?
3   How has your company extended its market reach through the Internet?
4   What knowledge products have you successfully sold over the Internet?
5   Does your organization participate in online communities? Does it offer community facilities for customers and potential customers?
6   How quickly can your customers find the information they need on your Internet website? Has this been validated by measurement and observation?
7   What strategies do you have in place to exploit m-commerce (mobile commerce)?
8   Has a study been conducted of business-to-business exchanges relevant to your marketplace? What are the pros and cons of participating?
9   Identify three dot.com start-ups in your industry. What lessons can you learn from them to improve your own e-business capabilities?
10 Look at all the systems involved for order fulfilment. How well are they each integrated with your Internet presence?

Notes

1   In such a fast changing market there are wide variations in the results of different surveys, and how broad the scope, e.g. US or worldwide,

business-to-business or all types of transaction. As an example, Gartner estimates $7.1 trillion (a thousand billion) for business-to-business e-commerce
worldwide in 2004.

2 *E-business Survey*, PricewaterhouseCoopers and The Conference Board (October 1998).

3 The first two chapters of *Electronic Commerce: Strategies and Models for Business-
to-Business Trading*, Paul Trimmers (John Wiley & Sons, 1999), goes into the
advantages in more detail and cites many examples.

4 'B2B: 2B or Not 2B', Technology Research Report, Goldman Sachs (April
2000). The first study was published in fall 1999 and is updated every six
months: http://www.gs.com/high-tech/research/

5 'Big Blue gets wired', Ira Sager, *Business Week e.biz* (3 April 2000).

6 NUA Internet Surveys (http://www.nua.ie). NUA provides weekly sum-
maries of surveys carried out by the major Internet research companies.
UFB Locabail surveyed 90 000 companies in Germany, France, Italy and the
UK.

7 Drkoop, like many dot.com start-ups, ran into cash flow problems in mid-
2000, as their initial funding ran out, and sufficient revenues were not generated. Nevertheless, there seems an insatiable appetite for health information,
and other companies will surely fill any gaps left by Drkoop, should it not be
in business by the time you read this.

8 *Blown to Bits: How the New Economics of Information Transforms Strategy*, Philip
Evans and Thomas S. Wurster, Harvard Business School Press (1999).

9 The asymmetric version, ADSL, works on the basis that most users want to
download more than they upload. A typical speed split is 6 Mbps down
and 640 Kbps up. Actual speeds are very dependent on the distance from
the user to their local telephone exchange and the quality of the copper
wires. By mid-2000 there were an estimated 30 million subscribers around
the world (mostly in Europe, US and Japan).

10 An auction of five 10-year licences in the UK in Spring 2000 attracted 20 bidders, with the winning bids totalling £22.5 billion ($35 billion) – more than five
times that anticipated, and roughly equivalent to £2000 per subscriber. A little
later, the licences awarded in Germany cost even more – over $40 billion.

11 WAP stands for Wireless Access Protocol, which is optimized for low bandwidth devices. However, early problems of handset compatibility and the
success of i-mode phones means that the precise formats that will be successful are not yet certain. In any case, Web pages need to be rewritten in the
appropriate markup language – WML (Wireless Markup Language for
WAP) and cHTML (compact HTML) for i-mode – and optimized for the
characteristics of the device.

12 Yahoo stands for 'Yet Another Hierarchical Officious Oracle'.

13 A growing problem is that an increasing proportion of Web pages are not
available to indexers. They are generated on-the-fly from databases, held in
non-indexable formats (e.g. PDF), or are only accessible through use of password dialogues. The overall number of Web pages is reckoned to be close to
10 billion (mid-2000).

14 Berlecon Research maintains an online database of B2B marketplaces. In September 2000, it contained 1213 profiles of which 736 were categorized as vertical and 412 as horizontal. 628 were categorized as exchanges, 441 as catalogue and 329 as auction sites. http://www.berlecon.de/services/b2bdb/en/eingang.php.

15 Figures from Forrester Research (June 2000), IDC (September 2000), Lehman Brothers (August 2000) cited in NUA Internet Surveys http://www.nua.ie.

16 The brand name was one of its largest assets at the time of collapse. This and other assets were bought by fashionmall.com at a small fraction of the several hundred million dollars put into the company by investors and creditors.

17 A survey of Web mergers showed that in the first seven months of 2000, out of 238 dot.com start-ups, 41 collapsed, 29 were sold, and 83 withdrew plans for going public. Cited in 'Model from Mars', Marcia Vickers, *Business Week*, p. 58 (4 September 2000).

18 Readers letters, *Internet Magazine* (June 2000).

19 This is one of the reasons why Amazon.com fell out of favour with analysts during 2000, since it was not even covering its ongoing cost of sales.

20 Their IPOs were oversubscribed 30 and 9 times respectively. Although both are leaders in their markets, they have yet to prove themselves as long-term winners (see the comments on Amazon.com on page 66).

21 'F1 Grand Prix Racing', *Internet Magazine* (June 2000).

22 Things, of course, look different in 2000. eToys that peaked at $86 in October 1999 was down to $7 in May 2000. Volatility is clearly one of the main features of Internet stock valuations.

23 Cited in 'Dot.com bubble will burst by June', Vicki August, *Computer Weekly*, p. 5 (3 February 2000).

24 One such analysis is given in 'Valuing Internet business', Chris Higson and John Briginshaw, *Business Strategy Review*, Vol. 11, No. 1, pp. 10–20 (Spring 2000). They ask if Internet stocks are a bubble waiting to burst. One such bubble was that when tulips were brought into Holland, and the price of a single bulb, just before the market collapsed in 1637, was 5200 guilders – the price of a house and 20 times the annual average artisan's wage.

25 Gartner Group (September 1999).

26 By Spring 2000, traditional retailers' share of the market had grown to over 50 per cent at the expense of dot.com only companies. (*Source:* Jupiter Communications).

Chapter 3

K-business:
new markets,
new models

Imagination is more important than knowledge.

(Albert Einstein)

The first two chapters have introduced the two main themes of this book – knowledge as an exploitable asset and e-business as an important new way of conducting business. The next few chapters draw these themes together by examining in more detail the strategies and practicalities for building an online knowledge business, a k-business. As we have seen, trading on the Internet is a tricky challenge. You can end up much richer or much poorer. How do you start to plan a course through this exciting but hazardous territory? Two of the early strategic decisions that have to be made are: (1) what role to play in the overall knowledge trading system; and (2) what online business model to adopt. This chapter evaluates the options.

We start by reviewing the different potential knowledge roles that can serve as the basis of your k-business focus. These can be in any part of the knowledge supply chain, from content creator to knowledge shop. There are also many positions for intermediaries such as aggregators and market makers. If your organization has completed a knowledge management audit (see page 11), it will have already identified some knowledge domains and value-adding knowledge processes in which you excel. Any of these or a combination can serve as the basis for market positioning. What must be borne in mind is that the Internet changes the dynamics of knowledge value systems, leading to the emergence of innovative roles or combinations, such as a collaborative community for new knowledge ventures.

The second part of the chapter analyses the different ways of generating revenues from knowledge through the Internet. These are divided into two main groups, fee and free. The wealth of free information on the Internet has conditioned many users to expect free content. Yet, if it has value and has taken time and effort to create, how can the supplier generate revenues from it? Advertising and affiliate marketing are possibilities. What content can be sold directly over the Internet for a fee? The answer to the fee vs. free dilemma is not easy, and depends very much on individual factors. This chapter concludes with some guidance on what might influence your business model decisions.

What kind of k-supplier are you?

Various ways of generating revenue from organizational knowledge were introduced at the end of Chapter 1. Your organization may have specialized knowledge that has value to a particular group of customers. It may have developed competencies in particular knowledge management processes. Knowledge businesses are part of a wider knowledge value system, in which knowledge flows from creator to consumer. At each step in between, knowledge is processed, perhaps being converted into new forms or being combined with other knowledge. Figure 3.1 shows a simplified model of such a system, depicted as two linear value chains, one for the knowledge supplier and one for the customer. In the supply

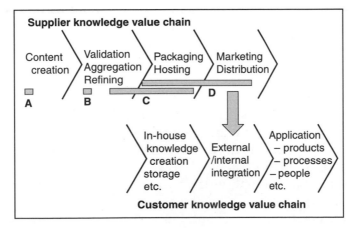

Figure 3.1 Supplier and customer knowledge value chains showing some possible positioning options

chain, content is created, processed in one or more ways, packaged in a form suitable for hosting on the Internet, then marketed and distributed. The customer integrates this knowledge into their own value chain and uses both internal and external knowledge to improve their products, processes, the skills of their people and so on.

This linear value chain representation is an oversimplification of what happens in practice, but it does provide a useful perspective for considering where to position your k-business. Your aim should be to build on your strengths and add value to the knowledge systems of your target customers. Few organizations have the capabilities to perform well in all aspects of the value system. You will probably need alliances with other suppliers. These may vary according to the type of customer and their knowledge needs. It may be that you are a good knowledge creator, but need partners to help with marketing and distribution. Or you might be a good knowledge aggregator, but need access to quality content creators. You may concentrate your efforts on one activity, such as suppliers A and B in Figure 3.1, or combine several activities, such as suppliers C and D. Let's now consider some k-business opportunities for each part of the supply chain. As we go through these options, you will note that many of them should already be receiving attention as part of your organization's knowledge management programme.

K-creator

Knowledge creation is a very diffuse activity. It takes place all the time in many situations. Much is generated as part of another activity, but little thought is usually given as to how to capitalize on it further. Knowledge consumers seek knowledge that addresses their immediate concerns. It follows that this knowledge is most valuable when it is readily usable in its new context. Creators of knowledge can add to its value by explaining its utility and areas of application. They also add value by presenting it in a form that can be applied with the minimum of effort by the user. Good packaging – a topic covered in detail in Chapter 5 – therefore plays an important part in enhancing the usefulness and value of knowledge. For an Internet-based business, compelling content is one of the main ways of attracting people to a website. This creates a strong demand for quality content, written and presented in a meaningful and attractive manner.

Knowledge creators such as authors and composers have traditionally relied on agents, large publishing houses or distributors to gain outlets for their work. Because of the time and investment involved, most creators have had to hand over publishing and marketing rights, usually on an exclusive basis, to those further along the supply chain. In return they receive royalty payments, typically amounting to only 10 per cent of sales. The ease of publishing on the Web and its much reduced costs of production and distribution alter the relative balance of power in the supply chain. If you are a well-known creator like Stephen King, then you may be able to publish and receive payments directly on your website.[1] For most creators, other online channels, such as broker or syndication sites, auctions and knowledge markets offer attractive outlets.[2]

> **Do you have a good story?**
>
> The idea behind goodstory.com is to give writers better access to buyers and agents via the Internet. Details of short stories, articles or books are posted on the website. The writers have to give permission to potential buyers to download the material, which is digitally watermarked to prevent copying. It was recently taken over by Creative Planet who provides similar facilities for creators in the movie, TV and music industries. Direct publication of eMatter (online content 'longer than an article but shorter than a book') is offered by MightyWords. In this arrangement, authors can receive up to 50 per cent royalties. Further along the value chain, Rightscenter.com is an online global rights exchange for agents, scouts and publishers.

K-mediary

At one time the Internet was hailed as an effective way of cutting out intermediaries. Manufacturers and creators can sell directly to consumers and avoid paying wholesalers, distributors and other organizations in the traditional supply chain. The result, experts argued, would be widespread 'disintermediation'. The reality is somewhat different. With millions of creators and millions of consumers, intermediaries can still play an important role in connecting those who seek knowledge to those who can provide it. At one level, an intermediary may just provide a meeting point, such as community or trading space. At another level, an intermediary may be more actively involved in attracting key participants to a trading hub and structuring its activities. Unlike an intermediary in a physical supply chain, a k-mediary is less likely to stock and distribute knowledge themselves, but simply connect buyers directly to the creator's knowledge repository, from which they can download the most up to date knowledge objects.

The primary added value of a k-mediary is in meta-knowledge – knowledge about knowledge. Yahoo!'s popularity stems from its structured hierarchy of information. Users can quickly converge on the section of index that interests them, and be directed rapidly towards relevant sources. K-mediaries can add more value for the consumer by evaluating knowledge quality from different creators. Examples of different types of k-mediary now follow.

K-aggregator

A knowledge aggregator consolidates knowledge from multiple creators, and brings it together in one place. It may be repackaged for resale under the aggregator's own brand name, but in many cases the original content creator already has a powerful brand name. Highly popular online information services such as Dialog initially positioned themselves as such one-stop-shops. Many also add value to the consumer by providing a consistent user interface (cf. the Northern Light screen of Figure 2.6).

News is one of the most popular types of information that is aggregated. NewsEdge and Moreover.com aggregate news from thousands of sources daily. Each story is categorized, usually by sophisticated software plus a small element of human editing. Users receive in their email or on their personal news page, headlines and synopses filtered and sorted according to their profiles of interests. As well as for news, there are aggregators for many other types of information including financial analyses, market research, company information and scientific discoveries.

Aggregators face two main challenges. The first is ensuring that they have a good spread of con-

> **One-stop business research**
>
> Powersize.com aggregates business research from over 10 000 sources, including newspapers, magazines, trade journals and newswires. Free access is provided to some 2400 sources, with access to others being offered on a subscription or pay-per-view basis, typically $2 to $5 per article. Users can search by category, company, industry or within a given date range. A free daily *Editor's Choice Newsletter* is sent by email. Each issue focuses on a particular theme and gives hypertext links to featured contents as well as free downloadable samples. Each month 12 million newsletters and alerts are emailed, providing an attractive audience for advertisers who can link offers to the topic of the email. Founded in 1997, Powersize's customer base grew rapidly and reached over 600 000 at the time of its announced acquisition by Hoover's Inc. in July 2000.

tent. Often this requires access to all the principal content creators in the relevant knowledge domain. The second is establishing a viable revenue model. The traditional revenue model, as exemplified by NewsEdge, is to charge the buyer, normally a corporate purchaser, and pay the content provider (who may be a publisher) a royalty based on usage. Moreover.com is attempting to turn this model on its head. By attracting thousands of end-users with free content, it hopes to attract revenues from publishers for connecting potential buyers of their products and services into their website – a form of advertising or referral fee.[3] Aggregators also generate revenues by providing services based on their aggregation expertise, such as customizing content for corporate intranets. This is another example of commercializing specialist knowledge processing know-how.

K-portal

Aggregation is just one facet of a much more broad-ranging portal. A portal is a gateway to knowledge. Former directory and search engine websites, such as Yahoo! and Lycos, have transformed themselves into generic portal sites. They offer categorized links, searches, shopping and online communities. The pulling power of these generic portals – AOL attracts over 100 million visitors a month worldwide – means that they can command significant advertising revenues. But for others who want to take advantage of this popularity, the cost can be high. Drkoop.com, for example, is reported to have agreed to pay AOL $89 million over four years to be one of its main health content providers. However, such high payments now seem questionable in view of Drkoop.com's own declining health from mid-1999.[4]

Alongside these mass market portals are many industry- and profession-specific portals. These offer users various combinations of basic information, detailed resources, news, job information and links to related sites.

Top 10 visited websites

The following are the most visited Web properties for August 2000. The survey is compiled from analysis of usage of a sample of households with Internet access in 13 countries (US, Canada, eight countries in Europe and three in Australasia).

	Website	Number of unique visitors
1	AOL	61.3 million
2	Yahoo!	61.2 million
3	MSN	51.2 million
4	Microsoft	48.9 million
5	Lycos	33.0 million
6	Excite	26.4 million
7	Disney (includes Go)	20.0 million
8	AltaVista	17.1 million
9	About.com	16.1 million
10	Time–Warner	15.2 million

The figures are dominated by the US, where eBay makes it into the top 10. These figures show the overall popularity of portals, which account for nine out of ten of the top sites.

Source: Nielsen/NetRatings. With acknowledgements.

By becoming the preferred home page of the specific audience they are targeting, they hope to attract high numbers of well-qualified users and therefore generate revenue through advertising, sponsorship and online sales.

Legalportal Canada (http://www.legalportal.ca) is an example of a niche portal. While its home page lacks the visual appeal of its mass market counterparts, it crams in over a hundred categorized links. There are links to legal directories, law firms, legal publishers, recruiters, precedents, discussion lists and a Cyberlaw encyclopaedia. One click on Canadian Legal Resources takes the user to another categorized list of 1100 entries covering conferences, courts, law schools and other categories. The home page also has many generic entries that are useful to any small professional business – local maps, airlines, lists of couriers, search engines and so forth. Primarily the effort of a single lawyer, Alan Gahtan, it is a natural point of call for those involved with Canadian legal matters, and a way of attracting clients. Gahtan comments: 'It's been really good for raising my profile in the legal community and for getting new clients. More than that, I use it to keep references to interesting material that I need in my own practice.'

K-refiner

One of the problems of many portal and aggregator websites is that the hyperlinked content is not validated for quality. On some portals the selection and prioritizing of items depends on payments by the creator, rather than its quality or value to the user. Many organizations' knowledge initiatives recognize the value of knowledge refining. This is where a subject matter expert, or knowledge editor, selects the best content, reviews it and may also create an abstract of it. One of the main selling points of subscription-based online information services is that users can be more confident in the quality of the content. Others have sorted out the wheat from the chaff for them. Of course, this is only true if some items have been filtered out, which is not true for those services that claim to be comprehensive.

> **Portal B™ – a scalpel for information searching**
>
> Following a survey of knowledge management professionals and librarians, which showed that search engines were regarded as 'blunt objects', the developers of Portal B (a service of Data Downlink) set about creating a portal for high value business information. Editors are used to select suitable content and websites, and a team of 70 Web indexers – professional librarians – scour the sources and categorize the material. The information professionals review, write abstracts, rate and index the links to over 10 000 websites and databases by hand. The human element in evaluating and refining is seen as a crucial role in 'breaking the search barrier'.
>
> *Website:* http://www.portalb.com

An interesting question is where and how k-refining is best carried out. Is it by the customer, for example by staff in their knowledge centre, who manage their intranet? Is it by independent third parties? It is interesting to note, that whereas at one time, some generic portals gave sites within sub-categories star ratings, many now simply list the 'top sites'. There is a general trend to peer review where other users, rather than editors, give ratings and comments. From a k-business perspective, a knowledge refiner must be certain that the extra costs associated with refining can be surpassed by the additional revenues generated. This may only be possible in specialist fields where the refiner has an established reputation as a subject matter expert.

K-packager

On websites, which supply information from multiple sources, users expect a degree of consistency in presentation and expect to be able to find what they want quickly. Having a good classification scheme and index usually helps faster retrieval. If a piece of information can only be viewed after payment of a fee, then the buyer rightly expects the description of that information to be clear and accurately indicate its content. In packaging terms, this is known as the wrapper. A wrapper can be as simple as the first few lines of text, such as the results returned by a typical search engine. It could also have more structured information like a bibliographic record, which includes title, author, publisher, creation date and abstract. As the supply of knowledge objects on the Internet becomes abundant, the wrapper must also act as a sales tool, enticing the reader to buy it rather than alternatives. Portals and aggregators may also have their own standards on structure, appearance, and content quality that need to be independently verified.

> **About.com – the human Internet**
>
> About.com is one of the fastest growing websites (now in the top 10 most visited sites). Its popularity comes from its structured directory, listing over 1 million entries in 50 000 subjects grouped into 36 channels. A key feature of the business is the use of 750 trained 'guides' operating in 20 countries. They review and create links for content in their specialist subjects. In return, they receive 30 per cent of the advertising revenues derived from their pages.
>
> *Website:* http://www.about.com

The k-packager role sits between the knowledge creator and portal or aggregator. Traditionally it is carried out by an editor and typesetter at a publishers or even the creator. But online knowledge needs better presentation and packaging if the full functionality of the Internet is to be exploited. This is therefore an emergent intermediary role that has not been fully developed, although some of iqport's guilds undertook this role on behalf of the creator (see page 113).

K-broker

A knowledge broker is another kind of intermediary between creator and aggregator. One type of knowledge broker seeks out content and creators. They use their personal networks to find world-renowned subject matter experts and highly saleable content. This is analogous to a commissioning editor at a publisher. Another type of broker acts as the human intermediary between a knowledge seeker and various knowledge sources. They respond to a client's request, questioning them intelligently about the knowledge and how they intend to use it. They then use their knowledge of different sources to select the most appropriate knowledge for their client. Teltech, a Minneapolis-based research company, is a good example of a k-broker that also adds features of other knowledge intermediary roles (see below).

Teltech: human brokers connect people to knowledge

At Teltech, a Minneapolis-based research organization, the broker role is performed by staff called knowledge analysts. Teltech's knowledge-based services combine the best of human assisted research with the best computer techniques. Its scientific and technical knowledge resides in thousands of online databases (many externally sourced) and its extended network of 3000 experts. These include retired industrialists, academics and part-time professionals. Teltech's core added value comes from the way it structures knowledge, its brokering expertise and its quality of service. Knowledge sources, both human and explicit, are classified using Teltech's 30 000 term thesaurus called KnowledgeScope™. Clients with research queries and problems contact Teltech's knowledge analysts, whose knowledge of all the sources at their disposal allow them to quickly identify the most relevant knowledge.

Teltech's approach has been extended to an online service with the launch of Teltech.com in September 1999. Developed around a set of 19 vertical industry portals – including petrochemicals, rubber and plastic, food and aerospace – its main features are:

- A directory of links to websites that have been selected for their relevant content.
- In-depth analyses of topical issues.
- The Northern Light search engine that connects users to high quality content, both on the Web and in specialist publications.

- Real-time news feeds for the specific industry.
- Online events where industry experts speak on a topic and answer users' questions.
- Access to leading experts, available for telephone consultation.
- Access to Teltech's knowledge analysts to offer user guidance or carry out research on the user's behalf.

On offer to clients is a combination of computer-held and human knowledge resources and do-it-yourself online research, assisted by human analysts and experts where appropriate. Such a combination helps researchers find relevant information more quickly. According to a survey cited by Teltech, researchers find what they want only 34 per cent of the time when directly searching the Web. With Teltech.com its survey of early users indicated that 90 per cent of respondents saved research time, while 74 per cent of them found more relevant information than other Web directories.[5]

K-publisher

A knowledge publisher coordinates several activities within the value chain to create the finished product. Established publishers, whether of books, periodicals or reports, have existing resources that they can make available on the Web. However, many have been cautious in what they offer online, so as not to jeopardize their existing hard-copy sales. Many publishers' websites are still rather limited, not allowing access to full text material. Even if you are enticed to check out contents of an archived magazine, sometimes all you see is a list of unhelpful links to 'Issue No 3 (July 1998)', 'Issue No 4 (August 1998)' etc. You can often get better information about the contents of a publisher's site from a search engine like Northern Light. Furthermore, if you want to buy a book from their online shop, you generally get a better deal from Amazon.com. And if you like a particular writer, there's a good chance that there is more up to date and stimulating material on the writer's own website. In short, many traditional publishers have been slow to adapt to the Web environment.

In contrast, publishers of E-zines and E-journals, created specifically for a Web audience, have had no such constraints. As well as benefiting from the lower costs of Web publishing, their publications can be kept continually up-to-date, and new material published in a timely manner, without regard to production schedules. The Web also lends itself to a different style of publishing, with shorter pieces and links to related material. News can be linked to library resources; analysis can be linked to online discussion groups and so on. The investor's website Motley Fool gives its viewers news, analysis and discussion boards. In addition, it encourages its users to sell their knowledge by making available reports at soapbox.com. The reports are rated by readers and the creator receives 60 per cent of the cover price (typically $10–100).

Effective use can also be made of multimedia. The BBC has exploited its vast reservoir of knowledge resources, from programme archives to real-time news, to create one of Europe's best content sites. Its news pages include audio and video clips, as well as links to earlier news on the same topic and to related stories, analyses and programmes on its other media (sound broadcasting and television).

K-mall or k-shop

This role is that of a retailer, offering an electronic shopping area on the Web. The 'shop' is stocked with appropriate selections and provides e-commerce facilities for ordering. Naturally, where information products are involved, the same unit of stock can be sold and delivered many times over. Unlike a real shop, the online shop can also display a much wider selection of goods. Bookstore Amazon.com boasts 2 million titles compared to around 30 000 in a typical book store. A shopping mall brings several shops together in one place. Early shopping malls on the Web tried, generally unsuccessfully, to transplant the real-world model into the new media. They would have a wide range of independent stores, which the user would browse to select their purchases. Many did not even aggregate the purchases into a single shopping basket.

There are, of course, many sites that sell knowledge in one form or another. There are information stores, such as the Economist Information Unit's online shop (EIU.com) and MightyWords.com mentioned earlier. Other sites, such as keen.com and ideaRocket.com, offer knowledge in the form of online advice, while you can seek out consultancy services at eTrask.com and Marketing Unlimited. Knowledge is also sold from many specialist portals. These wide-ranging examples raise the question of what a knowledge shop really is.

A few websites specifically position themselves as knowledge shops. Knowledgeshop.com was one of the earliest. Started in 1997 by Know Inc. its main focus is products and services for knowledge management, including seminars and courses. It also hosts expert communities and has a platform for knowledge networkers and entrepreneurs to co-create new knowledge businesses – knowledgecreators.com (see page 124). Knexa, on the other hand, offers knowledge over a range of subjects.

These and other websites positioning themselves as knowledge shops have had very hesitant starts. This suggests that knowledge is too broad in scope and too complex to be sold in online shopping baskets like many other products. Without significant investment, it is unlikely that a k-shop as broad-based in scope as Yahoo! or Amazon.com will emerge. Possible scenarios are:

- K-shops that specialize by knowledge domain, and are therefore likely to be an adjunct to a specialist portal.
- K-shops that specialize by type of knowledge – information, online advice, consultancy assignments, contracts etc.
- The addition of knowledge products to well-established existing online stores or auction sites, such as Amazon.com or eBay.

Creating a k-shop is challenging. First, you have to select your focus, such as a knowledge domain, or a type of knowledge product. Second, you have to do everything that a portal does to attract buyers and sellers. Finally, the nature of many knowledge products does not lend them naturally to being sold as standard items in a shopping basket. Therefore, an equally likely scenario to those above is that most online knowledge sales will take place within some kind of knowledge market. A knowledge market brings together knowledge providers and knowledge consumers in a more dynamic way than a portal or shop. Potential buyers and sellers share details of their wants and offers, and through a variety of bidding and negotiation mechanisms agree their sales contracts. A typical knowledge market is simply a form of business-to-business exchange, where the product is knowledge. Despite the challenges of selling knowledge, several knowledge markets have been launched and there is a growing interest in them as environments for knowledge trading. The potential importance of knowledge markets is such that the whole of the next chapter is devoted to examining them in more detail.

K-community

A knowledge community is the epitome of the early culture of the Internet. Through newsgroups, Internet chat rooms, email discussion lists and Web conferencing (message boards), people who share common interests freely exchange knowledge online.[6] A community of practice (see page 13) is an example of a knowledge community within an organizational setting. Cutting across departmental and geographic barriers, they are often one of the most important elements of a knowledge initiative. A community lets people tap into deeper personal knowledge than is readily available

on Web pages, documents or databases. Communities also add
vitally important social and relationship dimensions to knowledge
exchange.

> **E-vis.com – collaborating communities**
>
> E-vis.com brings the community concept with
> a difference to manufacturing supply chains. It
> provides collaborative workspace for project
> teams. Participants collaborate using a wide
> variety of tools – threaded discussion
> forums, 3-D visualization (useful for reviewing
> product designs), project management tools,
> Webcasts and online training. Users pay a
> modest monthly subscription fee.
>
> *Source:* http://www.evis.com

The value of communities has
frequently been overlooked by
businesses when building their
Internet presence. Yet the success
of Geocities, now part of Yahoo!,
was based entirely around providing facilities for their users to
create and grow their own communities. As well as discussion and chat
groups, communities have libraries of resources and participants can
create their own home pages. Much of Compuserve's revenues, before it
became part of AOL, derived from usage payments for its thriving professional forums. Businesses such as Topica and Egroups have been built
around the provision of community software and services.

Communities exhibit a property that many website owners aspire to –
'stickiness'. Their members return repeatedly to keep up-to-date with
the latest community developments and the evolving dialogue. A k-
community is a natural enhancement for a business-to-business website
or specialist portal. Product developers can access community knowledge
to test out new product ideas. Marketers can use them to sense what's
important to their customers. Unless you have particular influence in
bringing together a group of industry or professional peers from many
organizations (which independent analysts, consultancies, publishers
and membership organizations frequently do), then your ability to raise
revenues from community membership fees is severely limited. However,
the value that they bring in terms of attracting site visitors and gaining
community knowledge far exceeds any monetary return.

K-processor

To identify knowledge needs and sources in an organization, knowledge
managers are trained to ask: 'knowledge for what?' By understanding
how the recipient of knowledge will use it, the provider can make it
more relevant. It becomes even more useful if it is seamlessly integrated
into the recipient's work activity. Sometimes this integration is provided
in the form of an interactive dialogue. At the Virgin Wine website, users
can work their way through Wine Wizard. According to their answers,

they are then directed to the wines that are most likely to appeal to them. In the field of knowledge, Karl Erik Sveiby helps you assess your intellectual capital with his intellectual assets monitor calculator at http://www.sveiby.au.com. After your results are calculated, suggestions are given as to how to increase it, such as converting some human capital into structural capital.

Games and simulations are another way of conveying knowledge more effectively than simply through static information. The drug pipeline game by Searle Health puts you in the hot seat of a pharmaceutical manager steering a new drug from research and development through its clinical trials to launch.[7]

At the moment k-processing is normally a secondary role to one of the others. Adding some k-processing, such as Novartis does with its hypertension calculator, is a useful facility to add to any website, but not necessarily a k-business in its own right. However, in just a couple of years, applications service providers (ASPs) have emerged as distinct businesses for high volume generic products, such as finance and inventory management. Already many professionals manage their calendars and PC backups through Web-based services. These are the precursors of businesses with a k-processing focus.

K-franchiser

Franchising is already well established in many business areas, but what about knowledge? Methodologies and training courses are common ways in which knowledge is routinely franchised. Although the name franchise might not be used, any business that sells rights or licences to knowledge, such as business methods, can be considered knowledge franchising. The techniques of Neuro Linguistic Programming (NLP) have moved from the writings of two academics to a fully franchised knowledge business, where practitioners are licensed and accredited. Franchising offers a way of replicating knowledge where the supplier does not have to invest heavily in developing a delivery network, but provides the tools in the form of training, business methods and copyright material, for others to build their own knowledge delivery businesses. In return they receive registration and licence payments, fees for materials, and usually a percentage commission or royalty on sales.

As online knowledge demand increases and online knowledge business models become proven, we can expect to see online k-franchising become a recognized business. The idea of franchising knowledge management programmes has already been explored by Victoria Ward,[8] while First

Tuesday represents a method of knowledge networking that has become replicated around the world and is indicative of the k-franchising opportunity (see below).

First Tuesday: knowledge networking through franchising

First Tuesday is an example of a thriving knowledge network in action. It was started as a meeting of friends, and friends of friends, in London's Soho Alphabet Bar in October 1998 by venture capitalist Julie Meyer. It quickly became a regular event with a buzz. Ideas bounced around and connections were made between potential Web entrepreneurs and financiers. As a result several dot.com companies emerged from these meetings. These include several knowledge intensive businesses – Moreover.com (customized news), edreams (travel site offering expertise for a fee) and the now defunct clickmango.com (health products and advice). Over $150 million in seed capital has been raised from introductions at these meetings, where participants put coloured dots on their name badges – red for investors, green for entrepreneurs and yellow for professional service providers. The format has expanded to 98 cities world-wide and membership now exceeds 70 000. A challenge that Meyer faced in early 2000 was how to commercialize on the success of this network. Although licence fees for the local networks were one potential source a much more valuable one would be to take a commission of just 2 per cent from any venture capital deal that originated from a First Tuesday meeting. In Spring 2000 she had already gained $1 million initial funding to franchise First Tuesday, and reported that some venture capitalist firms had already accepted her commission proposal, based on the quality of new ventures that have emerged. Other potential ways to capitalize on this networking knowledge include publications, events and courses. In the event, First Tuesday was sold to Israeli seed-stage venture capitalist Yazam for $50 million in July 2000. Its basic format, though, continues to thrive and replicate.[9]

K-anything

The knowledge role of a k-business does not have to be any of those that have been discussed so far. Anything that enhances the usefulness of knowledge, how to find and use it, brings value to the consumer. New mechanisms and models are continually emerging as innovators combine knowledge elements in a myriad of different ways. The number of different pathways through a knowledge value system multiples as knowledge

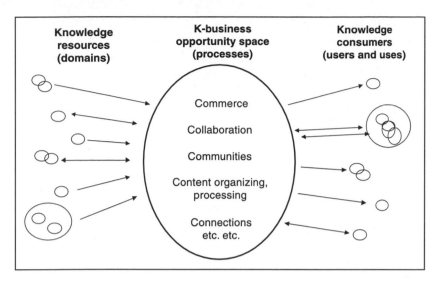

Figure 3.2   K-business opportunity space

moves from person to person, and changes between explicit and tacit. A k-business can focus on specific knowledge domains or applications, on specific knowledge processes, or any of the infinite number of possible combinations.

This vast opportunity space is depicted in a simplified way in Figure 3.2. Every element or pathway represents a potential k-business. Analysis of this space is the kind of activity that should be addressed by a knowledge management programme. Looking outside-in (at customer knowledge and unmet needs) and inside-out (what you have to offer in terms of knowledge content or process expertise), as discussed at the end of Chapter 1, are good ways to seek k-business opportunities. You can use the proven knowledge management technique of matching a problem/needs database with an idea bank, to help to identify and prioritize opportunities. Use your intranet as a planning tool by creating communities based around new business ideas. You might even incentivize participants by offering shares in any businesses that emerge. Above all, your intranet can be an ideal test-bed for your new k-business.

From fee to free

We now turn our attention to different business models that an online knowledge business can pursue. Despite all the red ink on the profit and loss accounts of dot.com companies, many Internet businesses do make a healthy profit. This is because they have developed a viable revenue-generating model for their business as a whole. One of the difficulties facing information and knowledge providers is the expectation of many consumers that information on the Internet is free. This is now true even for patent information, which was previously available only through a costly subscription to a proprietary online service. There are several reasons why such information may be provided free:

- the provider is a public sector organization such as the European Patent Office which offers a public service and does not have to recoup costs;
- the supplier is a patent attorney, such as Australia's Phillips Ormonde & Fitzpatrick, using free information as a marketing tool for its legal services;
- the information is provided by a university professor who wants to share his or her knowledge more widely.

But this is not all. The entire contents of *Encyclopaedia Britannica*, which cost millions of dollars to compile, were made available on the Internet at no charge in October 1999.[10] $20 million was reputedly spent in promoting the relaunch of its website as a free reference resource. Why? It needed to recover lost ground following a dramatic decline in sales caused by the introduction of lower cost CD-ROM encyclopaedias such as Microsoft's *Encarta*. *Encyclopaedia Britannica* therefore decided to reposition itself as a knowledge portal, and base its future on its trusted brand name and authoritative content. It expects to generate healthy revenues from online advertising and e-commerce, selling related products and services and syndicating content.

With the growing abundance of quality free material on the Internet, how viable is it for a k-business to charge fees for online knowledge? As we shall see later (page 92), fees for online knowledge are far from uncommon. Buyers will pay for something distinctive that gives them extra value. This may be additional or unique knowledge, better search options, customization or additional services. Various ways of enhancing the perceived value of a basic online knowledge product are covered further in Chapter 5.

Like *Encyclopaedia Britannica*, most Internet business models will have a component of information or knowledge that is free to the consumer. The basic premise behind this strategy is that it attracts buyers to your fee-paying products and services. The Internet is used to build presence, convey quality and establish your reputation. Free information generates sales leads and should make it easier to convert visitors into revenue generating customers. This is the marketing technique of progression, one of the ten Ps of Internet marketing that is covered in Chapter 7. Other reasons for providing free information are:

- To encourage wide readership, thus making the website attractive to advertisers.

- Because it has been superseded by more up to date information.
- To provide an indication of the quality of knowledge available from the same source.
- To act as a marketing hook for other fee paying information or services.

Useful knowledge

The main reason why professional people visit websites is to gather information.[11] They seek knowledge that will help them do their job better. Amongst the most sought after content is news and analysis, market surveys, product information, 'how to' guides and reference material.

A k-business website that is not a recognized portal must have content that is unique or world-class to attract significant numbers of visitors. It also needs to be well referenced by search engines and other websites covering similar ground, or well marketed (see Chapter 6). Take the field of knowledge management as an example. Few knowledge professionals will not have visited *Sveiby on Knowledge*, the website of knowledge management guru Karl Erik Sveiby at http://www.sveiby.com.au. It features on virtually every list of KM resources, has received many favourable reviews in the knowledge press and has links from many other KM sites.

Remember too that the Internet is more than just the Web. The Web is predominantly a 'pull' medium. As such, users must consciously access it to retrieve information. A complementary strategy is to use email to 'push' information to your target market. These emails can be regular newsletters or occasional alerts about new information, products or services. These emails can include hotlinks to your website thereby making it easier for readers to browse items of interest. Irish Internet service company NUA illustrates both these points (see below).

> ### NUA: 'making free content pay'
>
> NUA is a Dublin-based company with a New York office that specializes in the delivery of Web publishing solutions. Founder Gerry McGovern believes very much in the notion that free content is valuable. He personally writes a weekly thought-provoking email called *New Thinking* which is described as 'contributing to a philosophy for the information age'. Since 1996 NUA has distributed *NUA Internet Surveys* – 'The Number One Resource for Statistics' – a summary of Internet surveys carried out by research companies across the world. Each edition provides a summary of survey results and hotlinks to the respective research websites. A recent addition, in Spring 2000, was *NUA Knowledge News*. With a combined readership of over 250 000, these free email newsletters keep the

name of NUA prominent amongst its target audience. They complement the website, which archives the content by topic and gives additional summary information.

In describing his original motive for starting *NUA Internet Surveys*, McGovern comments: 'I figured that getting information was the key reason people used the Internet. We wanted to target journalists who were researching articles on the Internet and managers who were planning major Internet developments. Both these groups needed statistics on the Internet, but in 1996 these statistics were hard to come by. Our idea was to summarize surveys and other reports, to categorize them very well, and to make them easily searchable, thus creating a useful resource. The objective was to become the No. 1 website that people would use to gather such information, and I think we've pretty much achieved that objective.'

The website itself is not a main revenue earner. No referral fees are paid by the companies whose surveys are featured although the website does generate revenue from a limited amount of advertising. McGovern states categorically that the newsletters mostly help in branding and marketing: 'I believe that quality information is the foundation of brand-building on the Internet.' He points to clear evidence that it has helped NUA gain customers for its Internet implementation services: 'We have won customers such as Lucent Technologies, Procter & Gamble and Thomas Publishing because managers from these organizations were using our information to put together their Internet business plans, and then decided to contact us when they wanted to implement them.' The NUA website also acts as showcase for its Web publications expertise, offered as NUA's Web Publishing service. Another benefit arises from the process of gathering information on Internet developments: 'It keeps NUA sharp and up to date on our marketplace.'

For NUA, delivering free information has proved to be an effective strategy in helping to build the business to the size and reputation it is today, with over 100 employees and cited in *Fortune* as amongst the world's top Internet companies.

Source: Gerry McGovern, Founder and CEO, NUA.
Website: http://www.nua.ie

Relationship building

Attracting visitors to your website is the first stage of developing a relationship with them. Your aim should be to strengthen that relationship through knowledge exchange and ongoing commercial transactions that benefit both parties. There are several ways of using the Internet for relationship building:

- *Frequently Asked Questions (FAQ) pages.* Providing answers to common questions shows that you understand customers' concerns and have addressed them. Of course, FAQs also save you time and money by allowing the customer to get answers themselves, rather than calling your telephone advice or support lines.
- *Automated email responses.* These can provide a rapid response when potential customers want more detailed information on specific products and services. An email also gives information in a form that they can easily forward to colleagues. If you think that an automated response is too impersonal, then you can always send a personally composed follow-up email.
- *Offer multiple ways of contacting your organization.* If every Web page is identified with a contact for enquiries, potential customers can make immediate email contact to the most relevant individual. Many organizations fail to recognize that many potential customers may find it more convenient to use other methods. Making contact name and address, telephone and fax numbers prominent on key pages will broaden the communications channel with your marketplace.
- *Registration forms.* These can be used to capture data on your visitor's main areas of interest. Keeping them simple and not too onerous, and offering some tangible benefits in exchange for completing them (see page 212) will increase their effectiveness.
- *Email alerts.* By customizing these to a visitor's interests, you can make them aware when your website has important new information or when you have products and service announcements to make.

As relationships develop with a particular organization or community, then you can customize Web pages for them. This can extend to providing customers with a tailored version of your website to run on their intranet. Dell does this with its Premier Pages for its preferred customers. Product selections, pricing and purchasing conditions can all be customized. While such arrangements do not necessarily generate revenues directly, they make it easier for customers to buy from your website. You are also enhancing your relationship and customer capital, which may well have marketable value.

Free exchange?

An important part of the ethos of the Internet is free exchange of information and knowledge. That's what happens in online communities. But such exchanges are not recorded as transactions, since a thriving community relies on reciprocity. On one occasion you contribute your knowledge and on another occasion receive knowledge, usually from somebody completely different. These knowledge transactions are not tallied up as 'I owe yous', although you may make a mental note that you are putting in more than you are getting out, and therefore spend less time contributing in future. But what if such exchanges were tallied up in a favour bank, where units of value are assigned according to user ratings? This is, after all, only formalizing some mental models that already exist.

Now consider this type of exchange. You want to make people aware that you have valuable knowledge for sale. You decide to make it visible on a knowledge portal. In return for your entry, though, the portal provider demands that you evaluate two other knowledge contributions. This 2:1 reciprocity already happens on the net at GarageBand.com. Here the product is music rather than knowledge. Hopeful rock bands can upload a song in MP3 format, provided that they listen and rate two others selected randomly and sent to them for evaluation. Similarly, formalized exchange without fees is how some advertising banner networks operate. Your advert will be posted once each time you post two others (work that one out!).[12]

Even though there are online advice sites that do charge a fee, many carry on the Internet tradition of offering free advice. One of the first was www.allexperts.com that has thousands of volunteer professionals, who generally answer questions within a day. More recent additions include Ask a Librarian, run by a consortium of British libraries, Ask An Expert and Askme.com.[12]

From free to fee

What ways can revenues be generated from a knowledge-intensive website? The most obvious way is to offer knowledge products and services for sale. For knowledge that is packaged in well-defined forms such as pages of information, booklets and reports, this may not be too difficult. But what about more valuable knowledge in the form of expertise, consultancy services and the like? Not too long ago it was thought that only low priced items, costing no more than around $100, could be sold directly from a Web page. Today, we know that expensive cars can be sold this way, although for payment and contractual reasons the sale is usually completed with a signed hard-copy contract. Consumers are prepared to buy expensive items when they know the product well and they believe that they are getting value for money. They may have already gained sufficient product knowledge by sampling them in the real world, such as test-driving the car they plan to buy. Or they may have received recommendations from friends. The reputation and after-sales support of the supplier is also important.

In the case of knowledge products and services, the potential customer may find it much more difficult to evaluate them. For a start, it is not necessarily a standard product that can be precisely described. Only when knowledge has been pre-packaged into well-defined and under- stood elements is a sale straight from a Web order form likely to occur. Buying a place on a scheduled public course is such an example. For many other products and services, such as consultancy, a significant amount of sales effort goes into dialogue between buyer and seller – under- standing needs, demonstrating how the knowledge and its delivery can satisfy the user's needs, and coming to a mutual agreement on the details of the offer. In these situations, the best that can be hoped for from the Web pages is that they do enough to stimulate this dialogue. They need to convey the nature of the product or service, show samples of output, and refer to real case examples that relate to the customer's needs and inspire confidence. All this can be carried out online, although it does need more than a Web order form to complete a sale! In my own business, I have undertaken many short assignments, including consultancy and running client workshops, as a result of such a process. Clients have discovered about the services we offer from our website. An ensuing email dialogue has clarified their needs, leading to proposals that are then refined through negotiation culminating in a sale – all done over the Internet. Sometimes the first indication I have had that the engagement is real rather than virtual is when somebody greets me at a distant foreign airport!

Subscription vs. pay-as-you-go

Selling knowledge in the form of information online is generally an easier proposition than selling expertise. Database hosts like Dow Jones and Dialog have been doing this for years. The basic revenue model of such ser- vices is a subscription fee which gives users unlimited access – at least for a specified number of simultaneous users – to their information databases. This works well for librarians and others who know that a subscription costing $10 000 or more will be well used. Where it acts as a disincentive is where end-users, such as engineers and marketers, want access to specific information on an ad-hoc basis during a project. They prefer to buy specific pieces of information, which typically cost $2 to $25, on a pay-as-you-go basis.

Even for end-users, subscriptions have their place. Consumer Reports Online (CRO) has a thriving following of over 480 000 online subscribers who typically pay $24 a year.[14] In the field of business, the *Wall Street Jour- nal*, whose annual subscription is $59 a year, has over 250 000 subscribers.

In contrast, the *Financial Times*, that initially charged subscriptions (at least for its back issues), is now completely free.[15] In another twist, mad.co.uk gives access to several sources, and offers pay-per-view, even though some of its providers offer their information only on a subscription basis.

> **The human genome – free and fee**
>
> In July 2000, the first sequencing of the human genome was announced. The once strong rivalry between the publicly funded Human Genome Program and privately funded Celera Genomics, founded by Craig Ventner, was smoothed over. While the basic DNA sequences – some 3.5 billion of them – will be posted on the Internet free, there will still be many opportunities to create fee-based services. Celera charges subscriptions to corporate subscribers for access to its database that contains additional information. DoubleTwist charges for software processing tools that help scientists analyse and interpret the basic genome information.

In practice, suppliers would do well to offer a mix of both models. Pay-as-you-go information will attract first time buyers or occasional users, while those who turn into regular buyers will benefit from subscription. By segmenting a market into different groups of users who buy different amounts with different frequencies it is possible to increase overall revenues. This requires gaining understanding of the volume-price curve for the knowledge on offer. Up-front subscriptions represent a threshold that many customers will not be prepared to jump without some encouragement.[16] On the other hand, thousands, perhaps even millions, of busy professionals will be prepared to fork out small sums even for unfamiliar items. As a seller of information, would you rather have 100 subscriptions at $10 000 or sell 1 million individual items at an average price of $5? Or better still – both!

Advertising

Selling products and services is only one way of generating revenues from a website. Web advertising is doubling every year. Jupiter Communications predicts that advertising revenues will grow from £4.3 billion in 1999 to over $27 billion in 2005.[17] Most revenues come from banner advertisements placed prominently (usually at the top) on content pages. For each thousand advertisements seen by visitors the site owner receives a payment, typically $10, though targeted and portal sites can command prices over $50. Unfortunately for advertisers, the 'click-through' rate, i.e. the proportion of times that the viewer clicks on a displayed ad – has declined rapidly over the past few years to less than half a per cent on average. Many organizations have now embarked on professional Web campaigns to improve the targeting and appeal of banners. With strap lines such as 'Takes the anal out of analysis', a campaign aimed at UK

What sized banners?

The banner got its name from its long rectangular shape which frequently adorns the top of a Web page. Other shapes and sizes are gaining in popularity, but there is wide variation. The recommended standard Web advertisement sizes are:

Full banner – 468 × 60 pixels
Full banner with vertical navigation bar – 392 × 72 pixels
Half banner – 234 × 60 pixels
Vertical banner – 120 × 240 pixels
Button 1 – 120 × 90 pixels
Button 2 – 120 × 60 pixels
Square button – 125 × 125 pixels
Micro button – 88 × 31 pixels

Another popular size for a full banner is 460 × 55 pixels.

Source: Internet Advertising Bureau; http://www.iab.net

---

private investors by financial site TheStreet.com, saw its click-through rate increase from 0.4 to more than two per cent.[18] An interesting experiment at MIT shows how the use of cooperating intelligent software agents can enhance click-through rates. In one experiment an agent was used to select banner ads for a website. It achieved a click-through rate of 4.5 per cent. However, when several agents shared information cooperatively, they were able to achieve 8.6 per cent click-through.

As indicated in Chapter 2, not all advertising needs to be as blatant as banner advertisements. Promotional links, entries in directory listings, extra payments for bold or extended entries are other ways of generating advertising revenue. Sponsorship is a related form of advertising, in which a sponsor pays a fee for being associated with a given site or particular Web pages. It is commonly used in professional email lists, where each emailed newsletter carries a few lines of advertising from that edition's sponsor. Having a well-respected company as sponsor can also add credibility to a website.

One of the problems in seeking advertising revenues is that placements are concentrated in just a few highly visited sites. Fifteen sites, such as Yahoo! and ABC Sports, account for 75 per cent of all advertising revenues.[19] As in the real world, there are a whole host of advertising support services that will help you sell advertising, place or swap banner ads, and even give detailed analyses of visitors and click-through patterns.

For most k-businesses, selling advertising on your site is generally not a big revenue generator (see Table 3.1).[20] If you can attract the right sort of advertiser (e.g. your business partners) without much effort, then it is a worthwhile addition. B2B portal VerticalNet generated $18 million from advertising in 1999, 90 per cent of its total revenues. Unless you too have

Table 3.1 Advertising terminology and revenues

Hits	Number of accesses to your server (a common statistic but not relevant to advertisers, since each image on a page needs a separate access)
Page views or impressions	The number of times a specific page has been selected by viewers
CPM (cost per thousand)	Terminology carried over from conventional advertising (the M is the Roman symbol for 1000). Usually refers to impressions. Typical CPM for broad based advertisements is $10 and declining
CTR (click-through rate)	The percentage of page views that result in a click on the advertisement (typically 1/2 to 2 per cent)
Revenue generated from 100 000 visitors	100 000 views × $10 CPM = $1000 less agency fees, discounts etc. Equivalent to $2 per click-through. The advertiser must convert these into sales. If the conversion rate is 5 per cent, i.e. this percentage of referrals result in sales, then the cost is $40 per sale. Does your site attract the right type of person that this is a worthwhile cost for the advertiser?

created a portal that is a 'must visit' for a specific audience, or have some intelligent agents on your side, then don't count on getting rich on advertising. You may also need to be careful about who you let advertise on your site, especially when using banner ad networks. Ask yourself: would you let this organization advertise in your product catalogue?

Affiliate programmes

In affiliate programmes the website owner gets a fee for referring users to the affiliate sites. Amazon.com was an early pioneer of affiliate marketing. It has thousands of affiliates who earn referral fees by directing users from their websites to Amazon.com. The affiliate adds an identifier code to the Amazon hyperlink on their site, so that the referral can be tracked. An affiliate earns fees when the visitor to Amazon makes a purchase. They receive 15 per cent of the purchase price where the link takes the buyer to a specific book, or 10 per cent of sales where the link is to the Amazon site in general. Affiliates receive regular statements showing how many referrals were made from their site, and which resulted in purchases. Once a quarter they receive their fees. A slightly different affiliate programme is run by EGroups.com, a website for online communities.

It offers $300 for each successful referral of a list with more than 250 members.

As with advertising, a site needs to generate a significant amount of traffic to see any sizable revenue for low-ticket items. In common with advertising, there are affiliate marketing programmes, such as that from LinkShare, that help you identify and create appropriate affiliation deals.

Affiliate revenues for a Web page with 100 000 visitors a month:

$$100\,000 \text{ visitors} \times 2\% \text{ CTR} \times 5\% \text{ conversion rate (sales per referral)}$$
$$\times \$20 \text{ item} \times 10\% \text{ commission} = \$200$$

If, on the other hand, the referral is to a consultant who receives an assignment, even a 5 per cent referral fee can be worthwhile. Finders' fees are not at all uncommon in the consultancy business among individual consultants or small consultancies. When they cannot address the needs of a potential client, they pass on the lead to others in their network who offer complementary skills. However, the referrer's reputation is at risk if the recommended consultant does not satisfy the client. Affiliates therefore need to be doubly sure that they link to reputable organizations. The online affiliate model has yet to develop for professional services, although referral fees of good candidates for recruitment sites and headhunters are not untypical (although not widely publicized online).

Commissions and revenue sharing

Each role covered in the first part of this chapter – aggregator, shop, portal etc. – can generally be used to seek some form of revenue sharing from business partners. A shopping site will add its mark-up or take a commission. These are usually smaller than the equivalent margin for physical goods in retail store. An aggregator may charge either buyers or sellers. Who pays what to whom depends on relative market power, who processes the transaction, and who takes the risk. Some market sites charge for listing products while others charge only on sales. Some business exchanges may charge buyers to go through a pre-qualification process. Band-X, a telecommunications bandwidth exchange, takes a 0.625 per cent commission from whichever party posted a bid or offer. Since the final negotiations take place party-to-party without Band-X involvement, it gives a quarter of its commission to the responder so that they 'remember' to report a deal.[21] Some sites pay users up to $10 an hour simply to surf the net, in exchange for allowing banner advertisements in their browser window.[22] The popular email software product Eudora has two prices – free if you have non-removable pop-up adverts in your mail window, and $50 if you don't.

We noted earlier how Freeserve started the avalanche of free Internet Service Providers in the UK. Until they arrived on the scene in 1998, an ISP connection would cost typically £10 ($15) a month. Freeserve spotted the opportunity to negotiate with BT, the UK's main telecommunications provider, to share the telephone call charges that Freeserve subscribers incurred by going online. After all, Freeserve attracted new users and encouraged more surfing, giving BT revenues that they might not otherwise have gained.[23]

> **SciQuest.com – from free to fee**
>
> A dramatic shift has taken place in the sources of revenue for life sciences e-marketplace SciQuest.com. In 1998, most revenues came from advertising. By mid-2000 90 per cent came from e-commerce commissions (typically 10 per cent) of goods sold through its website. It is also expecting to create new revenue streams from software licences and the sale of information, such as supplier's quality and delivery times.
>
> *Source:* 'Who will profit from the Internet Agora?', Robert D. Hof, *Business Week e.biz* 5, June 2000

Knowledge buyers and sellers need to be alert to revenue sharing opportunities and topsy-turvy business models. You might expect to receive payment for your knowledge, but with busy professionals struggling with information overload, what if you have to pay them to consume it? It already happens in some professions. Graduates in subjects ranging from archaeology to marine biology pay to go on 'digs' and expeditions where the number of applicants far exceeds the number of available places. You could view paying consumers as a form of marketing expense. Pay them to take some of your knowledge, but have in reserve some more highly valued knowledge for which they pay you.

Karl Erik Sveiby, one of the first people to analyse know-how industries,[24] has examined the various ways in which knowledge industries can charge for knowledge (see below).

Fourteen ways to charge for knowledge: Karl Erik Sveiby

What is the value of an idea that comes in the flash of a second but is based on a life of experience? It is hardly the time spent on it. Basing the value of knowledge on time spent can never be correct; still it is the most common. What other ways are there to charge for knowledge? Let's look at how the knowledge industries charge for their knowledge. They are ranked from one to fourteen, with the most attractive on my personal ranking list listed as number one.

1   Take intangible revenues into account
The most challenging and most creative way to charge for knowledge is to take the intangible revenues into account. With very few exceptions authors of management books do not get rich from the royalties. So

why do consultants spend long unpaid hours in front of their word processors? Because a published book generates publicity and credibility among potential clients. Intangible revenues are flows of knowledge and they come in three forms – revenues that add to the External Structure (e.g. customer relationships), to the Internal Structure (e.g. business processes) or to the competence of the employees. Intangible revenues are seldom made explicit, yet they are often the major reason why a project or an assignment is undertaken.

2   Link royalty to financial output or outcome

The oldest and most established method is the 'royalty'. Authors, software developers, designers and inventors, tend to be paid for their intellectual property rights in the form of a percentage on the long-term revenues from their creative efforts, particularly if they are independent professionals. Royalty is a simple and good method, because it links the output directly to the input. But it is simple only if the creative effort has been formalized into a product or tangible/visible outcome that is protected by law.

3   Link success fee to non-financial outcome

A success fee can be linked to a non-financial outcome. The most common today is its negative counterpart: a penalty if certain conditions are not fulfilled, e.g. if a deadline is not met. A more positive approach is to link a success fee to pre-determined non-financial indicators, e.g. quality of output or customer satisfaction. Obviously, if one links a success fee to survey results the survey methodology has to be impeccable.

4   Create insurance premium

This might be the oldest knowledge charging system in the world! In ancient China the patients paid a monthly fee as long as they were well but they expected to be treated for no cost when taken ill. The charges and the taxes that finance community services are financed in the form of an insurance system. You pay when you are healthy or have a job or a house for times when you are ill, jobless or the victim of a fire.

5   Transfer price

Transfer pricing is common practice in team sports. Soccer clubs and basket ball clubs 'buy' and 'sell' their stars, sometimes at incredible prices. The star usually also receives a share of the price. Transfer prices are not common in other industries, often because civil law does not allow it. The laws are the legacy of the industrial era, and were installed to protect workers to be exploited by employers. Today's professionals are more like the sports stars and perfectly capable to care for themselves, so it is likely that transfer prices will become common practice in professional services and other knowledge organizations.

6   Let the supplier pay

How is it possible to charge the supplier instead of the customer? It is much more common than one might think. Why is most of the content on the Internet free? How can it be that the commercial channels on TV do not cost you as the viewers anything? Because there are more people with a message to tell than there are people who want to listen. So the market forces have created a market on which the suppliers of information pay, not the consumers.

7   Charge for a team

Some big consulting firms charge a fixed amount per team inclusive of expenses, rather then per consultant. It is a method pioneered by the strategy consulting firm McKinsey as an approach of creating more flexibility for planning their resources. The client should in principle not have to care about who is assigned to the project; whether they are flown in or locally based. For the knowledge company the method has the nice added benefit of allowing for lifting the charges of the lowest paid associates and for the seniors to spread very thinly on many assignments. There are not many firms in the position to use this method, though. It requires a high level of concept standardization and very high project management skills.

8   Package the solutions

The dilemma facing most knowledge sellers is that the offering cannot be made visual or real until it has been delivered. Moreover, the customer often contributes to the solution. This amplifies the pricing problem. One approach to reduce the problem is to make the offering a 'product'. Most service firms sell their service as packages, for instance travel, hotels and airlines. The knowledge company's equivalent is the 'Concept'. Much of the conceptual developments made by management consultants belong in this category, such as 'total quality'. The latest trend is to trademark the concepts in order to gain more protection: EVA, Intangible Assets Monitor, IC-Index, to mention a few examples.

9   Commission

A well-established method is to pay a 'commission'. Commission is similar to a royalty in that it is generally tied to the commercial value of a transaction. The advantages are that it is easy to negotiate and simple to follow up. The major disadvantage is that commission is a one-off, thus does not encourage long-term relationships.

10 Link fee to other vehicles

The financial services industry charges by using 'spread' (difference in buy/sell prices) or commission on the capital raised. Union membership fees are often linked to the salary. Needless to say such practices can be very profitable for the vendor, because they conceal the real cost, but they are increasingly being phased out in the banking industry and it will be interesting to see how commission fees will hold up in the onslaught of the Internet.

11 Buy into customer

Instead of charging a fee in cash, the knowledge company might transfer the whole or part of the fee into shares in the company they work with. This is similar to profit-sharing, although the involvement and the risks become much greater. It is the backbone of the revenues for the venture capital industry, the most valuable and rarefied knowledge of which is their managers' ability to pick and back successful entrepreneurs.

12 Link fee to input

To charge a percentage on the input is a fairly simple method and has been used by knowledge companies for a long time. Head-hunters often charge a percentage of the salary of the new employee. The method is simple, because generally the input is easier to establish than the output, but it is not a very good approach. The method is rightly regarded with suspicion by customers since it has a built-in incentive to increase their costs.

13 Retainers

Retainers are common practice in the consulting industry, particularly for small consulting firms for which it adds a sense of security. It is like being employed part-time. Retainers are also used by vendors to a large corporation that take over outsourced internal departments like recruitment, facilities management, IT department. Even if retainers do not have to be linked to time spent, they are no remedy to the fee-for-time problem.

14 Tender

Tender has long been established practice in technical consulting where projects are well defined. The vendor offers a fixed price irrespective of the time involved. Engineers and Architects are used to it. The advantage from the clients' point of view is of course that they can compare similar offers. The problem from the vendors' point of view is that the tendering process is a risk-reducing exercise so it reduces the incentive to come up with creative solutions. The yardstick tends to be the price offered, so the offering is commodified to such an extent that it becomes unprofitable.

Which is the best model?

What these methods indicate is the difficulty in choosing an appropriate pricing mechanism for knowledge. Where knowledge is explicit and in standard packages, the Internet can provide a marketplace where price comparisons can be made. As in other markets, price transparency can lead to commoditization, where there is pressure to reduce prices. For tacit knowledge it is easier to charge based on inputs, such as time spent, rather than the contribution of knowledge to outputs and outcomes. However, this can limit earning potential, whereas an efficient knowledge business charging a fixed price or price based on output could make more profit through taking less time.

Whatever the attractions for a supplier in seeking to generate revenues from selling knowledge, it is important to bear in mind that there will always be others willing to give similar knowledge away free.[25] Similarly, in the real world many expensive lawyers give a proportion of their time for 'pro bono' work. In the virtual world, free and fee go hand in hand. Who pays what to whom depends on many factors. What is good for one supplier in one market for one type of knowledge may be totally inappropriate in another. A good approach is to review evidence of other models at work in your market space, then think creatively about new ones. Having got several options in place, review your business model against the following ten criteria:

1   Does it leverage other existing revenue streams?
2   Does it minimize cost? How easy is it to increase efficiency?
3   How easy (and costly) is it to scale – by a factor of 10, 100, 1000?
4   Are there appropriate incentives for others in the customer's knowledge value system?
5   What are the business risks? Are they limited or open-ended? How predictable is the outcome?
6   What stops it becoming sustainable in the medium to long-term?
7   How novel is it for consumers? Are there existing practitioners or analogues in related markets?
8   Does it increase your customer knowledge?
9   Does it increase your customer's knowledge?
10   Does the model increase your own knowledge and intellectual capital at minimum cost?

The Internet and markets for knowledge are full of potential surprises – and consequently opportunities for innovative business models.

Summary

This chapter has considered two key components of a k-business strategy. The first is the positioning of the knowledge business in the overall knowledge value system. This was done from both a supplier and consumer viewpoint. Many different knowledge roles are possible. These include being a k-aggregator, k-portal, k-refiner and k-franchiser. Selecting the most appropriate role or roles depends partly on your organization's distinctive knowledge competencies, but also on other market participants and what alliances you can negotiate.

The second strategic element considered was that of finding a viable business model. Two main groups were explored – fee and free. The first are those models where selected information or knowledge is given free to the consumer. This approach is used to create market awareness and for reputation and relationship building. The second set of models are those where fees are generated though a website. These fees may be for the direct selling of knowledge itself, but can also be for advertising, affiliation and sales commissions.

The main conclusion to be drawn from the variety of possible approaches is that there are no clear rules for success. What works in some cases may not work in others. The Internet is a place where topsy-turvy business models abound. Therefore, the k-business's primary emphasis should be on experimentation and innovation – adding to their own knowledge of their k-business environment.

Points to ponder

1 What unique and sought after knowledge does your organization possess that could be the basis for a k-business?

2 In which knowledge activities do you have well developed competencies, perhaps evident through the activities of a formal knowledge management programme?

3 Are there existing portals or aggregators for the knowledge domains in which you excel? If so, could you become a preferred business partner of one? If not, could you rapidly establish one yourself?

4 Examine what knowledge you currently sell (whether offline or online). How well is it packaged and described to potential buyers?

5 What kind of sampling methods do you have in place for consumers to gauge the quality of the knowledge you have to offer?

6 Look at the Teltech case on page 80. Could you provide a similar service for your focused domain?

7 Consider your organization's website. Does it have active online communities? If not, what kind of community could you host to create a focal point for potential or existing customers? If you already have communities, are people in the organization using them to increase your organization's intellectual capital?

8 What free information or knowledge is available at your organization's website? Is it well used compared to comparable sources? Could better information be provided to increase the number of visitors?

9 What information or knowledge products are currently sold from your website? Are there some other knowledge products that could be packaged and sold profitably with minimal investment?

10 Does your organization have in place a guiding set of principles for advertising and affiliation, both on what it spends and on what it buys?

Notes

1 In July 2000, Stephen King launched the first chapter of his e-novel, *The Plant*, exclusively on the Web. His promise to readers was that if 75 per cent of them paid $1 then he would continue to write and publish further chapters. http://www.stephenking.com.

2 'Author's new online route to publishers', Joia Shillingford, *Financial Times, FT-IT*, p. XIV (7 June 2000).

3 'Content is advertising; only eyeballs matter', *Information World Review*, pp. 43–44 (December 1999).

4 'Greed disease', Nelson D. Schwartz, *Fortune*, pp. 63–68 (29 May 2000).

5 Teltech was acquired by UK software and systems company Sopheon in September 2000.

6 The earliest communities were formed around bulletin boards and Usenet newsgroups, but are not widely used in business. For most professionals today the email discussion list, in which messages can be batched into a daily digest, is the most common technology used by inter-organizational communities. Liszt.com (now part of Topica which hosts many professional email lists) has provided a list of lists since 1995, and seen the number recorded grow from 20 000 in 1997 to over 90 000 by mid-2000. Web message boards are also popular since the messages can be structured to show threads of conversation (new topic, reply, reply to reply etc.). For communities internal to an organization, groupware products such as Lotus Notes are also common.

7 The drug pipeline game is at http://searlehealthnet.com/pipeline.html.

8 'Is franchising the business model for KM?', Victoria Ward, *Knowledge Management Review*, p. 5 (March/April 1999).

9 'Schmooze Tuesdays', William Echikson, *Business Week e.biz*, pp. 54–55 (15 May 2000). Updates from the First Tuesday website http://www.firsttuesday.com and 'Matchmaker, matchmaker', Caroline Daniel, *The Business – FT Weekend Magazine* (16 September 2000).

10 In its heyday, *Encyclopaedia Britannica* made revenues of $650 annually from sales of its hard-copy volumes. Now they are only a tenth of that. The *Oxford English Dictionary* is following quite a different strategy. Its online version, part of a 17 year £34 million programme to develop the new third edition, is available only by individual subscription (£350/$550 a year).

11 In a Nielsen/Internet survey respondents were asked what they used the Internet for. Gathering information was the most common activity, cited by 76 per cent of respondents; next was collaborating with others (55 per cent).

12 Popular banner ad exchange networks are the BannerAd Network and Link Exchange (part of Microsoft's bcentral http://www.bcentral.com). They also collect fees for placing banner ads, hence squaring the 2:1 mismatch.

13 Ask a Librarian is at http://www.earl.org.uk/ask/index.html; Ask an Expert, with a slant towards children's education, is at http://www.askanexpert.com. Askme (http://www.askme.com) has 120 000 experts on its books. They receive

points for answers and the top points winners each month get small cash prizes.

14 'ConsumerReports.org: surviving on subscription fees alone', *Content Exchange Newsletter* (18 September 2000). http://www.content-exchange.com

15 *Wall Street Interactive* at http://interactive.wsj.com. Financial Times at http://www.ft.com.

16 Free trial periods, say of 30 days, is a common encouragement.

17 'Global online ad revenues to skyrocket', *Jupiter Communications* (19 June 2000); http://www.jup.com. There is a strong bias towards North America that accounted for over 80 per cent of the global spend in 1999, although this proportion is predicted to decline to only 60 per cent by 2005.

18 'The Top 50 UK online advertisers', *Revolution*, Online Advertising Report (2000). Based on results from Forrester Research's *Internet AdWatch Spending Monitor*.

19 Advertising survey, *Jupiter Communications* (November 1999); http://www.jup.com.

20 Useful guidance on banner advertising can be found in *Guide to Marketing on the Internet*, Dan Janal (John Wiley & Sons, 2000). Regular analyses of the prevailing rates and effectiveness of online advertising is provided in *Web Marketing Today*, Wilson Internet Services; http://www.wilsonweb.com/wmt/. See for example Issue No. 85 (1 July 2000).

21 'A Nasdaq for bandwidth', John Browning, *Wired*, London (April 1998).

22 A pioneer of this was AllAdvantage.com. Its business model ran into trouble on two counts. It paid consumers, whether it had sold the ad or not. It also had a multi-level marketing scheme where it paid extra for introducing others into the scheme. To stem outgoings it reduced surfing fees but to compensate introduced a daily $50 000 sweepstake. (*Source:* 'Sweeping costs aside', Tim Jackson, *Financial Times*, p. 15, 5 September 2000).

23 In the UK, local calls are not free but charged by the minute.

24 His early writings include *The Know-How Company* Karl Erik Sveiby and Tom Lloyd (Bloomsbury, 1987), The Know-How Company, *International Review of Strategic Management*, Vol. 1, No. 3 (John Wiley & Sons, 1992). More recently, he is well known for his work on intellectual capital measurement described in *Measuring and Managing Intangible Assets*, Berrett-Koehler (1997).

25 In one survey, 44 per cent of respondents said that they were unwilling to pay for information over the Web, since what they wanted was free elsewhere. *GVU 9th WWW User Survey*, Georgia Institute of Technology, http://www.cc.gatech.edu/GVU/user_surveys/ (1999).

Chapter 4

Online knowledge markets

*In a few years' time, e-commerce in tangible goods will be dwarfed by
e-commerce in knowledge.*

(David Brett, CEO and Founder, Knexa.com)

Online knowledge markets are a natural evolution of some of the Internet
buying and selling methods discussed in the previous two chapters.
Online communities facilitate the exchange of specialist knowledge. Business-to-business exchanges are trading hubs for specific industries or
classes of product. Why not combine these ideas by creating marketplaces
where buyers and sellers trade knowledge? Knowledge markets are
attracting a lot of attention and investment as the benefits become more
apparent. Most are still largely embryonic, but some valuable lessons
can already be learnt from pioneering marketplaces and from their conventional e-commerce counterparts.

The chapter starts by describing the characteristics of a knowledge
market and its potential benefits for buyers and sellers. A taxonomy of
the different types of market is then introduced. Two main dimensions
are used: the type of knowledge – from human capital to intellectual property; and the type of trading model – from auction to exchange. These
categories serve as the basis for a more detailed analysis of the markets
that already exist or are likely to emerge. The next part of the chapter
addresses the question: what makes a good online knowledge market?
Knowledge market creators and users face a number of challenges,
caused in part by the unique characteristics of knowledge. These are

examined with some suggestions as to how they might be overcome. The chapter concludes with an assessment of the types of products and markets for which knowledge markets are most appropriate.

Do knowledge markets exist?

A knowledge market is a place where knowledge is traded. In many fields, knowledge trading is already an established activity. There are vibrant content industries like publishing and broadcasting.[1] Other examples are people-based industries like management consulting (selling the know-how of people) and recruitment agencies (trading in human capital). For some of these knowledge businesses there are active markets in the sense that buyers and sellers go there to trade. Recruitment agencies act as market brokers for jobs. Other brokers for human capital include speakers' bureaux, literary agents and professional associations that offer a referral service, putting enquirers in touch with their members who have the required expertise. There are also markets in intellectual property, such as copyrights and patents.

However, there are many situations where knowledge markets barely exist. The personal nature of much knowledge means that human and social factors loom large in many areas of trading and exchanging knowledge. When professionals and managers seek advice, their first port of call is usually someone in their knowledge network, for example a work colleague or a peer in another organization. If their knowledge needs are greater or not easily obtained through their network, they tend to go first to people and suppliers they already know and trust. Established relationships count for a lot. Much existing buying of knowledge, especially that which is more people-based, takes places through established supply chains.

Now think of a traditional marketplace. It is more dynamic. It brings together buyers and sellers who do not necessarily know of each other. It allows participants to compare what's on offer and learn more about what products and services are available. It engenders competition and innovation. It also fosters cooperation in that suppliers get together to address common concerns. In the real world, trade exhibitions and competitive tendering for services are situations that show some of these characteristics. Conferences are other occasions where professionals can top up their knowledge for a fee. Between such events, professional workers seeking knowledge have to rely on their network or other means, which do not necessarily get them the best knowledge at the keenest price.

Within organizations, the need for continuous access to knowledge has spurred the development of various knowledge initiatives. In particular, two common practices have created one-stop-shops for knowledge – knowledge centres and intranets. Stocked with the right knowledge (or links to knowledge) these should ideally be the first port of call for knowledge seekers rather than the place to try as a last resort. In effect, they act as a knowledge market. Knowledge from various suppliers has been brought together in one place. Knowledge seekers can browse what's on offer, do directed searches for specific knowledge and in many cases seek advice from a knowledge broker, such as a librarian, on where to go for additional knowledge. Knowledge suppliers can make their knowledge more visible and accessible.

Several pioneers in knowledge management have recognized the existence and benefits of knowledge markets within organizations. Prusak and Davenport devote a chapter to them in their book *Working Knowledge.*[2] They point out the existence of market pricing and exchange mechanisms, even though money is rarely the form of payment.[3] They suggest three main factors at work, the most significant being reciprocity followed by repute and altruism. Reciprocity means that knowledge suppliers can expect to benefit when they become knowledge recipients in the future. Repute gives recognition to the supplier as a knowledgeable person willing to share their expertise. Altruism is where the knowledge supplier is motivated by reasons such as their love of their subject, and their desire to pass on their knowledge to others. When an internal knowledge market operates efficiently both individuals and the firm benefit. Knowledge flows more freely. The organization gains efficiencies and applies knowledge more effectively, generating the kinds of benefits shown in Table 1.1 (page 3). Professionals get the knowledge they need to succeed in their job. They also increase their level of competence and skills, which should help them progress in their careers.

Outside the organization, similar knowledge trading mechanisms exist in knowledge networks, whether these are professional societies, special interest groups or informal networks. Knowledge is

---

HP's internal knowledge market

In most organizations, internal knowledge is shared freely. But at HP, some kinds of knowledge are now charged for and help to pay for knowledge management services. Users of HP's internal search engine pay $3 a month to access. Payment is made with HP's NetCard, an internal electronic charge card. The electronic accounting system can handle even small sums efficiently, such as 12 cents for a report from another department. The aim of using the NetCard, which can be used for a wide range of inter-office services, is to help knowledge providers recover their costs in serving their users. NetCard is part of a broader initiative to expand internal e-commerce services.

Source: *Knowledge Management*, Freedom Technology Media Group, March 1999

also exchanged as part of everyday business conversation. The more aware individuals are of the value of the knowledge they possess, the more care they will take in giving it away freely outside of their close network or a formal trading relationship. The growing importance of knowledge means that the time is ripe for the creation of more one-stop shop mechanisms to improve the flow of knowledge and to increase the efficiency of knowledge exchange and trading. The Internet provides the right facilities for this to happen.

From real to virtual

The pervasiveness of the Internet has already started to shift existing knowledge markets into cyberspace. Examples include:

- *Intellectual property trading.* Copyright material, patents and designs are increasingly traded online, widening creator access to a broader market base. Trading sites can also serve as rights clearing houses. The Alba centre in Scotland has an online trading infrastructure where integrated circuit designers can find out if certain functional designs exist, and if so buy licence rights to use these 'blocks of virtual intellectual property', rather than design their own.
- *Recruitment agencies.* Many types of recruitment, such as computer contracting, are fast shifting into online mode. The pool of job seekers and recruiters is larger. Computerized testing and profile to job matching helps both parties more quickly find mutually beneficial matches. Portal sites such as Careermosaic.com give hints on writing CVs, links to recruitment fairs etc.
- *Management consultancies.* Their business is knowledge, but they are increasingly packaging it, both for internal use (on their intranets and knowledge bases) and externally, such as Arthur Andersen's Global Best Practices and Ernst & Young's ERNIE.
- *Research companies.* Market and industry researchers, such as Nielsen and Gartner Group now deliver much of their material over the Web or transfer it to clients' intranets. Market size data are usually provided ready for use in spreadsheet format. The problem-solving broker Teltech (see page 80) now offers its service online.
- *Public sector tendering.* Under European law, large public contracts must be open to tender by companies in all member states. You will find more RFPs (requests for proposal) for management consultancy being announced over the Internet by government departments and public sector agencies.

Other developments are also influencing the creation of online knowledge markets. One is the growth of the Internet as a vehicle for e-commerce and knowledge exchange. As noted earlier, many of the models of e-commerce, such as online malls and auctions, can be adapted to the marketing of knowledge. Business-to-business exchanges, in particular, offer significant potential for increasing the efficiency of buying and selling. The popularity of online communities demonstrates the high interest in seeking and sharing knowledge with like-minded people. Here the same factors that apply in internal knowledge markets – reciprocity, repute and altruism – are also important. But many knowledgeable people who are not active in these communities may be encouraged to do so too if they were recompensed financially for their time and expertise. If monetary exchange was introduced into these communities, could they adapt?

Key ingredients

A knowledge market needs buyers (knowledge seekers), sellers (knowledge providers) and a set of market making mechanisms. There is no shortage of seekers for knowledge. As mentioned earlier, virtually every professional needs a constant flow of fresh knowledge to maintain success in his or her job. The question is, how much of that is readily obtainable through their normal channels, including their organization's knowledge centre, and how much must be sought externally? Even where they are well served through their personal networks and contacts, they will sometimes need to validate quality and value through market testing. In many specialist areas, such testing may reveal the benefits of external sourcing. A good knowledge market will also give buyers access to knowledge that is more obscure or second opinions that challenge an organization's groupthink.

Participation in an online marketplace by sellers enables them to serve more customers. It saves them costs in creating their own e-commerce website, an attractive proposition for many individual creators. Even where they do have their own e-commerce website, a thriving marketplace may well have more pulling power. The existence of a market may encourage suppliers to commercialize more of their knowledge, since much of the marketing and trading infrastructure will already be in place. A market also lets them test new ideas for knowledge products and services.

Apart from buyers and sellers, markets need a market-making mechanism to work. Often, human brokers provide this. In internal knowledge markets, the brokers are 'gatekeepers' and networkers who help to connect knowledge seekers with knowledge providers. In conventional knowledge markets, this may be the head-hunter (in the recruitment market) or the rights agent (for intellectual property). In the online environment, many of these functions may be automated. As a minimum an online website will need facilities to capture and process details of needs and offers. It may add intelligence that includes matchmaking capabilities and a set of business rules. These rules may filter out specific matches, based on personal preferences of buyer and seller, or they may include rules for dynamic pricing to maximize revenues. If the market is a full trading hub, as many of them are, they need order processing and account management facilities. They may even host various delivery mechanisms, including online knowledge repositories and communities. In return for providing these facilities, the market maker will seek revenues from one or more sources, such as commissions from buyers and/or sellers, advertisers, sponsors, or from affiliate fees for successful referrals to complementary websites.

Online knowledge markets pose some special challenges for buyers and sellers alike. Unlike most markets, the product of exchange – knowledge – has some unique characteristics. It is mostly intangible, making it difficult for the buyer to assess and value beforehand. Its value is context-dependent, making it difficult for the supplier to price it in a transparent marketplace of multiple buyers with varied applications.

The bleeding edge?

Many of the online knowledge markets cited on page 118 are not open to all-comers. Participation is often restricted and needs and offers are not visible to all parties. Several are asymmetric, in that they are biased

Figure 4.1 Knowledgeshop – a pioneering knowledge website

towards either buyers or sellers. Recognizing the potential of the Internet to create totally new kinds of online knowledge trading environments, several independent knowledge shops and markets were created in 1997–8, although their fortunes have been very mixed. Knowledgeshop, a Canadian venture, even two years later had fewer than 100 products for sale. IdeaMarket, which acted as a market for reports and other documents, has ceased trading. Much earlier efforts, such as Coordinet, to match freelance teleworkers to those seeking their skills did not take off, although a new German venture Telinex is revisiting this opportunity.[4]

Perhaps the early pioneers were ahead of their time, or lacked the investment to raise their profile and attract sufficient buyers and sellers. The same cannot be said about a more recent and ambitious venture, iqport.com. Started by NatWest bank with a sizeable investment, and receiving support from Arthur Andersen and Lotus, it closed shop in February 2000 at the end of its market trial. Promoting itself as 'the knowledge market for people in the know', its window of activity gave a glimpse of what a knowledge market of the future might look like as well as some salutary lessons for market participants (see below).

iqport.com: a knowledge trading platform

Launched as a market trial in 1999, iqport.com promoted itself as 'the place where you can buy and sell knowledge'. It appealed directly to individual knowledge providers and users. Conceived by Freddie McMahon and colleagues at UK's NatWest bank, it positioned itself thus: 'modeled on the US stock market, the iqport.com system allows members to leverage intellectual capital as an asset to be bought, sold, and/or exchanged for shares'. In its case, the shares were tokens with a value of US$1 each. At the end of a trading period, if you sold more in value than you bought you could 'cash in' your tokens for real money. Conversely, if you bought more than you sold, then your credit card account was debited.

iqport.com was probably the first initiative that brought together all the desirable facilities that a knowledge trading platform needs. It provided a managed knowledge repository, an e-commerce platform and a business and community infrastructure to support its members. Its main features included:

❑ *A classified repository of knowledge assets.* These assets were categorized with user-defined keywords and identified the intended audience and application of each asset. Potential buyers could search different classes of assets, such as those that were 'branded' by guilds (see below), or met a certain accreditation level, such as 3-star. An advanced search facility allowed users to narrow their searches to a defined industry, discipline or other categories.

- *Asset wrappers.* Each asset had a 'wrapper' that described its contents, so that potential customers could gain a good idea of what it contained before committing to purchase. The wrapper provided an abstract of the content, its format (e.g. Word document, presentation, video etc.), author details, price, content structure (e.g. number of pages) etc. Branded assets were highlighted with their guild and accreditation rating. The rating criteria differed from guild to guild. Typically a 1-star asset gave generic advice and met minimum standards of readability; 2-star meant validated by subject matter experts and may be based on real cases and research; 3-star signified 'cutting edge', 'thought leadership', and was endorsed as original. One guild (O2 Solutions) rated according to the degree of multimedia content, with 1-star being predominantly text, and 3-star being rich in multimedia.

- *Pricing.* Pricing of knowledge assets is notoriously difficult. On iqport.com prices ranged from $2 to over $200. Often, very similar items varied in price by a factor of five or more, a common feature in many markets. The benefit of a system like iqport.com is that these comparisons can be made quickly and easily. For those planning to sell assets, the guilds had good guidelines on how to set price based on factors such as originality, relevance, uniqueness, and size.

- *Division of revenues.* A key feature of iqport.com was that the value of an asset was divided into 100 shares. Naturally, iqport.com took their percentage cut, but the rest could be apportioned in any way between guilds, assessors (who provide the star rating) and any others in the supply chain. Thus a person or organization could have an 'interest' in assets that were not directly owned or authored. The creator, unlike many other traditional knowledge supply chains, such as publishing, would typically take a 50 per cent share.

- *Simple and easy payment.* This was one of iqport's strong features. Like many e-commerce sites, it had a secure trading platform. But it offered much more besides. On joining, members who wanted to trade gave their credit card details, and the system maintained an account. As well as seeing the status of their account, account holders could also view detailed summaries of transactions, such as viewing which assets were selling the best and who the purchasers were.

Guilds: communities of knowledge

One of iqport.com's unique features was its guilds – communities with a difference. Whereas many online communities provide discussion facilities and library resources, the aim of the iqport.com guilds was to build businesses around areas of specialized knowledge. They helped sellers 'wrap' their knowledge, advised on pricing and accredited content. For buyers they acted as specialist portals and offered related services. As well as featuring their branded assets, a typical guild would have links to community search, library, chat room and interest groups. Some had voting facilities, and special facilities for people wanting to collaborate on developing knowledge assets (see Futurizing.com below). Many restricted some of the facilities only to their members. Iqport.com provided central facilities to join the guilds. For some membership was automatic after you had submitted your basic details. Others sifted applications through a human validation process. Here is an overview of the main guilds that addressed the interests of the knowledge community.

- **Futurizing.com and ICUniverse.com**

These two closely related guilds were the inspiration of Leif Edvinsson (formerly of Skandia) and his colleagues. Futurizing.com provided a space for its participants to identify 'emerging intellectual capital opportunities' (see knowledge co-creation later in this chapter – page 124). Its membership was by invitation only. ICUniverse.com was the corresponding open community that develops just-in-time knowledge businesses, i.e. that create one based on a specifically identified need with a potential client. Again, the stock market analogy is used: 'So just like you can invest in futures in the stock market, you can invest in knowledge being created in the knowledge bazaar. For your investment you will get shares in the asset. If the asset is as good as you believe then the price will go up and you will get a good return on your investment.' ICUniverse 'Global Minds Shaping the Future' is now a knowledge agency of Knexa.com.[5]

- **Bright**

Bright (http://www.bright-future.co.uk), 'the network for smarter networking', put its emphasis on a range of topics such as virtual working and personal development skills to help knowledge workers be more effective. It had a thriving Web-based discussion space under the name of Bright Talk. It also recruited some high profile management experts as part of its guru and accreditation network. Although Bright is in a dormant state, its initial main backer ISP continues to do business in e-commerce ventures and uses some of the knowledge gained from the iqport.com experience.

- **O2 Solutions**

The focus of O2 Solutions (http://www.o2solutions.com) is management and human resources. Among its content providers are *The Wall Street Journal* and the London School of Economics. It included several assets from knowledge management pioneers, such as 'How to improve business performance by effectively managing knowledge' by Kent Greenes (BP) and Hubert Saint-Onge (Clarica). O2 Solutions continues to sell knowledge assets as a knowledge agency of Knexa.com (see page 119) and from its own website.

- **Other guilds**

Other guilds on iqport.com included:

- ❑ Advantage Hiring – providing software and tools in the area of employee selection and assessment.
- ❑ Fount – community of business professionals committed to business improvement through learning development.
- ❑ Knowledge Guru – providing knowledge in law, business and management, travel and tourism.
- ❑ Millennium Leadership Community – taking leadership into the next millennium.
- ❑ The Risk Guild – risk knowledge.

Several of these were created especially to capitalize on the iqport.com platform. Most were backed by one or more existing knowledge businesses that still use the net as a sales channel, albeit without all the advantages of iqport.com.

Although most of iqport.com's assets were information, there was nothing inherent in its design to prevent the selling of online training, consultancy and other people-based knowledge. During its trial, the only visible case was a senior consultant priced at $75. Unfortunately its wrapper gave no clarification what time the price covered (presumably it was an hourly rate), no description, no author, in fact no information other than a 2-star rating. So it is doubtful that there would be any takers. However, several guilds had considered the revenue opportunities of organizing online 'master classes' and providing chat rooms for online consultations.

End of the experiment

After nearly of a year of its market trial and a delay in the original planned full commercial launch date, a short announcement was sent to all participants in January 2000: 'In the context of NatWest's wider e-commerce strategy, a decision has been made not to proceed to full scale commercial trading with iqport.com.'

Iqport.com had many desirable characteristics that participants seek in a knowledge market, so why did it not go ahead? NatWest is, of course, primarily a bank, and it could be argued that knowledge markets were a peripheral activity to its main Internet banking and other e-commerce services, which it continues to develop. However, participants found several deficiencies with iqport.com, mostly in terms of implementation, rather than the core concept.

Iqport.com's primary problems were to do with usability and performance. Although its menus and sections were well laid out, it relied heavily on frames, which most Web developers now use with caution. One effect was that if you inspected a wrapper of an asset that you were contemplating buying, you could not backtrack but had to search again. Since searches were often frustratingly slow (45 seconds or more), this put off all but the most determined buyer. The website was difficult to navigate. Screens were inconsistent. Some wrapper screens were incomplete, omitting the price. It was not easy to contact the developers. All 'contact us' hyperlinks, including 'email us' led back to a single form, which when completed frequently did not elicit any response from iqport.com. At one time, following a server reconfiguration, almost every link had a '404 file not found error' for days on end. In short, iqport.com was let down by poor technical implementation. No doubt these flaws could have been put right with more investment and the appropriate expertise, but this did not happen. Despite its demise, iqport.com offers some valuable insights into the opportunities and challenges that face knowledge markets.

The next generation

Despite the setbacks and hesitant starts during 1997–9, the interest in online marketplaces for knowledge has subsequently grown enormously. Scores of new ventures have been created, many receiving substantial investment from individual 'business angels', venture capitalists and large corporations. Clearly many feel that the time is ripe, even though they still face many challenges in gaining critical mass and developing a profitable business. Datamonitor predicts that just one type – people-to-people information exchanges, where people seek answers from other people at a knowledge hub – will be a $5 billion business leveraging over $50 billion of sales by 2005.[6] An indicative list of knowledge market initiatives is shown in Table 4.1.

The majority of recent initiatives involve the marketing of human knowledge in different-sized chunks. These can range from a few words of advice, through to individuals selling their time, to full-time jobs and large consultancy projects. Knowledge markets are innovative in the variety of e-business models they use, including auctions and exchanges. Analysis of over 50 knowledge markets by the Kaieteur Institute for Knowledge Management (KIKM), has resulted in a classification scheme in which knowledge markets are divided into ten distinct categories. These are shown with some indicative examples of each type in Table 4.2.[8]

Table 4.1 Examples of knowledge markets

Type of knowledge	Example	Launch date	Key characteristics
Human capital	eTrask	July 2000	European exchange for professional services, e.g. legal, accountancy, marketing and business advisory services
	Elance.com	Dec 1998	Targeted at freelancers offering services, using a similar approach to eBay. Auctions, project bids; also project work space for virtual teams. Buyers pay a percentage of project fees
	IQ4hire.com	July 2000	An exchange for large IT consultancy projects (in excess of $250 000)
Information	MightyWords (formerly eMatter)	Sept 1999	Aimed at giving a wider market for creators of short documents. Authors receive royalties of 50 per cent
Intellectual capital	Yet2.com	Feb 2000	Licensing proprietary R&D. 13 founding sponsors, including 3M, Dow, Du Pont, SAIC, who between them account for 10 per cent of all US commercial R&D
	Rightscenter.com	Oct 1999	Global publishing rights exchange used by publishers and agents in a closed user group. 300 active rights sellers, 5000 buyers in 56 countries[7]
General	Knexa.com	Sep 1999	Wide range of knowledge assets covering broad range of subjects. Number of times an asset is sold can be restricted

Table 4.2 Categories of knowledge market with examples

Category	Examples	Types of knowledge
1 Knowledge auctions	Knexa	All categories.
2 Knowledge stores or malls	Knowledgeshop	Intellectual capital (KM focus)
3 Expert knowledge or question and answer exchanges	KnowPost	General consumer categories
	InfoMarkets.com	Business, technology, careers and education, personal
4 Intellectual property exchanges	Patent & Licence Exchange (www.pl-x.com)	All types of intellectual property
	TechEx	Technology and intellectual property in biomedical industry
5 Stockmarket or investment knowledge exchanges	iExchange.com	Stock tips by individuals
	Equity Engine	An automated virtual incubator
6 E-education or e-learning exchanges	Emind	Professional development courses
	GKE (Global Knowledge Exchange)	Exchange for distance learning materials (degrees and certified programmes)
7 Community oriented or social capital networks	Community of Science (CoS)	R&D professional network
	KELP (Knowledge Exchange and Learning Partnership)	A community of African post-secondary institutions in sustainable development
8 Intellectual capital exchanges (human capital, work, job, project, fee agent or professional services exchanges)	BrainBid.com	Freelancers for project work
	Ework Exchange	Freelance contractors, e.g. business services, software development, writing
9 Vortexes – vertical or industry-specific knowledge markets	IdeaLive	Listings and placement service for artists in film, music and art
	Oil & Gas Knowledge Exchange (OPPIS)	A global networked forum of companies sharing offshore production knowledge
10 B2B knowledge exchange	EBrainx.com	Knowledge services in professional areas, such as sales and marketing, legal

Source: The Kaieteur Institute of Knowledge Management, *Knowledge Markets Metaportal Site*, with some changed examples. http://www.kikm.org/portal/page2.html

With the embryonic and fluid state of these markets, it is likely that the names of many of the individual examples listed above will change, even as the distinct categories become more widely established. Several of these ventures are based on the models described in Chapter 3, such as auctions and business-to-business exchanges. Some, such as question and answer networks and intellectual property exchanges, are attempting to establish markets where none previously existed or were very inefficient. Now follows an overview of the unique characteristics of each category:

Knowledge auctions The most common form of auction, often found on advice sites (category 3), is a reverse auction where a knowledge seeker asks for bids to provide knowledge. Sellers vie with each other to get the business, although the buyer may not necessarily buy from the lowest bidder. Other subjective judgements enter the equation, such as the reputation of the seller and the expected quality of the advice. Sellers who announce availability of knowledge may invoke auction mode, such as selling their time to the highest bidder, but for packaged knowledge that can be sold again and again, the auction site may simply provide the appropriate vehicle for selling knowledge at a fixed

---

How to auction your knowledge

Five steps to success:

1 Personal knowledge profile – build your profile to help buyer's evaluate your credibility in your area of expertise.
2 Category selection – choose the most relevant category for your content.
3 Describe your knowledge – provide a well-written and clear description that will attract bidders and avoid numerous email queries later.
4 Set a price – consider setting a minimum bid a little lower than the price you think it will sell for, to get the auction going.
5 Set your auction parameters – set price increments and time intervals to dynamically change the price to increase revenues.

Source: Auction Sellers Guide, Knexa.com

---

price. Knexa.com (see Figure 4.2) provides facilities for the seller to dynamically change their pricing based on a set of rules. For example the price may be increased by a specified increment after so many successful sales or be decreased if unsold for a given time interval. Knexa.com takes a 20 per cent commission on sales.[9]

Knowledge stores or malls These are k-shops described on page 82. Know Inc.'s Knowledgeshop sells various knowledge products, including information and courses. Sellers are charged placement fees (typically $100 to $200 an item) and a 15–25 per cent commission on sales.

Expert knowledge or question and answer exchanges Knowledge seekers post questions for which they seek answers. Some websites link through to a

Figure 4.2   Knexa.com – a knowledge marketplace

panel of experts. Others have open bidding arrangements. The advice may be delivered in a variety of forms – pre-packaged answers (TWI), live phone calls with experts (Keen), online chat, streaming audio and video (MindCrossing), or email replies (InfoRocket). Technology is increasingly used to automate the process as much as possible, For example, TWI (The Welding Institute) is experimenting with artificial intelligence techniques to replicate as far as possible a live human expert in answering many of the 25 000 detailed technical questions it receives each year. MindCrossing has a multilevel approach in which the user's queries can be answered from information in an expert's MindStore, email questions and answers or live audio streaming.

Intellectual property exchanges These match buyers and sellers for different types of intellectual property such as publishing rights, patents and designs. R&D departments of organizations are finding these an attractive way of exploiting their inventions (see Yet2.com below). For digital rights, samples can be supplied which include watermark technology to limit copying or render them unusable after a short evaluation period.

Stockmarket or investment knowledge exchanges   As their name implies, the knowledge traded is investment knowledge. iExchange.com provides stock picks from various providers, who supply additional material such as analysis reports. The performance of each recommended stock is monitored and ranked so that buyers can gauge the track record of the knowledge provider. An emergent category is information and access to venture capital for start-up business in the form of virtual incubators.

E-learning exchanges   These capitalize on the growing interest in distance education and online learning resources. Some simply list the resources or suppliers, while others provide the mechanisms for exchanging resources online.

Community oriented or social capital networks   These are knowledge communities (see page 83) where knowledge is freely exchanged; it is traded for social, rather than financial capital. One such community is CoS (Community of Science). It provides a hub where scientists can seek sources of research funding, post their expertise profiles, and have a customized workbench that gives them access to databases and discussion forums.

Intellectual capital exchanges   These mostly deal in human capital in all shapes and sizes from freelance work for individuals through to large consultancy projects. The basic model follows that of all exchanges with buyers posting details of their requirements and sellers posting details of their capabilities. They particularly appeal to individuals and small companies who do not have the marketing reach or resources of larger firms. They vary in the degree of openness. Sometimes overviews of competitive bids are provided. In many cases, bids are passed privately to the other party with the originator retaining anonymity until the offer is shortlisted or accepted.

Vortexes – vertical or industry-specific markets   These are extensions of the k-portal (page 77) into mechanisms where knowledge trading can take place.

B2B knowledge exchange   This category covers B2B knowledge services and other exchanges not listed above. To some extent, they combine the features of question and answer services (category 3) and consultancy services (in category 8), but with a B2B focus.

As markets of all types grow beyond their initial critical mass, we can expect to see more segmentation along industry or professional lines. Thus, several of the above categories may converge and more industry segments emerge. There is an open question as to how the generic markets, such as advice sites, will fare in this environment. There may be more vertical market segmentation, at the same time adding functionality from other markets, such as consultancy and IP search. Another shift may be convergence towards the all-embracing consumer model ('the eBay for ideas'). One likely development is that of private exchanges, where participants are restricted to a group that meets certain criteria. These are likely to exist as private areas on existing exchanges that already have the matching and trading infrastructure in place. A similar situation exists in communities, where some are open to all-comers, some require users to apply for membership, others are by invitation only, whilst the most private ones do not even publicize their existence.

The attractions of markets

Online knowledge markets are creating opportunities throughout the knowledge value system. Like other Internet commerce initiatives, they open up new channels, reduce the costs of buying and selling, and introduce the convenience of shopping from your desktop. They are particularly attractive to individual creators who find it much easier to gain outlets for their creations than has traditionally been the case. Mighty-Words and Knexa.com give particular encouragement to submissions from individuals, who can expect to receive from 50 to 80 per cent of the asset's purchase price. Knexa.com's CEO David Brett describes people in career change as ideal suppliers – for example, a recently retired geologist who has knowledge of value to the oil industry.[10] By becoming essential hubs of knowledge exchange for particular groups of people, the market makers are ideally positioned to generate sustainable revenue streams. Primarily these will come from trading fees – a commission on sales and/or purchases. Also, high traffic and a well-profiled membership will be attractive to advertisers. Many aspire to become the Yahoo! or eBay for knowledge. Four particular features of knowledge markets make them attractive to participants – market access, precision matching, transparency and knowledge development.

Better market access

Online markets increase the market potential for suppliers. Take the case of intellectual property. Only a small fraction of new inventions – around 3 per cent – gets used by the firms who patent them. They often have more immediate relevance to firms in other industries. Yet finding potential routes to exploitation can be time consuming. Yet2.com was born out of Ben Du Pont's frustration at finding new uses for Du Pont's new technologies. Potential buyers pay membership fees on a sliding scale according to the level of detail they want to access. Yet2.com takes a 10 per cent commission on patents sold or licensed.[11] Now that intellectual property exchanges exist, more companies are likely to follow Dow Chemical's lead in actively managing its intellectual assets portfolio and seeking to generate revenues from it.

Online markets are seen by many as being particularly helpful for small businesses and individuals who often do not have the marketing resources to seek out potential customers. The more specialized that knowledge is, the more likely it is that buyers and sellers are widely distributed and isolated from each other. A market makes it easier for buyers to find sellers and vice versa. A *Harvard Business Review* article on the 'e-lance economy' (electronic freelancers) appears to have inspired ventures aimed specifically at individuals and small businesses.[12] Thus, eLance.com provides facilities for individuals to bid on projects. It also provides them with virtual project space. A similar site, but with a European focus (its founders are three Belgian entrepreneurs) is Smarterwork.com. It plans to introduce facilities that help individuals find partners to jointly bid for larger projects. By mid-2000, both had over 10 000 contractors and several hundred active projects, mostly in IT, media and business services.[13]

Precision matching

A market with a large number of buyers and sellers potentially makes it easier to find closer matches between buyers' needs and suppliers who can service them. The market can help at several levels. First, a good classification scheme should draw together the most likely matches. Secondly, good computer searching algorithms may uncover potential matches where buyer and seller are not in the same area of the marketplace. Thirdly, and probably the most effective in general, is the use of human brokers. The market maker may provide these, in the same way that a knowledge centre has staff who can help their users. Having knowledgeable brokers (such as those at Teltech.com – see page 80) may give the market a distinctive market advantage. Brokers are also typically found in communities. 'I don't know it myself, but I know someone who does' is a common response to questions posed in community discussion spaces. Last but not least, the facilities in most markets allow for dialogue between buyers and sellers so that needs and offers can be refined.

More transparency

Open markets give buyers and sellers more visibility of the range of services that are on offer and of prevailing market prices. Although this is
likely to put pressure on prices, the costs of the normal buying and selling
process can be significantly reduced. Consultants, for example, can be
more selective, and minimize the amount of travel for project scoping
meetings with prospective clients by doing many of the preliminary discussions online. Exchange sites vary in how much visibility they give to
rival bids. In the area of consultancy projects, Smarterwork.com just indicates how many bids have been received, while eLance.com shows the
actual bids and bidders' profiles. Such visibility quickly raises the knowledge of both buyers and sellers. In one case on eLance.com, a buyer seeking help to write a business plan for a start-up company offered 3 per cent
of equity. However, several bidders indicated that this was not necessarily
a desirable strategy, and offered instead fixed price bids. Furthermore,
unlike some exchanges, such information is visible to casual visitors as
well as people who have pre-registered.

Another interesting shift that sometimes occurs when individuals gain
increased visibility of other market participants, is that they switch role.
In one reported example on Smarterwork.com, a Web designer realized
that too many of them were chasing too few jobs, and that his rates were
five times or more higher than those of programmers from countries like
India who were charging only $12 an hour. He therefore 'reinvented' him-
self as a buyer, sourcing talent from the site to create project teams.[14]

Knowledge co-creation and development

Since knowledge markets act as a focal point for knowledge exchange, several entrepreneurs have seen this as an opportunity for market participants
to get to know each other and create new knowledge businesses. Knowl-
edgecreators.com, a venture of Know Inc. (the creators of Knowledgeshop), provides opportunities for the creation of new businesses through
a virtual organization structure. A virtual team comes together in a 'co-
creation area, a secure virtual space used for sharing ideas, having real-
time chat, and testing online products'. Know Inc. provides the essential
infrastructure, including videoconferencing and electronic whiteboarding,
project management, legal agreements etc. Each team operates rather like a
mutual fund, where team members and Know Inc. own equity in the
venture and share revenues. Futurizing.com, which started as one of
iqport.com's guilds, created a similar idea through its Knowledge Café
and Bazaar (see below).

The co-creation process at Futurizing.com

The aim of Futurizing.com is to create new knowledge businesses through what is described as 'an online intellectual capital commercialization process'. Two facilities that expedite the innovation process are the Knowledge Café and Knowledge Bazaar. The former is a creative environment where new ideas and opportunities are floated. The latter allows participants to view the discussions in the Knowledge Café and lets them make investments in potential knowledge assets and businesses. The website (http://www.futurizing.com) maps the various stages involved:[15]

- *Post research topic.* The Knowledge Café provides an informal environment for proposing and discussing ideas for new knowledge assets.
- *Facilitate network.* Facilitators from Futurizing.com create and nurture online threaded discussions according to asset themes.
- *Post research proposal.* Once a particular asset has been scoped in terms of content, contributors, likely customers and price, a proposal is posted on the Knowledge Bazaar.
- *Gain investor.* Investors buy shares (knowledge futures) in the yet undeveloped asset. New rounds of investing take place as required.
- *Develop asset.* The asset is created by the agreed contributors and then passed over to Futurizing.com's partner ICUniverse.com, the portfolio managers.

Futurizing.com illustrates the potential of collaboration to develop new knowledge businesses. Unlike the majority of communities, creation of intellectual capital with financial rewards for the knowledge developers is a key motivator for participants. Knowledge markets can act as the magnet for such activity, but few have yet shown the inclination. Futurizing.com is in its formative stages, although the surge of interest in Internet incubators (see page 231) suggests that it is only a matter of time before we see more virtual incubators for knowledge businesses along the lines of Futurizing.com. Even for established businesses, the potential of markets for accelerating knowledge development within a company should not be overlooked. The market is host to a wealth of knowledge that can be tapped both formally through trading, and informally though communications and networking.

What makes a good knowledge market?

Because they are relatively new, few of the knowledge markets mentioned so far have a sustained trading record. Indeed several have stalled, while others like iqport.com have come and gone. Analysis of their experience to date suggests a number of desirable characteristics that are needed if an online knowledge market is to succeed.

An easily locatable marketplace   Potential buyers must be able to quickly find a relevant marketplace, e.g. via a well-known portal site. The market space should be subdivided into areas or neighbourhoods according to the domain of knowledge, the types of product, seller or buyer.

Critical mass   There must be sufficient buyers and sellers in the same niche to actually establish a market, rather than a few lone buyers or sellers whose offers and needs do not match. This critical mass varies from market to market, and may depend on how location-dependent service delivery is. Is face-to-face involvement absolutely necessary or can knowledge be delivered virtually?

Well presented selling space   Buyers must be able to quickly understand the scope of what is available and then to hone in on their precise needs. Clear classification schemes and information hierarchies are essential. A common problem when markets are new is that too many subdivisions are created, resulting in many having no entries at all. A better strategy is to use broad divisions initially and subdivide as the number of entries grows. Additional benefits are gained when the selling space is customized to the customer's needs.

Good descriptions of knowledge assets   What is on offer must be well described, such as in a 'wrapper' that follows a standard format. Products or services that are difficult to describe, such as advice and consultancy, need special attention to convey their characteristics to the buyer. The experience of sites like Smarterwork.com is that many projects are ill-defined, making it difficult for potential suppliers to place meaningful bids. Marketplace owners are addressing these problems by helping participants with guides and advice.

Mechanisms to sample (try-before-buy)   Many market sites seem to put off potential participants by forcing them through a burdensome registration process. While significant detail is needed to conclude a deal, markets need to be welcoming to casual visitors. Sellers need to consider how potential buyers can savour their offering. In the creative sections of eLance.com, writers and designers can post samples. For more intangible knowledge services other approaches, such as testimonials or buyers' ratings, are needed.

Validation of supplier and product quality   Buyers gain confidence if a third party has validated the reputation of a supplier. Bright's accreditation process for iqport.com used a mechanism of peer review. Knexa.com does spot checks on suppliers' credentials. As with many knowledge transactions, the best guide is usually a customer testimonial, and many sites encourage customer feedback. IdeaRocket gives everyone visibility of user ratings of suppliers' earlier transactions.

Some guarantee of satisfaction   The market owner may guarantee payments, as eBay does for its clients through an insurance policy. But what about the more difficult situation where a buyer does not feel that the knowledge received was commensurate with expectations? This is where market owners may need to support some kind of independent arbitration scheme by relevant experts; after all, expert witnesses are used in legal arbitration cases.

A fair and transparent pricing mechanism   A problem with knowledge is that perceptions of value differ widely. Posting the prices actually paid for knowledge assets will increase transparency. Dynamic pricing is another technique that can be adopted in an online market, particularly if the asset's value is time-dependent, e.g. where its value decays as the information goes out of date, or where there are capacity peaks and troughs in the case of human expertise.

Simple and easy payment mechanisms   Most markets provide a range of payment mechanisms, including credit card payments for specific transactions or a trade account with monthly billing. Sales of low priced items, such as pieces of advice costing just $1 or so, will benefit when there are more universal micropayment systems (see page 214).

Effective reward mechanisms   There must be good incentives for individuals and organizations to develop new knowledge assets and knowledge businesses. If markets can show the sales potential and take only modest commission fees then suppliers will be encouraged to commercialize their knowledge. Many markets offer free postings in their early stages.

Ways of sharing knowledge between buyers and sellers, and different buyers   Providing community facilities is the obvious way to do this. Provision of closed communities can also be attractive to particular groups, such as suppliers trying to develop consortia or preparing joint bids for projects.

Sense of community   A marketplace is a social meeting point and has its own set of values and norms. Some may initially be set by the market provider. Thus eBay provides extensive guidance on good practice and etiquette for first time buyers and sellers. Once relationships develop, buyers and sellers develop their own groups and sub-communities. A marketplace that does not provide facilities for online discussion between buyers and sellers is likely to have a less loyal following than those that do.

Many of the foregoing are desirable in all online markets. The diversity and intangibility of knowledge makes several of them extra challenging. It should go without saying that a sustainable marketplace needs a robust and user-friendly e-commerce platform, and follow all the basic tenets of online marketing as described in Chapters 5 and 6. iqport.com, for example, had addressed many of the unique challenges of knowledge markets, but its cumbersome online platform, confusing channel marketing and lack of responsiveness to users contributed to its demise. Appendix B gives a market evaluation template.

Potential and pitfalls

Knowledge markets are more suited to some kinds of purchase than others. One way to consider different types of purchase is to consider them along two main dimensions, as depicted in the market space diagram of Figure 4.3. The horizontal axis indicates the level of knowledge that the buyer has of the market. How much does the buyer know about available products and services and their suppliers? If they have high market knowledge then they are more likely to purchase from the supplier (or their distributor)

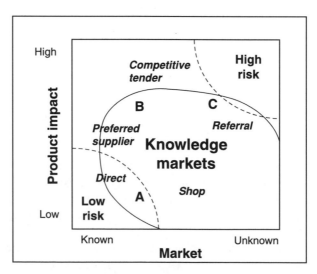

Figure 4.3   Optimum region for knowledge markets

directly. The vertical axis represents the impact on the buying organization. The impact is high where volumes or prices are high. It is also high if the purchase is complex and will therefore take significant time to evaluate. In these cases, buyers are likely to deal with preferred suppliers or go through a competitive tendering process. Knowledge markets are generally more suitable when the buyer has insufficient market knowledge and where the impact of a wrong purchase is low.

However, these boundaries are constantly being pushed into new territory as indicated by A, B and C in Figure 4.3. At A, the buyer may go to the market to test existing suppliers against competitors, especially to gain a more favourable price. Boundary B is where buyers go to the market to gain access to new suppliers, perhaps when there are doubts whether existing ones have the capability or capacity to meet their needs. Boundary C is approaching an area of high risk. Here buyers go into the marketplace to gain knowledge and minimize risk. The purchasing process is likely to be protracted and involve several iterations. As the buyer's knowledge increases, their position in the market space diagram in any case moves to the left. At this stage of knowledge market development, much more research is needed to refine knowledge market taxonomies and to evaluate their effectiveness for different types of knowledge purchase.

There are some pitfalls to be aware of when participating in knowledge markets. The first is to consider how balanced they are in terms of buyers and sellers. Regulatory authorities have expressed some concerns about B2B exchanges dominated by large suppliers with undue influence. Buyers need to check exchange ownership and openness to all suppliers to ensure that they are not being used by a few dominant suppliers just to bring in more bidders and reduce prices. Another potential pitfall concerns the rules of participation and flexibility. Participants need to be clear about how much control they have over displaying and changing their bids and offers. They must determine whether the market's policy suits them. Most importantly, a knowledge market must be viewed in its wider context. Participants must be sure that it best suits their needs. Are there other markets that should be checked out for specific purchases. Would direct approaches make more sense? The key to addressing all these potential pitfalls is knowledge management. By collecting and collating knowledge of all relevant markets and your organization's usage of them, you can determine how well they suit your own objectives.

Summary

Online knowledge markets have significant potential to change the way that knowledge is traded. Although some knowledge markets currently exist, such as the recruitment and rights agencies, many conventional knowledge markets are biased towards buyer or seller, and are inefficient. The Internet is already stimulating some significant changes. It allows more buyers and sellers to make contact with each other. Easy access to market information creates greater transparency and makes markets more efficient. Buyers and sellers are able to access more opportunities and compare offers and prices. These benefits are encouraging significant investment into several different types of online knowledge market. Among the ten different types identified are knowledge auctions, question and answer exchanges and intellectual property exchanges.

Based on lessons from pioneering knowledge markets, such as iqport. com, a set of desirable characteristics for a successful market is proposed. The intangible nature of knowledge means that particular attention should be given to providing ways in which buyers can sample or assess what's on offer. The marketplace should also be easy to find and use. Knowledge markets are not suitable for every kind of knowledge transaction. A market space diagram distinguishes purchases according to the buyer's knowledge of the market and the organizational impact of the purchase. Knowledge markets have potential in much of this space, but even where they are not the natural first choice, they can help buyers test prices against existing suppliers, find more suppliers who might meet their needs and expand their knowledge of the products that are available.

Knowledge markets have had a hesitant start, and like many B2B exchanges, the future of many of them is uncertain. However, the exchange model of an online hub that offers a wide range of facilities – community discussion space, private co-creation areas, and market information, seems to have good potential, although individual market makers may struggle to generate profits. Looking even further ahead, we can expect to see some of the features of financial markets, which like knowledge also trade in intangibles. Leif Edvinsson, former vice president of intellectual capital at Skandia, and the pioneer of measuring intellectual capital, has envisaged IC stock exchanges and even derivatives markets where IC options and futures are traded.[16]

Points to ponder (and practise)

1   What conventional knowledge markets can you think of which facilitate the process of buyer meeting seller (such as a recruitment agency)?

2   Next time you seek a significant piece of advice chart out the path you took before finding the advice you needed. What were the difficulties in finding what you wanted quickly?

3   What stops you from seeking such advice online?

4   Try out a question and answer network (e.g. Askme.com, Keen.com, infomarkets.com). What advantages or disadvantages did you find?

5 Convert a piece of your personal intellectual capital into a packaged knowledge asset. Place it on an auction site or shop (e.g. Knexa.com. MightyWords.com). What did you learn from the experience?

6 In the section 'The attractions of markets' four factors were mentioned – access, matching, transparency and knowledge co-creation. How important are these to you or your organization as a buyer?

7 Think of other factors that might be attractive to buyer, seller or market maker.

8 Review a vertical market or exchange from the perspective of a supplier. What benefits do they give you as a supplier relative to your existing marketing channels?

9 What factors other than buyer knowledge and product impact affect whether a knowledge market is a better way to trade knowledge than existing alternatives?

10 When would you not want to sell your knowledge through a market? Review your product line and consider how attractive a knowledge market would be for each product.

Notes

1 The European Commission estimates that the digital content industries in Europe account for over 5 per cent of GDP (€412 billion), more than that of telecommunications (€221 billion) and hardware and software (€189 billion) combined. (*Source: Euroabstracts*, European Commission, June 2000.)

2 'The Promise and Challenge of Knowledge Markets', chapter 2 in *Working Knowledge: How Organizations Manage What They Know*, Thomas H. Davenport and Laurence Prusak (Harvard Business School Press, 1998).

3 For the more obvious knowledge trading places like a knowledge centre, there is often payment involved. This may be in the form of an annual budget levy on departments that use the centre, or increasingly through charging mechanisms based on usage.

4 Telecommunications Links with Experts. http://www.telinex.com.

5 In Fall 2000 neither of these domain names – http://www.futurizing.com and http://www.ICUniverse.com – was operational, although because of the latter's agency status with Knexa.com this may change.

6 *P2P Ecommerce Information Exchanges'*, Market Analysis Report, Datamonitor (April 2000).

7 'Authors' new online route to publishers', Joia Shillingford, *Financial Times*, FT-IT Review, p. XIV (7 June 2000).

8 Details can be found at KIKM's *Knowledge Markets Meta Portal* at http://www.kikm.org/portal/page2.htm. At the time of writing, KIKM were planning a further round of research into knowledge markets through a multi-client research study due to take place in 2001. Another site, http://www.B2Business.net, gives a listing of what it calls knowledge eMarketplaces.

9 For more details on Knexa's dynamic pricing mechanism, read the seller's guide at http://www.knexa.com.

10 'From recipes to theses, it's a knowledge market', Andrea L. Nyland, *Knowledge Management*, pp.12–13 (Freedom Technology Media Group, October 1999).

11 'The new online marketplace of ideas', Tyler Maroney, *Fortune*, pp. 229–230 (17 April 2000).
12 'The dawn of the e-lance economy', Thomas W. Malone and Robert J. Laubacher, *Harvard Business Review*, pp. 28–36 (September 1998).
13 'Working together – separately', Jane Lewis, *Computing*, pp. 52–53 (1 June 2000).
14 Ibid.
15 These details were taken from the website in July 2000. See also note 5.
16 *Intellectual Capital*, Leif Edvinsson and Michael S. Malone, pp. 186–188 (HarperBusiness, 1997).

Chapter 5

Productizing knowledge

The best knowledge must be embedded into all products and services.
(Karl Wiig, CEO, Knowledge Research Institute)

So far, we have considered the various ways in which developments in electronic commerce and the Internet open up new opportunities for marketing knowledge. Although knowledge can be sold in an ad hoc way, such as offering expertise in response to a request for help, repeat sales can be gained by explicitly packaging knowledge products and services. This is the process of 'productizing', even though in most cases the 'product' contains a strong intangible and services element.

This chapter analyses strategies for developing a knowledge product and service portfolio. The two main types of product and service that can be developed are object-based and people-based. These are closely related to an organization's structural capital and human capital. An essential accompaniment to a knowledge product is its 'surround'. This is the bundle of related attributes and services that make it attractive to buyers and users. Many of these aspects, such as brand image, customer relationship, and access to expertise, are relatively intangible. They therefore need special attention when the product or service is marketed or delivered over the Internet. A related element is the product 'wrapper'. This is used to describe and promote the product.

The process of productizing evolves naturally from an organizational knowledge management programme. It is a good example of inside-out thinking (see Chapter 1), where internal knowledge is taken to the outside world in a potentially profitable way. The chapter concludes with a discussion of the stages involved in making this happen.

Knowledge in products and services

Every product exudes knowledge. It is knowledge that its designers and makers have used to create it – materials knowledge, scientific knowledge, production knowledge and so on. A medicinal pill is the result of applying knowledge of the pharmaceutical effects of chemicals, and the extensive knowledge gained from clinical trials with a large group of patients. Most product manufacturers today seek to add services to their products. This is because many tangible products are like commodities, where consumers have difficulty in discerning the relevant differences between one make and another. They therefore make their selection based on lowest price. Add-on services, such as leasing, warranties, training, repair and maintenance increase customer value and generate product distinctions. These services too are knowledge-intensive, many of them using the knowledge and experience of individuals at the point of delivery. Moreover, since they can be customized to each buyer's needs, they are generally more profitable.

Services pose an interesting marketing challenge in they are mostly intangible. You can't touch or feel a service before receiving it. Until you experience it at first hand, you do not necessarily have a clear idea of what it actually is. Furthermore, a service delivered by one person in one place is rarely identical to the same service delivered by another person elsewhere. These are some of the reasons that there has been a trend over recent years to 'productize' services. The financial services industry offers potential buyers a wide range of financial 'products', including loans, mortgages, insurance policies and investments. It is also creative at developing new products, such as index tracking funds, variable premium life-cycle insurances, and derivatives. By embedding service knowledge into a product, the offering becomes more tangible to the consumer, simpler to understand and easier to reproduce in volume.

The distinction between products and services is therefore steadily blurring. Many products include a large service element, and many services are productized. The result is a range of hybrid offerings that Michael Schrage has dubbed 'provices' and 'serducts'.[1] The knowledge in these is sold and delivered in several different forms.

Forms of knowledge

There are many ways of categorizing knowledge. One is according to whether it is personal, shared or public. Another is by type – factual (know-what), procedural (know-how), systemic (know-why), judgemental (know-that). Related but different dimensions are the level of abstraction and conceptualization. These range from broad concepts to systematically applied knowledge to automated knowledge, which is so embedded in a person's consciousness, that he or she uses it subconsciously.[2] Such categorizations are useful in helping one think more clearly about the nature of personal and organizational knowledge. The important points from a productization perspective concern where knowledge resides and how accessible it is.

In Chapter 1 a fundamental distinction was made between explicit and tacit knowledge, with the former residing mostly in documents and data-bases and the latter in people's heads. In reality, this is an over-simplifica-tion. Some knowledge, such as factual knowledge, can be made very explicit and precise. At the other extreme, deep tacit knowledge, such as judgemental knowledge and belief, is very personal and extremely diffi-cult to convey to other people. There is thus a wide spectrum of types of knowledge between these two extremes. Karl Wiig describes several manifestations of knowledge.[3] He distinguishes tacit knowledge that is capable of being made explicit and that which is not. He describes different forms of embedded knowledge – in products, systems, organizational structures and processes. A further category is implicit knowledge. This is knowledge that is inherent in other manifestations, but needs analysis

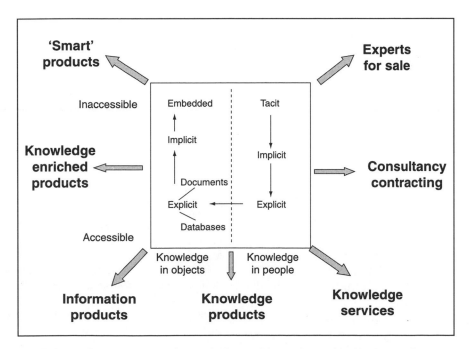

Figure 5.1 Different forms of knowledge and how they may productized

by knowledgeable people to extract it. An example is the assumptions used in product designs that may become evident through reverse engineering. Another is best practice guidance that is the result of distilling the pertinent knowledge from analysis of successes and failures.

Figure 5.1 portrays different forms of knowledge according to accessibility, and whether it is primarily held by people or in objects. Each of these forms is capable of exploitation in the external marketplace, as shown by the outgoing arrows. The arrows inside the box show the general sequence in which specific knowledge evolves from personal tacit knowledge through to more explicit and codified knowledge. At each stage, the knowledge can be used to enhance existing products and services or sold as knowledge products and services in their own right.

People-based services

Some of the most valuable knowledge-intensive services are those relying on personal knowledge. Specialist expertise is highly sought after. An expert is someone who has acquired deep tacit knowledge, insights and wisdom gained from years of experience. When their specialist expertise is in demand, it can command high prices in the marketplace. Some may even achieve the status of 'guru', a leading expert in their field. This status is sometimes exploited by the individuals keeping the knowledge to themselves and not sharing or productizing it. A good dose of self-marketing also helps to increase demand relative to supply and maintain premium prices.

Almost every organization has its world-class experts, but their unique talents are often insufficiently recognized or appreciated within the firm. Unless they are sufficiently rewarded and motivated, these experts may well be attracted to work for an organization whose primary business is based on selling expertise, such as a consultancy. Motivation studies show that knowledge workers relish working on challenging and different assignments that will help them enhance their expertise. Organizations can often improve their return on expert knowledge by

> **Porsche – car maker or knowledge contractor?**
>
> Porsche, renowned for its design expertise, started hiring out engineers in slack times to other car makers. It now also undertakes contract research and development to exploit this talent. At any one time, a third of its 2300 designers and engineers may be doing external contract work. Its non-manufacturing revenues grew 50 per cent in 1998 to $462 million, some 15 per cent of Porsche's total revenues.

deploying internal experts on direct revenue-generating activities. Any number of knowledge services can be created from this know-how and skill. Another route to exploitation of talent is to create outsourcing spin-offs. The highly successful IT outsourcing firm ITNET started as the in-house IT department of Cadbury–Schweppes.

One of the prime examples of a people-based service is that of contracting. Individuals and teams with specific expertise are

> **Online advice for start-ups**
>
> Management consultancy KPMG has teamed with MatchCo to offer online advice to entrepreneurs. For £1000 an entrepreneur can have their ideas evaluated, receive advice on marketing and legal issues and how to seek funding. MatchCo helps match the entrepreneurs with investors. KPMG's consultants advise on how to present their business case for funding. KPMG view it as a new way of delivering consultancy and gaining Internet based clients.
>
> *Source: Management Consultants News, Vol. 10, No. 9, 1999; http://www.matchco.co.uk*

contracted out to clients who have full access to their personal knowledge. As with any people-based service, the interaction between knowledge provider and user enriches the knowledge of both parties. In the case of contracting, this knowledge often moves around with the individual. More developed, in terms of exploiting expert knowledge, is the management consultancy market. Although predominantly people-based, most consultancies have developed exploitable organization knowledge. This includes knowledge about their consultants' capabilities, knowledge of clients, and skills to manage a consultancy assignment. In addition, some of the experience gained by individual consultants is codified into methodologies, computer systems and databases, such as databases of best practices. It then becomes object-based knowledge and part of the consultancy's structural capital – a reusable resource that leverages the knowledge of its consultants.

Because of this investment in structural capital, consultancies are tending to adopt new revenue and charging models. One is to base the fee on deliverables or results, rather than on a time and materials basis. After all, why should they not benefit from higher profits if their consultants can be much more effective because they can quickly access a wealth of packaged knowledge? Another is to take equity stakes in start-up businesses in lieu of fees for their advisory services. Their reward is thus more closely linked to the success of their client. Another strategy is to convert some of their knowledge into products for external sale. One way of doing this is to take an existing internal product, such as best practices databases, and adapt it for external resale. Alternatively, a knowledge product may be specifically developed by packaging various knowledge resources that already exist within the firm (see below).

Consultancies productize their expertise

Over the years, Arthur Andersen has built up an impressive set of databases and an intranet that its consultants regularly use. In February 1998 it launched KnowledgeSpace (http://www.knowledgespace.com) that offers clients versions of the sources used by its own consultants, including customized industry news sources, Arthur Andersen's own critical analyses and online conferences with experts. It also offers a version of its Global Best Practices database (http://www.globalbestpractices.com). Clients, who pay $395 for a basic individual subscription, can also email questions that are not directly answered by the online information. Other products in Arthur Andersen's portfolio include CountryNet, a detailed resource on 84 countries for business travellers and expatriates; Mastering Markets, a self-paced training course on CD-ROM for managing treasury risk that includes an interactive tool to try out sample situations; and tax software used by its own tax specialists.

Access to human expertise is the focus of Ernst & Young's ERNIE service (http://ernie.ey.com), which first went online in May 1996. Queries are directed to the appropriate specialist for an email answer. The question and answer, with confidential parts removed, is then added to a searchable database of previously asked questions. One of the interactive facilities is the Software Selection Adviser. It starts by asking the user about the nature of their company, their requirements and selection criteria. After narrowing the possible options, it then takes the user through a template that generates a request for proposal. It also makes additional suggestions, such as negotiating maintenance and upgrade agreements.

With over 1500 corporate subscribers, paying $3500 or more each, ERNIE now generates revenues in excess of $5 million annually.

By February 1999 Deloitte Consulting had completed over 200 customer relationship management (CRM) assignments. Some of the top consultants who had worked on these assignments pooled their knowledge of best practice and developed a diagnostic tool kit, which is now sold as a separate product.[4]

Object-based knowledge products

One of the main problems of offering purely people-based services is that revenue-generating capacity is limited by the available number of skilled people. This can be overcome to some extent by codifying people-based knowledge into packages that can be more easily replicated and used by less skilled people. Thus, once advisers refine a set of methods, they can be packaged into a methodology.

Table 5.1 Examples of knowledge packaging

Type of knowledge	Examples of packaging
Scientific and technical	Journal articles, patents, products
Engineering	Designs, drawings, products
Procedural	Procedure manuals, computer software
Organizational	Processes, procedure manuals, computer databases
Know-how	Guidelines, best practice databases
Specific expertise	Expert systems
Factual knowledge	Books, directories

Knowledge is regularly packaged into well-understood formats (Table 5.1). The resultant knowledge objects are typically the result of synthesizing many different elements of knowledge and applying a design and development process. Thus scientific knowledge about the therapeutic effects of a chemical is encapsulated into medical drugs. The price of the medicine more typically reflects the value of this knowledge, rather than just the value of its chemical ingredients. Knowledge of how to diagnose problems with equipment and repair them is garnered from the experience of engineers and packaged into repair and maintenance manuals.

Object-based knowledge is most commonly packaged into two main types of media – computer-based and paper-based. The former includes databases, Web pages and software. The latter includes documents and many other types of publication – reports, books, articles etc. Hard-copy publication has traditionally been a popular way of productizing and diffusing knowledge. However, publication is increasingly taking place through computer media, such as CD-ROM and electronic files accessible through the Internet. Publishing in digital format offers much more scope for repackaging and allows the user to adapt the content to their specific needs or to forward it to colleagues. Compared to the passive nature of a paper publication, computer-based knowledge can be interactive and intelligent, aspects that are explored shortly.

> **Online therapy**
>
> What was once done behind the psychiatrist's couch now happens routinely online. A recent Harris survey estimated that 24 million people have sought mental health information online. It can be supplied in the form of email consultations with professionals, online chat, video-conferencing and discussion groups. One of the pioneers, Birmingham (UK) based psychiatrist Dr Russell Razzaque, now offers an Employee Assistance Program for corporations for $36 per employee per year at http://www.CyberAnalysis.com.
>
> *Source*: 'Virtual couch', Rochelle Sharpe, *Business Week e.biz*, pp. 91–93, 18 September 2000

Package variations

Knowledge packages vary enormously in terms of formality, size, scope, quality and style. A patent, for example, is a formal piece of intellectual property protected by law. Procedure manuals may follow well-defined company or industry standards. International standards, such as the quality standard ISO 9000, represent codification of best practice into a common structure, that has been agreed by formally constituted committees. On the other hand much explicit knowledge may be packaged as documents or emails with minimal structure and little evaluation. Knowledge packages may be an indivisible whole, like a report, or alternatively a collection of many self-contained knowledge objects. A single object can vary from many pages of textual material to a single number in a database record. It may be an unvalidated piece of breaking news, or an item that has been validated for quality through peer review. It may be very generic in nature, such as a general marketing concept, or it may be very customized and specific, such as market sizing information for accountancy services in Northern England. The same knowledge is often packaged in different ways to meet the needs of different consumers and the different ways in which they will use it. Some of the different types of packages that people may need include the following:

- *à-la-carte* knowledge objects available on a pay-as-you-go basis, direct from originators;
- quality assured knowledge objects with 'wrappers' describing and validating their contents;
- *table-d'hôte* knowledge – basic packages of core knowledge, e.g. 'how to' guides, such as 'how to start your own e-business';
- customized knowledge packages – a tailored collection of knowledge objects assembled either automatically or by humans (knowledge brokers): 'one-stop shops' for knowledge;
- knowledge 'on tap' – access to expertise around the clock for specific knowledge on an 'as needed' basis.

Some packaging makes knowledge more open and accessible (e.g. conversations with experts). Other packaging, while encapsulating knowledge as easily reproducible objects, is less context specific and adds opaqueness between originators and end users. We now consider some of the different types of package.

Patents and intellectual property

Applying for a patent is a common way that many R&D departments aim to protect their organization's knowledge. Provided an invention or discovery meets the criteria of novelty, an inventive step, and capable of application, a patent will provide the holder with monopoly rights for a period of up to 25 years. IBM heads the league for the number of patents awarded. In 1999 it was awarded 2756 patents, 900 more than next in line NEC. Around a third of IBM's patents were for software technologies fundamental to its business strategy.[5] There has been significant growth in the number of patent applications covering software and business processes. In the area of electronic commerce, patents have been awarded to Priceline.com for its 'name your own price' method and Amazon.com for its '1-Click ordering'.

As well as being valuable in the development of an organization's products or processes, patents can be lucrative sources of revenue when licensed to others. IBM earns more than $1 billion annually in revenues from licensing its patents.[6] However, many organizations do not actively manage their patent portfolio. The case of Dow Chemical, who revitalized and exploited its patent portfolio, has been widely recognized as an example of good knowledge management that has delivered significant short-term benefits. According to Patrick Sullivan Jr, a pioneer in intellectual capital measurement, organizations need to think beyond the legal filing process and consider their knowledge assets as business documents. The documents should be chunked into sections which are analysed for knowledge that has commercial potential. Computer-based systems, such as SmartPatents, can help organizations map the knowledge within patents against other knowledge sources. Visual maps help identify clusters of patents and guide market exploitability.[7]

Knowledge-enriched products

Knowledge can be used to enrich a product in two main ways. First, it can be embedded as part of the product. Second, it can be used to surround the core product with complementary services. Knowledge may be embedded into a product in many ways, such as software algorithms, neural networks that learn from situations, or even in chemicals. A 'smart' product is one with embedded knowledge that has a degree of intelligence beyond that of a pre-programmed response to a stimulus. 'Smart' oil drills sense the rock immediately ahead and use computer simulation of the oil reservoirs to steer the drill to extract the maximum amount of oil. Miravant is working on intelligent drugs that distinguish healthy cells from diseased ones and act selectively.

The behaviour of many intelligent products comes from sensing and integrating information from multiple sources and acting on it appropriately. Here are two examples. Car navigation displays integrate current information of traffic flows, geographic position and your desired destination, to adjust the optimum route in real-time. Military researchers are developing intelligent uniforms that assess a soldier's injuries from data collated from the clothes' woven optical fibres (determining the location), a miniature spectrometer (to sense the amount of bleeding), sensors and microphones (to assess the extent of injuries including the penetration depth of bullets). When appropriate, the soldier's radio will automatically transmit this information back to paramedics, together with their whereabouts determined from a geographic positioning device.[8]

As these examples indicate, there are many potential sources of information and knowledge associated with a product that can be processed and used to increase its intelligence. Amongst all this technical sophistication, we should not overlook the fact that some of the best intelligence to add to any product or service is human intelligence. How many times have you been frustrated by poorly designed voice response systems, when all you wanted to do was to talk to a human?

Let's now consider the second way of using knowledge to enrich a product – surrounding it with related product knowledge. This comes from two main sources: that used in the development of the product but not actually embedded into it, and that derived from its use. An engineering company might commercialize some of the unused development knowledge by selling it as consultancy or training to users of the product. It might even sell this knowledge independent of the product, as in the case of Porsche described earlier (page 136). Knowledge of a product's applications is potentially an even richer source of revenue. A supplier is in a good position to collate applications knowledge from all its customers, and keep it updated in a knowledge base. This is an evolving source of knowledge that can be used as part of an advisory service. In addition, some of it can be packaged as training courses for users. Most organizations have an accumulated wealth of product and applications knowledge that remains under-exploited.

Information products

Packaging knowledge as information is a common and relatively straightforward way of productizing knowledge. Traditionally, publishers and database hosting services have provided this as a route to market for knowledge owners. The Internet has now made it easier for owners to sell information packaged in databases, documents, e-zines (electronic magazines), newsletters and many other formats. They can be made available through the creator's website, through that of intermediaries or via email.

Articles, white papers, reports, and even books containing valuable information are often published first, or even exclusively, on the Internet. These may be sold for a fee, but often they will be used as a marketing tool to generate interest in higher value knowledge-based products. In either case, packaging some knowledge as information is virtually a necessity for creating a

> **Packaged knowledge**
>
> KPMG's *Change the game, change the rules of the game*, was published as an instant e-book in 1999, available free on the Web. It took just five weeks from start to finish, much shorter than the conventional nine months or longer of a conventional publishing cycle. It acts as a marketing tool to demonstrate KPMG's expertise in business transformation.

successful k-business. Let's now consider some of the more common forms of online information products.

Online databases

Online versions of scientific, technical and business periodicals have for decades been a staple offering of proprietary online services such as Dialog. There are also specialist databases of business and financial information, marketing surveys, legal information and patents, many also offered in CD-ROM versions. A key feature of most online services is the ability to search across a wide range of sources. As the Internet has grown in popularity, the information seeker is now more likely to be a professional end-user, rather than an information or library professional who traditionally did this task. There has been a corresponding shift to more user-friendly interfaces, as well as content and features aimed at specific groups of end-user, such as financial analysts, product developers or marketers. Indicative of these developments is a business best practices database offered by Best Practices LLC, a North Carolina based consultancy specializing in benchmarking (see case study below).

Packaging best practices knowledge

Best Practices LLC started life as a consultancy in 1992. In 1997 it started to transition its products and services to the Internet. It always intended to offer a database of best practices to its customers, but only recently felt that technology was mature enough to allow this to be accomplished easily. Its first online database used Lotus Notes and was tested with internal customers. The externally available database was launched in 1999. Specifically targeted at senior executives and consultants, it draws on case material from leading practitioners and its own consultancy experience to provide information on over 3000 techniques classified by business function and specific issue. Users can also do free text searches. The resultant information is presented using standard templates so that regular users can quickly find what they want. Initially launched on an annual subscription basis ($4000), it is now also available on a pay-per-document basis (typically $3–$5 per item). This allows ad-hoc users to buy just the items they need. Best Practices have also productized its consultant's insights into benchmarking reports. These too are sold online. Because of conscious productizing, revenues from information services have grown rapidly and are expected to exceed those from consultancy revenues by the end of 2000.

Source: Keith Symmers, Best Practices LLC.
Website: http://www.BestPracticeDatabase.com

From documents to blocks

The document is one of the most common forms of knowledge package. Many are conventionally divided into chapters, sections and paragraphs. But few document providers consciously consider the information they contain as distinct structural elements, each of which is a potential knowledge package. The Economist Information Unit is one organization that now sells information in various sized units (see below).

> **Converting hard-copy to online**
>
> It is estimated that 95 per cent of the world's packaged knowledge is still in hard-copy form. To make it more accessible, Versaware has 700 workers in Pune, India, who use scanners to digitize 6000 books a month at an average of 500 pages per book. They can then be purchased online (e.g. at eBookCity.com) for viewing or printed on demand. Publishers see this service as particularly useful for out-of-print books.
>
> *Source: FT-IT Review, p. XV, 7 June 2000*

EIU – information sized to suit

The Economist Intelligence Unit (EIU) has a long tradition of providing high quality newsletters, research reports and economic forecasts for business executives. One of its important knowledge assets is its ongoing analyses of the business environment in 190 countries. EIU launched its online store (http://store.eiu.com) in October 1999. This gives customers the ability to buy 'byte-sized' business intelligence. They can purchase as little or as much information as they need. Users of the store website can search by category, including country, industry and best practice. They can select for purchase individual sections, articles, chapters or whole reports. As an example, one customer might just want a short extract from a newsletter that features a particular company. Such an extract might cost only a few dollars, compared to several hundred for a newsletter subscription. Several payment options are available. Customers can pay as they go for individual items, take out annual subscriptions for unlimited access to all information, or choose various options in between. The online store is supplemented by the general EIU website that has sections of frequently updated free information, and a section for corporate clients. EIU also runs the e-business forum that gives news, analysis, thought leadership papers and a discussion forum on electronic commerce.

As organizations become more conscious of the benefits of just-in-time byte-sized knowledge – use what you need, when you need it – documents will need to be reconsidered in terms of their structural elements and the relationship between them. The discipline of content management addresses such considerations. Defining structural elements in documents is not new. A level of structure definition already exists in documents created using SGML (the Standard General Markup Language), a forerunner of the simpler HTML (HyperText Markup Language) which is widely used for Web pages. HTML's structural tags are mostly concerned with logical blocks that determine layout and formatting, such as ⟨div⟩ for division, ⟨p⟩ for paragraph, ⟨ol⟩ for ordered list and ⟨table⟩ for a table. But it also includes tags like ⟨title⟩, ⟨blockquote⟩ and ⟨cite⟩ that are intended for specific types of structure. A more recent markup language, XML (eXtensible Markup Language), takes structural definitions a stage further by allowing tags to describe the content of a block of information. Thus ⟨author⟩ could refer to the author's name, ⟨company⟩ a company name, ⟨product⟩ a product description, and so on. The content can then be processed by applications, such as an e-commerce programme, or used to search for information within a given block (similar to searching within fields in a database record). These tags can be defined as part of each document's definition. Herein, lies the rub. Unless providers and users agree a common set of tags, then one person's ⟨company⟩ may be another's ⟨organization⟩. Without common agreed tag definitions and the rules for what they contain, we are back to many of the problems that have haunted computer systems for years – that of incompatibility. Fortunately, various standards bodies and trade associations are already addressing this problem.[9]

> **Knowledge nuggets from MeansBusiness**
>
> To help give busy managers just what they need, the 25 editorial staff at MeansBusiness scour business books for gems of knowledge. These are refined and packaged in various ways including extracts, concept book summaries, themes and concept suites. For example, a user search on a topic may generate a $15 summary that contains the best insights on the topic from several books. The material is reviewed by the authors, who along with the publishers receive royalties on sales.
>
> *Sources*: 'Distributing nuggets of knowledge', Dawne Shand, *Knowledge Management*, p. 98 (Freedom Technology Media Group, April 2000); http://www.meansbusiness.com

Typically, structural blocks are relatively small units, which when grouped and sequenced in a certain way create a Web page or document. Organizing information into well-defined blocks offers several advantages. In the field of technical documents, using such an approach has been shown to improve information quality and reliability. Users of the *Information Mapping*® method, developed by Robert Horn, have reported improvements in accuracy from 60 per cent to well over 90 per cent in fault-finding and repair manuals. The method has fairly strict rules on the nature and structure of information blocks. There are only a limited number of block types, such as facts, principles, processes and concepts. There are best practice guidelines for creating each kind of block. There are also general readability guidelines, such as breaking long lists into smaller groups.[10]

The more general advantage of a block-oriented approach to documents is that it provides a starting point for creating information objects that can be reused in different information products or traded as information objects in their own right. In the field of computer software, object-oriented approaches are becoming more common. For example, Java applets are program objects that are downloaded to your personal computer and execute a set of instructions when you browse particular Web pages. There are libraries of applets that are available for sale or free download. Looking to the future, there is likely to be a great demand for small information blocks that can be rapidly downloaded into mobile phone handsets.

Adding richness to information

Many information products are passive. The information they contain is merely presented to the reader. With hard-copy this is inevitable. But too many information providers simply transfer their products over to new media without exploiting its characteristics. *Encyclopaedia Britannica's* first CD-ROM had a disappointing market response, since it needed more than simply excellent content to be attractive to consumers. In contrast, Microsoft's *Encarta*, as well as a low price had attractively presented content, multimedia clips and links to online updates. By exploiting the functionality of the Internet and developments in multimedia, the richness and usefulness of information can be significantly increased (Table 5.2).

E-book – active reading

Electronic editions of printed books already offer readers a richer reading experience. First the reader downloads a book from the Net (for example from 00h00.com) into a PC or an e-book, a specialized book-reading device. The type size can be varied, footnotes can give hyperlinks, and additional background information is available as you read. The reader can highlight passages and return to them quickly later. The book can be updated easily by the author. Now imagine what can be done if publishers fully exploit the features of the new media in an intelligent publication (see page 149).

Table 5.2 Features that add richness and usefulness to information

Feature	User benefits
Structure	Information presented in logical sections increases readability. Use of common formats helps the user quickly find sections of relevance. Adding XML tags simplifies exchange of information between databases and applications
Hyperlinks	Users can quickly connect to reference material and related pages without revisiting index pages or searching
Expert contact	By including author contact details, e.g. via email hyperlinks, a direct communications channel is opened between reader and expert. This provides opportunities for clarification, feedback or ongoing dialogue
Multimedia	The use of audio, images and video stimulates more senses and enhances comprehension for many readers and for certain kinds of information
Interactive	By linking information to applications or searchable databases, users can select relevant pathways through information, simulate real environments for learning purposes, or more directly use information as part of a work procedure
Ready to use	The information can be slotted directly into an application, such as information ready for use by a database or spreadsheet
Adaptive	Displaying different information according to usage patterns tailors the information displayed to the user's immediate needs
Customized	Matching information content and format to the user's preferences makes it more directly applicable in the user's context. Offering multilingual versions also makes it more accessible to readers whose primary language is different from the creators
Communities	Linking users with common interests to each other allows them to share views on the usefulness of the information provided and to share experience and continually enhance their knowledge

Take as an example the use of multimedia.[11] BP Amoco finds that the occasional 30-second video clip of expert commentary inserted into an intranet database entry helps personalize the entry and aids assimilation. Modern digital compression techniques make it possible to package images, diagrams, audio, video and animation into relatively small amounts of space. For example, a TV-quality one minute video clip occupies just over 30 Mbytes, a small proportion of most hard disks today. Equally significant is the use of video and audio streaming. By accepting lower quality video on just a portion of their computer screen, many

Web users are now used to hearing conference speeches or interviews with business leaders that are streamed in real-time. Such facilities can also be used asynchronously. Thus, META Group's interactive research reports can be downloaded to a PC for later viewing. They include colour presentation slides and streaming audio as well as normal text and diagrams. With much higher online bandwidths on the horizon, the days of high quality real-time

.xls – ready to run

.xls, a service of Data Downlink, aggregates and cross-indexes data from more than 70 business databases from different suppliers. Users can search for economic statistics, company financial information, investment research and more. Discrete pieces of numerical information that are selected are downloaded directly into an Excel spreadsheet where they can be immediately processed.

Website: http://www.xls.com

video are not far away. Static information without the added richness of the features of Table 5.2 will become as obsolete as black and white computer screens are today.

On a cautionary note, many Web users still have limited bandwidth access, and everyone has different preferred styles of absorbing information. Packaging information only as a Powerpoint presentation or a 30-minute conference talk will quickly turn off those readers who want to skim the information quickly to pick out relevant items. Providers must cater for all levels of need and richness.

Knowledge hybrids

So far in this chapter we have described examples of people-based and object-based knowledge products and services. In practice, many offerings are neither solely one nor the other. They are hybrids that contain knowledge objects of various types. A knowledge object is a small element of knowledge. Its core might typically be a block of information, with links to people for additional knowledge transfer. On the other hand, a five minute consultation with a doctor could be defined as a knowledge object. As with other knowledge packages, some, like the first example, are highly codified and easily reproducible, whereas others are context-dependent. They can be sold separately as small discrete units of knowledge or used in combination as part of a more comprehensive hybrid offering. Hybrid knowledge products combine the reach of knowledge objects with the richness of person-to-person interaction. Let's now look at two examples: intelligent publications and e-learning.

Intelligent publications

An intelligent publication combines and deploys knowledge in several ways (Figure 5.2). Raw information, such as that gathered from the news sources, is refined through analysis and interpretation to provide higher quality content. Customer knowledge is then applied intelligently to provide a tailored output for the user. This might mean selecting only those sections of the publication that are relevant. The publication can be made dynamic through real-time updating, for example by using intelligent agents, or accessing databases held elsewhere. As the user accesses the content, intelligence built into an embedded algorithm may help them with navigation or generate small pop-up windows with related content (such as done by Kenjin – see page 51).

Human intelligence is added through various knowledge networks. One such network might be an expert 'answernet', where experts on the subject matter for each part of the publication are accessible to answer questions, either through email, a chat facility, voicemail or telephone. In turn some of their knowledge may be encapsulated into an 'expertnet', an artificial intelligence system that interacts with the user, providing answers where available and linking into the 'answernet' where additional help is needed.

Another perspective of an intelligent publication is that it is a dynamically changing set of knowledge objects and links. Unlike a conventional publication, which is sequential, the reader starts with a specific object and then goes via hyperlinks to related objects in no particular sequence. Mind mapping systems, such as MindManager and The Brain, already display information in such ways, with conceptual links between related chunks of information. Other than familiarity with the normal conventions,

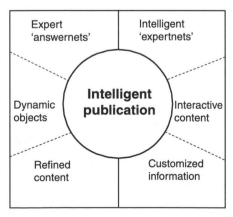

Figure 5.2 The elements of a typical intelligent publication

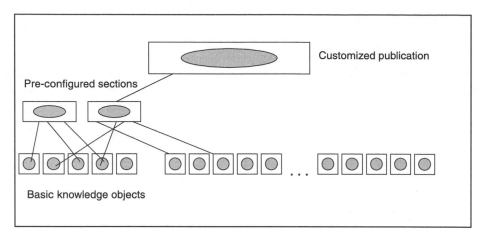

Figure 5.3 The architectural approach to publishing

there is no reason why publications should not be presented as a series of linked maps. Reading such a publication is closely related to Web browsing, although with a different interface.

A publication is traditionally a paper-based product, and paper is still a preferred medium for serious reading. With today's technology, it is possible for a reader to have a short question and answer dialogue with a computer, which then compiles a customized publication from various knowledge objects in its library. This is analogous to the architectural approach to product development, which is already successfully used in other areas. Here a common platform provides a base for connecting different modules together using standard interfaces. For example, numerous variants of hand-held power tools can be created from combining different bodies, motors and attachments such as drills and sanders.

Figure 5.3 indicates this approach applied to publishing. The publisher has available a wide range of knowledge objects appropriately classified by topic, audience etc. Selections of these are pre-configured into sections, which may be a few pages of text or sometimes as much as a chapter. A customized publication is then created by linking the relevant sections together in the appropriate sequence. The publisher may already have off-the-shelf publications appropriate to different situations and readers. The difficult part of creating a publication from individual information blocks is that of creating smooth transitions between them to produce a coherent document. This may require several variants of each knowledge object according to context and writing style. There will almost certainly need to be rules on sequencing and the insertion of linking sentences or paragraphs.

Such an approach does challenge conventional publishing processes and the style in which many writers are accustomed to writing. Shifts in mind set are already occurring, as some writers are now geared to writing in Web-style, with its shorter chunks of text and hyperlinks.

E-learning

Another example of a hybrid knowledge product is e-learning. This combines the techniques of distance learning with the Internet. Course material can be delivered on paper, CD-ROM or over the Internet. Email is used for correspondence between tutor and student. The business school of The Open University has exploited the Internet even further. It uses computer conferencing (FirstClass) in several modes – for student self-help groups, for student work groups which tutors can monitor, for communities of interest that connect students with world-wide experts and for tutor-to-tutor exchange of information and experiences. One organization that has identified e-learning as a medium to exploit its partners' knowledge is Scottish Knowledge (see below).

> ### Scottish Knowledge packaged for the world
>
> Scottish Knowledge is a consortium that markets one of Scotland's key intellectual assets – its universities. Its corporate shareholders include Scottish Power, Ernst & Young and BP Amoco. They have funded the transfer of course material into an online format, and in return get a 10–15 per cent commission on course fees. Its focus is in areas of Scotland's educational strengths – science, engineering, IT and telecommunications. Two of several degree courses on offer are an MA in project management from Aberdeen University and an MBA in entrepreneurship from Stirling University. Scottish Knowledge achieved sales in 1999 of £500 000, mainly through two large contracts with Malaya – one with Institut Technologi Mara and the other with Petronas, the national energy company.
>
> Source: 'Scots discover global market for learning', Ricky Dalton, Sunday Times, p. 3.11 (11 April 1999). Website: http://www.scottishknowledge.com

In these examples, the unit of e-learning is a course, itself a series of teaching modules. More useful in most on-the-job learning situations are much smaller learning objects. These can simply be small packages of knowledge, a few paragraphs or a page or two, that answer an immediate knowledge need, such as 'what is the best way of developing a knowledge thesaurus for my industry?' These information objects can include hyperlinks to related material and more substantial resources, including access to human experts and relevant online communities. Intermediate sized

Table 5.3 Distinctive characteristics of knowledge products and services

Characteristic	Example
Knowledge products	
The more you use them, the smarter they get	The more I use the voice input system on my computer to write this book the fewer mistakes it makes
The more you use them, the smarter you get	Regular use of a problem-solving database will result in a more knowledgeable customer support team
They adjust to changing circumstances	A car engine monitoring system adjusts key controls and 'knows' when essential maintenance is needed
They can be customized	Amazon.com remembers your preferences and makes suggestions of books you might like to read
They have relatively short life cycles	The database of business telephone numbers used in a sales management system needs regular updating
They enable customers to act in real-time	The traffic monitoring system in my car allows me to change my route to avoid traffic congestion
People-based knowledge	
Intangibility	I don't know why I prefer one particular service person to maintain my heating system, but I do
Inseparability	I can't buy an off-the-shelf diagnosis from my doctor. Production and delivery are simultaneous
Variability	When I consult railway enquiries for train times and connections, I get two different answers to the same query
Resource limited	The earliest I can get a piece of landscape design work done is in three months time, since local designers have a full workload
Object-based knowledge (online)	
Simultaneous use	I can be reading the same investment advice on *The Motley Fool* at the same time as thousands of other people around the world

Table 5.3 Continued

Characteristic	Example
Multiple reuse	Once I have used this advice, I and others can go back and use it again. Unlike a physical resource, it is not depleted
Always available	I can access emergency household advice at any time of day or night, without having to get the provider out of bed
Relevant and timely	I can access just the section I need from the repair manual to solve my problem. I am also confident that it has the most up to date solution
World-wide expertise	There is every likelihood that the knowledge offered is of high quality, since I am not restricted to experts in my locality

learning objects are short update training modules such as the familiarization tutorials now common in various software packages, and associated 'help' files.

Many organizations are sitting on existing content written by internal experts that can be turned into learning objects without too much difficulty. In fact, there may already be training courses whose content can be categorized and chunked. In common with other situations where content is packaged, the provider must see things from the user's perspective. They need to think about specific knowledge work activities and business processes, and what problems or common questions the content answers. The information may also benefit from restructuring along a typical learning sequence such as introduction, key concepts, distinguishing features, examples, guidelines and additional resources.

Special characteristics of knowledge products

It is useful at this point to summarize some of the key characteristics of knowledge products and services compared to traditional products (Table 5.3). The first six characteristics are those identified by Davis and Botkin.[12] The other sections of the table add characteristics of people-based services and of online products that have been discussed in this chapter. Each needs to be considered when developing a knowledge product or service. Some confer advantages that can be turned into a marketing tool, such as round-the-clock access to the best expertise. Others raise issues that need addressing, such as how to keep the product up to date and how to ensure a consistent standard of delivery where people are involved.

Completing the knowledge package

Creating the basic knowledge product or service is only the first part of the packaging task. A concept used by marketers is that of a core product and its product surround (Figure 5.4). For a k-business the core product is information or knowledge. This may range from a single item of information to a wide-ranging people-based service. As with conventional products, parts of the core product are hidden from view. These parts are used by the producer to make it work. Most people don't care what's underneath the hood of a car, or inside a stereo unit, as long as it works. Likewise, the average Internet user is not concerned about the HTML code buried in every Web page, nor the detailed routing header that accompanies every email. One use of the hidden area that is growing in importance is that of recording intellectual property rights information to ensure authorized use only (see page 156).

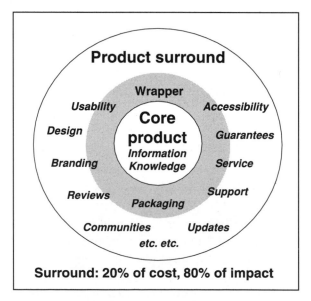

Figure 5.4   Core product and product surround

The highest value in many products lies in the surround rather than the core. This is particularly true for that information which is viewed as a low-cost commodity. In many cases the additional investment needed to create a product surround may be relatively small, while its impact and value to the customer can be much more significant than that of the core product. The surround includes a wide range of attributes, many of them intangible. The inner part of the surround for a knowledge product is sometimes called the wrapper.

Knowledge wrapper

The aim of the knowledge wrapper is to convey as clearly as possible the nature of the product's contents. It includes factual information, such as formats and size, and subjective information, such as reviews and quality rating, plus a good dose of promotional marketing. Typical elements that form a knowledge wrapper are shown in Table 5.4.

At first sight, some of these elements will be familiar to those who create metadata for documents or Web pages. A Web page META tag, that goes in the page's header, has tags for content, keywords and title, that are used by search engines as an indication of the page content (many also do frequency counts of words in the text). One of the most popular metadata standards is that used by librarians for bibliographic data and known as the Dublin Core (named after the first meeting of its originators in Dublin, Ohio). This has 15 core elements divided into three categories:[13]

1 *Content* – Title, Subject, Description, Source, Language, Relation, Coverage.
2 *Intellectual Property* – Creator, Publisher, Contributor, Rights.
3 *Instantiation* – Date, Type, Format, Identifier.

With the increasing emphasis on accessing and sharing Web content, there is currently much activity in developing standard metadata structures.

Table 5.4 Typical elements in a knowledge product wrapper

Title	Creator
Overview or abstract	How to purchase and open
Keywords	Instructions for use
Format	Quality rating
Size	Independent reviews
Unique features	Creation date
Applications and scope	Version number
User benefits	Last updated

Much of the standards work is being developed under the auspices of the W3C's Resource Description Framework (RDF). This work should help achieve better consistency of terminology across content providers.[14] As mentioned earlier in the context of XML, much of the standardization effort is work in progress. While standards will certainly help in conveying meaning for highly developed and more mature knowledge domains, achieving consensus in areas where knowledge evolution is fast changing will be a more difficult proposition. In any event, these developments are too important for any productizer of knowledge to ignore.

A good wrapper must offer much more than essential metadata. It must entice potential buyers to purchase, yet be informative and accurate. Unlike physical goods that can be returned if the buyer is not satisfied, the mere act of opening a knowledge object and viewing its contents means that knowledge has been transferred. To overcome these difficulties a knowledge provider may offer a free trial period of use, or a money-back guarantee if the buyer is not satisfied. But this still demands time and effort on the part of the user. Given the wide selection of alternative products a potential buyer will give greater weight to the views of independent reviewers and consumers. Wrappers might therefore contain summaries of these reviews (with pointers to the full reviews) or carry an accreditation rating, such as that given by an editorial team at an aggregator. Other information that may form part of the wrapper includes details of warranties, updating options, customer service and digital rights.

Digital rights

As copying of knowledge in the form of information becomes ever easier, digital rights are becoming an increasingly important part of a knowledge product's wrapper. As information objects are easily diffused, it is important that buyers and users understand any limitations on use or copying. The music industry has been particularly concerned about unlawful copying and distribution of copyrighted material over the Internet. Composers and other knowledge creators maintain that they need to gain a reasonable return on their intellectual investment, such as a royalty based on usage, in exchange for use of their creative output. Several tools now help protect digital rights. Digital watermarks, for instance, can be encrypted and embedded in images, yet are invisible to the naked eye, and can be used to prevent unauthorized copying and reading. Several systems are now being developed to automatically manage the tracking of products as they are sold and used. These also aggregate large numbers of small royalty payments so that lump sums can be paid periodically to the rights owner. As with other embryonic industries there are alternative approaches, software and service providers, and it will be some time before clear standards or favourites emerge. One of the most established is InterTrust Technologies whose software is used in a number of pilot services including the DigiHub service announced by Pricewaterhouse-Coopers (see below).[15]

DigiHub: an environment for managing digital rights

Using technology from InterTrust technologies, PriceWaterhouse-Coopers has developed DigiHub, an online business that provides a digital rights management environment. Initially focused on digital music, it not only validates users' rights but can track usage of the asset over its life cycle, both online and offline. Content creators use the services of a DigiHub to 'wrap' the asset, which as well as describing its contents adds business rules, such as pricing options. The resultant Digibox is a tradable item, where distributors can add their own rules. Consumers apply for an account which gives them a digital wallet that gives them access rights to the contents of a Digibox. A 'token' is loaded into their PC and gives them appropriate access depending on their product selection and amount of payment. They can choose the format they want. In addition, consumer preferences and reviews can be returned to the creator and others in the supply chain. One of the reasons for Price-WaterhouseCooper's involvement is that it is viewed as a trusted third party by suppliers and consumers alike.

Although we have described it as part of the surround, it is common for wrappers to be an integral part of the product, remaining as part of it or attached to it as it moves from seller to buyer, and from one user to another. This ensures that important conditions of usage and any rights information are readily accessible. Of course, the rights can be reinforced by clear identification of rights, such as copyright notice, on every page or screen.

The product surround

Outside the wrapper are the other elements that complete the product offering. These include associated services, brand image, after-sales support and so on. Although two suppliers may offer the same knowledge, intangible factors are an important influence on the buyer. These include the way that the knowledge is presented, the reputation of the supplier and the perceived level of service. In the online environment, the initial user experience can make or break a sale. Also significant is the way in which the supplier follows through with handling a user's queries and addresses their specific requirements. Many potential customers of goods sold over the Internet are let down by poor website usability, difficulty in finding what they want, and poor order fulfilment. Once bitten, twice shy. If visitors can find something similar elsewhere, it is extra hard to get them back. These usability and customer service issues are covered in more detail in Chapter 8 (page 237).

Other aspects of the product surround are self explanatory, but brand image is an important one worthy of special consideration. The importance of brands on the Internet is a topic of much debate. Traditionally a brand conveys a bundle of attributes that position the product, convey a level of quality, service, value for money etc. On the Internet suppliers change incessantly. Having a well-known brand name in the real world is no guarantee of success on the Internet. Even firms with a reputable brand have come unstuck on some occasions. Take well-known stockbroker Charles Schwab. It has come in for heavy criticism for not being able to carry out certain online trades within normally acceptable timeframes, especially during periods of volatile price movements. As a result, some clients have faced unexpected financial losses. How companies deal with such situations has a big impact on how well the brand reputation is sustained. On the other hand, successful brands have been created purely through the Internet. Yahoo! and Amazon.com are perhaps the best internationally known examples. Like their real-world counterparts, their websites have established themselves as places to visit again and again. Both, incidentally, have been around for over five years – an eon in Internet timescales – and have therefore had time to establish their online credentials. However, the lack of an established brand has not stopped many companies, or even entrepreneurial individuals, from trading successfully on the Internet. The quality of what's on offer and ease of doing business have often proved to be more important aspects of the product surround in the eyes of the potential buyer. Companies like Powersize, Moreover and Autonomy, unknown a few years ago, have all carved out knowledge intensive businesses on the Internet.[16] Autonomy is a good example of a brand associated with a product. The company who produced it was Cambridge Neurodynamics, but the success of Autonomy spawned out a new company with that name to align with the brand.[17]

The process of productizing

Developing new knowledge-based products and services draws on established principles of new product development. This involves a sequence of idea generation, scoping potential products, putting them through some kind of investment filter, then taking those selected through to prototyping, market testing and finally production. But even this traditional approach is being enhanced by the application of knowledge management and using the Internet. Let's briefly examine their influence on each phase in turn.

Creating product ideas　An established knowledge programme should already have provided a good starting point for this. A knowledge inventory or audit will identify knowledge assets. The only difference is that as information is collected, questions should be asked as to the likely exploitation potential of this asset externally. If the creators do not know, as often they will not, then some of the users will be able to articulate the benefits it gives to them. Other sources of ideas come from knowledge that is collated in idea banks. Close monitoring of what existing customers are asking about – from call centres, email requests to the website etc. – will also start to indicate potential candidates.

Selecting ideas to pursue　Formal methods involve putting ideas through some filter or sieve to see if they match certain investment criteria. However, with the Internet, there are so many uncertainties that it is often worth doing small 'proof of concept' projects. Communities can be very valuable at this stage. In order to protect commercial confidentiality product developers can set up closed user groups or communities. First, the ideas can be floated within these communities to gain feedback. Second, early prototypes can be given to community members to evaluate. The use of the Internet allows a wider range of opinion to be sought in a given time. Also, the nature of object-based knowledge products means that there are no physical limitations on having enough prototypes for users to test.

Developing the product　The beauty of many knowledge products is that there is no steep ramp up from prototype to mass production. You only need to make your website more accessible and ensure that your computer systems can scale up. Therefore, a process of continuous evolution can be adopted. In a recent new development I was associated with, the potential customers themselves urged a phased product launch: 'We'd rather that you gave us a bit at a time that works well, rather than trying to launch the whole product in one go.' Here again, the Internet provides an ideal mechanism for collaborative work with different developers, and for early user feedback. A good knowledge management technique to apply is that of maintaining a project history knowledge base. This provides a knowledge base of current status as well as maintaining a record of key decisions and assumptions.

Holistic evolution   In the knowledge and Internet environment, time-to-market is of the essence. An organization cannot allow the delays inherent in the conventional sequential process of product development. All the phases just described need to take place simultaneously and in an iterative fashion. It is as if the portfolio of knowledge products – each with its core, wrapper and surround – is prepared in outline, and gradually infilled. Again, the techniques of knowledge management can be exploited for sharing and maintaining an evolving knowledge repository. Then, at certain times, the packaged knowledge is deemed suitable for publication.

More is said about the process of knowledge product development in Chapter 8 (page 235).

Summary

Knowledge comes in many forms, from the deep tacit to the very explicit. In any situation knowledge evolves, often becoming more codified as it does so. But at each stage there are exploitation opportunities. The expert with deep tacit knowledge can contribute to a revenue earning advisory service. Some of their knowledge can be delivered as training courses. In general, there are two types of knowledge products and services – people-based and object-based. The latter is where knowledge is codified into more explicit form. This chapter reviewed a range of knowledge products with varying emphasis on each of these forms. The advantage of the people-based knowledge is that it can be tailored to its context and can generally command a premium price. Object-based knowledge, on the other hand, can be easily replicated and sold many times over.

One of the common types of object-based product is information, as sold in databases or publications. Unlike hard-copy publications, digitized ones can be enriched in many ways, including the addition of hyperlinks, interactivity and multimedia. Digitization makes it easier to reconceptualize publications as customized combinations of knowledge objects. Some of the most interesting developments in online products are likely to be in knowledge hybrids that blend both computer-based information and the human element. Routine knowledge is provided by the information elements, while more specific knowledge is provided through answernets, where experts impart their knowledge via email, chat or audio streaming.

An important aspect of any knowledge product is its surround. These are the attributes, such as service and brand image, that add value to the core product. One part of the surround is the 'wrapper'. This describes the contents of the document, which as well as some basic metadata elements can also include rights information, and information on applicability and usage. The chapter concluded with a short overview of how the Internet and knowledge management is making the product development process for knowledge products and services more iterative and evolutionary. Products evolve and adapt as knowledge flows more readily between developers and users.

Points to ponder

1   Who are the best internal experts in your organization? How is their talent exploited in revenue generating knowledge products?
2   Consider people-based services that you buy and use. What features make them an attractive purchase?
3   Look at your company's product portfolio. What is the knowledge content of each main product group? How could it be enhanced to command higher prices?
4   Would you consider any of your products 'smart' or 'intelligent'? In what way?
5   Consider five information products or services – reports, books, online information etc. – that you have used in the last few days. What sized chunks did you have to buy them in? Would you have preferred a different sized amount?
6   Look at your office bookshelf. How often do you use each item? Estimate what proportion of the information has now been superseded.
7   How much licensing revenue does your company earn from its intellectual property? What does this translate to in terms of revenues per employee? Could it be easily increased?
8   Take a substantive document that you have written recently. How could you turn it into an intelligent publication?
9   Consider what new knowledge or skills you have learnt during the past year. What were the most effective means of learning for each? Which would most easily lend themselves to an e-learning approach?
10 Consider a knowledge product or service you have bought or used recently. What were the key elements of the product surround that influenced your decision?

Notes

1   'Provices and serducts', Michael Schrage, *Fast Company* (August 1996).
2   'Approaches to categorizing knowledge', Chapter 5 in *Knowledge Management Foundations*, Karl Wiig (Schema Press, Arlington, TX, 1993) describes various dimensions and their relationships.
3   Ibid.
4   'Knowledge management', Clive Cauldwell, *Management Consultancy*, p. 12 (December 1999).
5   'IBM: Awarded record number of US patents', Tom Forenski, *Financial Times, FT-IT* (12 January 2000).
6   Ibid.
7   Patrick Sullivan Jr, a partner of ICM Group, was associated with the development of the human, structural and customer capital model of intellectual capital (alongside Gordon Petrash of Dow Chemical, Leif Edvinsson of

Skandia, and Charles Armstrong of S.A. Armstrong). His recent work on patent exploitation is described in outline in 'Earning more from intellectual property', *Knowledge Management*, p. 82, Freedom Technology Media Group (October 1999). SmartPatents' Intellectual Property Management System (IPAM) is described at its website http://www.smartpatents.com.

8 'Clever uniforms help casualties' Sean Hargrave, *Sunday Times*, Innovation, p. 13 (29 June 1997).

9 XML.org (http://www.xml.org) acts as a clearinghouse for XML schema proposals. In an attempt to get some coherence amongst the many independent standards for different industries, the CommerceNet sponsored eCo framework project (http://www.commercenet.net/projects/currentprojects/eco) is defining a common framework for the burgeoning number of specifications. Microsoft's BizTalk® Framework initiative (http://www.biztalk.org) is developing guidelines for defining and using XML schemas in applications. There is no shortage of activity, but which schemas will emerge as widely adopted standards is as yet unclear.

10 Information Mapping Inc., Waltham, Massachusetts. http://www.infomap.com.

11 'Electronic publishing in Europe' at http://www.elpub.org is a website sponsored by the European Commission that provides advice and resources on electronic publishing. A related website http://www.cordis.lu/ist/ka3 provides information on ongoing research and development programmes in the field of interactive publishing.

12 'The coming of knowledge-based business', Stan Davis and Jim Botkin, *Harvard Business Review*, pp. 165–170 (September/October 1994).

13 The first specification was published in September 1998. Details can be found at http://purl.org/DC/.

14 RDF uses XML tags to describe the properties of an information resource. For example, the tag <DC:creator> refers to the Dublin Core metadata element Creator. Work is also being carried out in related areas of schemas and ontologies – vocabularies of terms and relationships between them – see, for example, http://www.ontology.org.

15 DigiHub is explained in 'The next frontier: digital assets and the customer', E-Business Perspective No. 8, PriceWaterhouseCoopers. Providers of watermark and digital rights management solutions include Cognicity, Content-Guard and Blue Spike for music and Digimarc for images.

16 Success, of course, attracts attention. Hence, Powersize has now been acquired by Hoovers, a bigger and more established company.

17 The original neural networking activities continue with the rest of the former company, now renamed Neurodynamics. http://www.neurodynamics.com.

Chapter 6

Marketing revisited

The Internet changes everything.

(Larry Ellison, Chief Executive, Oracle Corporation)

The frequently cited quote that opens this chapter, although not to be taken too literally, is a stark warning that organizations must revisit all facets of their operations when going online. Marketing is no exception. The Internet is a powerful new tool for the marketer, opening new channels of communication between buyer and seller and making it easier to develop long distance relationships. It can significantly reduce promotional costs as well as allowing offers to be customized. This chapter looks at Internet marketing and assesses how it differs from conventional marketing.

The basis of all marketing is meeting, or ideally surpassing, a customer's needs and wants with your products and services. The marketer's starting point is the acquisition of good knowledge about potential customers: their success factors, individual requirements, buying patterns and so on. On the Internet this is initially difficult, since a potential customer visiting your website is 'invisible'. On the other hand, the very nature of the Internet means that its users leave tracks as they click from Web page to Web page. By using tools that analyse these 'click streams' marketers can build up a detailed picture of each user's online habits and interests. Another strand of analysis that is needed is a critical review of your own company's capabilities. What are its core competencies? What are its strengths and weaknesses for those factors that customers consider important? By evaluating these alongside the capabilities of competitors, your organization can position itself in the marketplace in terms of the types of customer it wants to serve and the products and services that it offers.

Good marketing strategies are based on these 3Cs of marketing – customers, company, competitors – the topics of the first part of this chapter.

The marketing mix is the name marketers give to a set of tools that are used to influence the marketplace and gain customers. It is usually described in terms of four Ps – product, price, promotion and place. The 4Ps of marketing have been the foundation of marketing teaching for over four decades.[1] With the advent of the Internet and its distinctive characteristics, now is a good time to reassess the elements of the marketing mix. The 4Ps do not go away, but they do change considerably. How they do so is discussed in the second part of this chapter. What the Internet also does it to open up many more possibilities for enriching the marketing mix. These constitute what I call the 10Ps of Internet marketing, the topic of the next chapter.

What's the same, what's different?

Marketing is defined as 'the management process responsible for identifying, anticipating, and satisfying customer requirements profitably'.[2] If your organization is in the public sector or is a 'not for profit' organization, you may not like the use of the word 'profitably'. But you still have customers to serve (even if you don't call them customers), and you are usually competing for limited resources. Therefore you may want to substitute 'cost-effectively' for 'profitably'. At the heart of this definition is the customer. You will recall from Chapter 1 that customer knowledge is generally considered to be the most important knowledge that an organization has. Knowing your customers and potential customers is the basis of marketing knowledge products and services on the Internet, just as it is for any other product and media.

Marketing is a very broad term and covers several different types. Distinctions are commonly made between consumer marketing, industrial marketing, business-to-business marketing and services marketing. Other types of marketing are stakeholder marketing (such as marketing inward investment plans to governments) and internal marketing (promoting the capabilities of your organizational unit to other parts of the organization). Each has a different emphasis and set of 'customers'. Internet marketing adds a further dimension onto each of these types. Whatever type is involved, certain fundamentals do not change:

- There are customers with needs and wants to satisfy – the 'customer' may be an individual or, for larger and complex purchases, several people; some of their needs are explicit; many others, especially emotional needs, are implicit.

- The buying process is similar – potential customers express their intentions, search for suitable products and suppliers, qualify them according to a set of criteria, select from a range of choices, and complete their purchase; some of these phases may not be as distinct or explicit as others.
- The sales cycle is similar – potential customers progress through a sequence: awareness, interest, desire, action, commonly known by its acronym AIDA; in other words, they go from being unaware that a supplier or its products exist, right through to completing a purchase and becoming a customer.
- A satisfied customer is one for whom the products and services supplied meet or exceed expectations; they deliver visible benefits to their business and offer good value for money.

In summary, the overall marketing approach remains unchanged. As a supplier, you need to identify and target specific customer groups and individuals. You need to understand their intentions, motivations, needs and level of spending authority. You need to guide them through a buying process that matches their needs with your products and services so that they can be more successful.

In Internet marketing, the 3Cs and 4Ps of traditional marketing still apply, though with changes of emphasis:

- *Customers.* On the Internet they come from a wider geographic area and cultural backgrounds. You must know about their needs and expectations and how they feel about your Internet presence.
- *Competitors.* In the Internet environment they are often not who you first think of. Try typing in some keywords related to your products in a search engine and see whose names pop up!
- *Company.* You must be critical about your innovative and online capabilities. With hundreds, even thousands, of other companies offering similar products and services, you must be clear about your distinctiveness.
- *Product.* Which of your products will you sell online? Some or your entire portfolio? Which of them will you deliver online?
- *Price.* Know what your customers value. Remember that on the Internet many expect information to cost much less. If you don't price appropriately, they will quickly find another supplier who does.
- *Place.* Although the Internet provides a single place to do business globally, you may still have to adhere to local trading laws, taxes and import procedures or restrict your geographic coverage.
- *Promotion.* This is an area where it is generally best to start afresh. Abandon your existing glossy brochures, even your existing marketing agency if they are not Internet savvy, and embrace the techniques of Internet marketing (see Chapter 7).

The main differences between Internet marketing and conventional marketing are due to the specific features of the Internet that have already been discussed in Chapter 2. First among these is the Internet's richness and reach. You can exploit multimedia and interactivity. You can reach a global market place. Then there is the 24-hours-a-day, 365-days-a-year opening hours and the reduced costs of marketing and order processing. Another difference is that in many circumstances the supplier's size does not matter. Small companies with a well designed website, who are responsive and give a high level of service, have often proved more successful at marketing via

> **From Ipswich to the world**
>
> Timber trading company KDM International recognized that the Internet was changing the nature of its business and that if it did not respond it might go out of business. It recruited Web programmers and designers to create the world's first forestry and timber e-market, TimberWeb.com, launched in 1997. Today this small company of 50 employees in Ipswich, England has hundreds of online customers from over 100 countries and a world-class website that attracts over a million hits a month.
>
> *Source:* Case Study,
> http://www.ukonlineforbusiness.gov.uk

the Internet than their larger counterparts. Also, as indicated by many of the examples cited in earlier chapters, new marketing methods are continually being developed. Online communities, interactive catalogues and online knowledge markets are all innovations that the Internet has made possible. Let's now consider the 3Cs and 4Ps in more detail, outlining their particular features and challenges for the Internet environment.

Know your customer

The starting point of Internet marketing is to know more about your customers and potential customers. Out of the 300 million or so users of the Internet how do you know which ones you can most easily convert into customers? You don't unless you develop a systematic approach for collecting and analysing information about your website visitors and customers. Figure 6.1 shows the inverted triangle of customer knowledge. As you drill down through the layers, your knowledge increases from aggregated information about the wider Internet community down to in-depth knowledge of an individual customer.

It has already been noted (page 61) that as the Internet matures, the demographic profile of its users becomes closer to that of the general population. Even so, there remains a digital divide between younger, more affluent and well-educated people and those who are poorer and older. Similar differences in uptake are found between larger and smaller businesses and between different sectors of industry. There are also significant national differences and regional differences within countries.

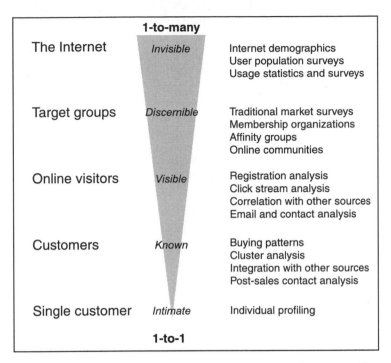

Figure 6.1 The inverted triangle of customer knowledge – from invisible to intimate

Several research companies, such as NOP, Gallup and Nielsen, carry out regular surveys of Internet access and usage among the general population and among specific professional groups. Such surveys will indicate what proportion of your target audience use the Internet and how they use it. A recurring finding is that, despite the popularity of the Web, email remains the most common use. Good use of email should therefore be an important element of any online marketing activity. Surveys also indicate that the primary use of the Web is to seek information. This again reinforces the importance of useful and compelling content.

The next level of customer knowledge is that about your target market segments. In marketing terms, a segment refers to a subset of the overall buying population that shares some common characteristics and needs. A common type of segment is a customer/product combination, such as small businesses seeking e-commerce advice. Conventionally, a well-defined segment is easy to reach with targeted promotions in specialist magazines or via direct mail. On the Internet, targeting using profiled databases is not so well refined, as any recipient of email spamming will assert! However, things should get better as organizations collate email addresses with customer information from other sources. In the meantime, discussion lists and communities provide a ready-made focus for reaching certain segments and quickly sensing their current issues and needs.

From invisible to visible

When an online user first visits a website, little is known about them individually. Collectively, they do share some general characteristics:

- They have been referred to your site by something else that has caught their attention. This may be a hyperlink from another Web page, a referral by a respected colleague, or perhaps they saw your URL in print.
- On average, they spend 20 per cent of their time using search engines.
- They generally have a few favourite pages that are visited time and time again. Most Web users spend the majority of their online time at just eight or ten websites.
- They expect immediate gratification and are 'click happy'. In this respect a Web page is like an item of direct mail. A typical reader will spend only two to three seconds before deciding whether to dwell a while, or go elsewhere.
- They use a variety of Web browsers, access devices and connection speeds to access the Net. In other words, the invisible majority, as opposed to the highly visible techno-enthusiasts (among whom are those who probably developed your website), will not have the very latest technology or the highest speed connections.

For these reasons, you need to work assiduously at making your website visible in specialist portals and search engines, display highly relevant information near the top of your Web pages and make them easy to download and read in a wide range of environments.

The moment that visitors reach your website and click their way around it, new sources of customer information come into play. You can trace their pathways through your Web pages, you can gain an impression of what they value, and you can capture individual preferences through registration forms. Let's look at a couple of the most important tools and techniques – log file analysis and personal profiling.

Log file analysis

Every time a Web user clicks on a hyperlink, an entry is made in the log file at its Web server. Several software programmes, such as WebTrends Log Analyzer, HitBox and SuperStats, collate raw data to provide periodic reports that contain a series of informative analyses. Figure 6.2 shows some extracts from a monthly log file report from the *Knowledge Connections* website at http://www.skyrme.com.

Date & Time This Report was Generated, Monday October 02 2000 -- 23:44:55
Timeframe, 09/01/00 00:00:00 -- 09/30/00 23:59:59
Number of Hits for Home Page, 2694
Number of Successful Hits for Entire Site, 173177
Number of Page Views (Impressions), 45591
Number of Document Views, 45591
Number of User Sessions, 13509

-------->> Most Requested Pages <<--------
Pages, Views, % of Total Views, User Sessions, Avg. Time Viewed
----
1 http://www.skyrme.com/, 2694, 5.9%, 2222, 00:01:46
2 http://www.skyrme.com/ insights/22km.htm, 893, 1.95%, 859, 00:02:41
3 http://www.skyrme.com/ insights/, 793, 1.73%, 631, 00:01:56
4 http://www.skyrme.com/ resource/kmres.htm, 783, 1.71%, 716, 00:03:03
5 http://www.skyrme.com/pubs/ kmreport.htm, 652, 1.43%, 620, 00:02:12
6 http://www.skyrme.com/pubs/ on97full.htm, 589, 1.29%, 546, 00:03:06
7 http://www.skyrme.com/updates/ , 508, 1.11%, 415, 00:01:49
8 http://www.skyrme.com/ insights/3lrnorg.htm, 507, 1.11%, 448, 00:02:29
9 http://www.skyrme.com/ insights/24kmeas.htm, 464, 1.01%, 440, 00:03:00
10 http://www.skyrme.com/site/ know.htm, 440, 0.96%, 402, 00:02:07

-------->> Most Active Countries <<--------
Countries, User Sessions
----
1 United States, 4025
2 UK, 1086
3 Australia, 528
4 Malaysia, 275
5 Canada, 246

-------->> Top Search Engines <<--------
Engines, Searches, % of Total
----
1 Yahoo, 784, 49%
2 AltaVista, 533, 33.31%
3 Lycos, 164, 10.25%
4 GoTo, 45, 2.81%
5 Excite, 38, 2.37%

-------->> Top Referring URLs <<--------
URL, User Sessions
----
1 No Referrer, 5415
2 http://www.skyrme.com/, 342
7 http://www.sla.org/membership/ irc/knowledg.html, 115
16 http:// informant.dartmouth.edu/, 62
33 http://www.bpubs.com/ Management_Science/ Knowledge_Management/, 35
38 http://www.cio.com/archive/ 060196_uneasy_1_content.html, 31

Figure 6.2 Extracts from WebTrends Log Analyzer report

The first section of the report contains summary aggregated information including the number of 'hits' and user sessions. While some people publicize the number of 'hits' their website receives as a promotion gimmick, this is generally a meaningless statistic. A 'hit' is every page element that is downloaded – every image, even a small icon, is separately fetched from the server and constitutes a hit. More meaningful are other statistics shown in this section – the number of user sessions and the average number of pages that are viewed during each user session.

The following sections give more useful information about site usage and visitors. The first is a ranked analysis of individual pages accessed. The home page is naturally high, if not top, in this list, but it is the other high entries that indicate the main topics of visitor interest. On the *Knowledge Connections* website, latest updates and overview articles on specialist subjects frequent many of the top positions. Resource pages, on this site covering knowledge management (entry 4 – resource/kmres.htm), are also invariably very popular. The next analysis gives a ranked list by country of the visitor's ISP or Internet gateway. As expected, the USA dominates the list, usually accounting for more than half the visitors. This particular analyser denotes all .com suffixes as USA, but it must be remembered that .com is also widely used by companies located elsewhere to demonstrate their international perspective. This analysis gives an important indicator of market potential by geography, although with proposals for many new top level suffixes like .shop, .pro, .ltd its usefulness may decrease.[3]

Later sections of the report show referral analyses, first from search engines, then from other domains. Careful analysis of the former against their general popularity will show where extra effort is needed to improve your visibility. More interesting are the other referrals. Many are from another part of the host website, and have been omitted in the figure. The more interesting ones are those from other sites, since these constitute the web of influence for your readers. The content creators and editors for these sites need nurturing, as do those from sites that are missing but which you would expect to be represented.

These basic analyses, while informative, have several limitations. How do you know whether there are more user sessions than those recorded, since some of your popular pages may be cached in visitors' PCs or at their Internet service providers? How you know what proportion of visits were made by automatic spiders, competitors or students as part of a set assignment? How you know which visitors may already be customers? To address some of these issues, there are more sophisticated analysis packages and companies that specialize in doing more detailed site audits.[4]

Customer profiling

One way of increasing your knowledge about visitors is to encourage them to provide you with information directly. This is commonly done using a registration form that asks for basic contact details and areas of interest. Registration forms should be simple, voluntary and offer something of benefit in return for their completion. Common inducements are offering the visitor more in-depth information such as a 'white paper', a regular email of latest promotional offers, or a more personalized website experience. A word of caution, though. One survey showed that nearly 60 per cent of visitors declined to register to enter a website. Of those that continued, 6 per cent gave up before the end, and 19 per cent gave false or incomplete information.[5]

A further, often untapped, source of visitor knowledge comes from analysis of emails and other online enquiry forms. Email communications can be encouraged by inserting email hyperlinks ('mailto:') into Web pages. Most browsers will let you pre-insert subject headings, which you can assign uniquely to different pages to find out what triggered an enquiry. As well as giving individual richness, email responses can be accumulated in a database and textually analysed, using text mining software.[6] This can reveal useful insights into their needs.

The best knowledge comes from integrating information from multiple sources and this is where the latest generation of eCRM (electronic Customer Relationship Management) packages can help. A traditional CRM package provides tools to analyse data culled from sales and other transactions, both at an aggregate and individual level. Typical analysis functions include sales analysis, call centre analysis, loyalty analysis, cross-selling analysis, campaign analysis and customer profiling. eCRM systems add facilities to do e-commerce transaction analysis and click stream analysis. Broadbase, for example, integrates data from both online and legacy systems. It can be used to correlate Web page responses with that of off-line marketing campaigns. Blue Martini's customer interaction system will integrate visitor profiles from registration information with their click patterns. Such analyses can reveal customer micro-segments –

How Marriott knows its customers

The Marriott hotel chain is renowned for its depth of individual customer information. It uses this to give guests their preferred type of room when checking in. Marriott's marketing people can monitor hotel capacity and focus promotional offers to optimize capacity utilization. Conference organizers can deal more easily with Marriott knowing that they have all their needs on file. Marriott's leading edge use of customer knowledge in its CRM is reported to have generated an additional $55 million in sales.

Source: 'How Marriott never forgets a guest', Amy Borrus, *Business Week*, p. 83 (21 February 2000)

groups of users sharing similar profiles and click patterns. By combining this information with the buying patterns of existing customers, a set of business rules can be developed, such that relevant product offers can be presented to website visitors. Forrester Research estimates that the proportion of companies using micro-segmentation on the Internet will jump to 60 per cent in 2001.[7]

The ultimate in customer knowledge is detailed knowledge of a single customer, the so-called segment of one. Today's CRM systems allow you to track all of a customer's interactions and sales transactions with you, as well as their preferences. The growing sophistication of eCRM systems and website analysis tools gives marketers unprecedented scope to understand and exploit customer knowledge. Even so, there remains a tremendous gap between the potential and reality as e-businesses struggle to meet customer expectations – a theme we return to in Chapter 8 (page 240).

Expect unexpected competitors

Competition is the second of the 3Cs of marketing. The Internet further blurs industry boundaries that were already blurring due to changes in the business environment. The reason is simple. The Internet makes it easier to access information and knowledge. These are the sources of competitive advantage for most businesses today, not bricks and mortar. Whatever the market, knowledge about it can be used to create new businesses and compete with established ones in the same field. For example, you might have initially considered Amazon.com a bookseller. In reality, it is essentially an information and knowledge business. Its primary initial assets were databases of information about books, alongside a set of codified business processes and an Internet website. The physical distribution of books was initially outsourced, a secondary element in its overall business model. Today, Amazon.com has extended this model to enter many other markets including music, software and even tools and kitchenware. Take another example. James Richardson runs an industrial design business in Connecticut. It supplies millions of electronics products with a staff of just two. In essence, it runs a virtual factory that contracts with assemblers and engineering suppliers, coordinates the physical supply chain and delivers to customers, all done using the Internet from its small office.[8] This business too is based on knowledge – specialist design knowledge plus knowledge of the market, suppliers and customer's needs.

These examples are not intended to suggest that knowledge is everything. In some businesses, access to raw materials, sales and distribution channels may be more important. The crucial question is to what extent critical resources such as these are controlled by dominant market players as opposed to being readily available for purchase in the open market. A new market entrant, who has knowledge of all the resources and processes that go into creating the final products and services, and has ready access to the physical elements, can compete on equal or even better terms than established suppliers. If they are agile at collecting and refining this knowledge, and combine different elements in innovative ways, they can quickly alter the dynamics of the market. Established suppliers, having built up their physical supply chains over many years are often loath to disturb them. They may therefore lack the agility against those businesses whose primary raw materials are information and knowledge. On the other hand, they have already made an investment in a proven supply chain and its established relationships that might take time and money for the Internet start-up to create from scratch.

A new competition framework

One of the most enduring competitor analysis tools is the Porter five forces framework.[9] This examines the interplay between five forces of competition – rivalry between existing competitors, the bargaining power of customers and suppliers, the threat of substitutes, and the attractiveness of the industry to new entrants. Monitoring existing competitors is a common starting point. They are usually very visible, and opportunities to gather intelligence about them abundant. All the evidence of Internet markets is that established rivals are probably the last place to look for competitors. They are stuck in their traditional modes of operation, and many lack the innovative capability and agility to transform their existing business into a thriving on-line business. Well-known market leaders in many sectors, such as Barnes & Noble in books, Toys 'R Us in toys, and Merrill Lynch in stock broking, lost out in the first round of online business growth to newcomers Amazon.com, eToys and E*TRADE respectively. Now, in the second wave, many of the larger established players have woken up to the opportunities of e-commerce, frequently by acquiring one of the pioneers that stirred them into action.[10]

Porter's model also considers suppliers and customers as competitors or potential competitors. The connectivity of the Internet means that a much broader range of interactions is possible within supply chains. It also makes it easier to bypass intermediaries. The Internet's reach means that marketers need to analyse information and knowledge flows along the whole length of the supply chain from suppliers' suppliers to customers' customers and beyond. In terms of new entrants, the Internet has seen many. Unlike a business that relies heavily on physical resources, such as plant, machinery and raw materials, the barrier to entry for an Internet knowledge-based business is relatively low. All that is needed to get started are a PC, an Internet connection, a good idea and the creation of a few Web pages.

Porter's model helps companies analyse sources of competition and profitability based on relative bargaining power and the economic laws of supply and demand in physical supply chains. For online knowledge businesses, the factors that sustain success are so different. Therefore, something quite different is needed to anticipate and analyse competitors. In the broadest sense competition is anything that gets between you and the customer. Apart from cash and a need to be fulfilled, the potential customer has two main resources that they use in making a purchase decision – time and knowledge. Therefore, relative competitive strength depends on such factors as speed or agility, and managing knowledge flows. A better model of competition is based around these factors (Figure 6.3).

Competition arises from those people who have the relevant knowledge, can assemble it quickly and accurately, and deliver it in a timely fashion. Knowledge creators, aggregators and others who own or control knowledge resources are core competitors to monitor. Central to the diagram is knowledge space, represented by the Internet and your customer's

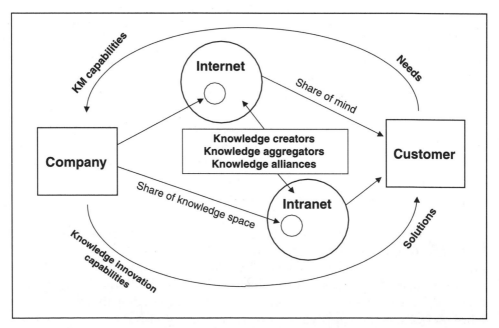

Figure 6.3 A competitive framework for Internet and knowledge-based businesses

Table 6.1 Comparison of traditional competition and online competition

Factor	Traditional	Online
Focus of analysis	Existing competitors	Who has the knowledge and connections
Location and numbers	Often few, specific geographies	Many and may be anywhere
Relative power	Strengths and numbers of suppliers and customers	Knowledge capabilities and alliances
Analysis strategies	Strengths and weaknesses in business processes, products, customer base etc.	Strengths and weaknesses in online and knowledge capabilities, knowledge uniqueness and agility

intranet. Here you need share of knowledge space as well as share of mind. These are related to the efficacy of your knowledge resources, their connections on the Web and how closely your marketing touches the right chord from the customer's perspective. Customers have their in-built knowledge filters, which should be regarded as competitive barriers to overcome. Time is also an important dimension in terms of time-to-market: how quickly can a new idea be converted into a viable knowledge business proposition? Important factors here are good anticipation of needs through knowledge management, good knowledge innovation processes and appropriate knowledge alliances.

These critical success factors for a knowledge business mean that competition in its traditional sense is less of a concern than having the relevant knowledge capabilities that can be rapidly combined and deployed. The rate of innovation in online knowledge businesses is such that there may be no competitors to emulate. Customers and capabilities should be the focus. Merely responding to an existing competitor's strategy is a recipe for mediocrity. Innovation and breakthroughs in thinking and approach are what will create new successful knowledge businesses. The challenge is one of rapid development and deployment of knowledge assets to meet the needs of specific customer segments. Since some of this knowledge may already exist with those that are regarded as competitors, it is not surprising that we will see more and more examples of co-opetition (collaborative competition).

If there are other organizations you regard as competitors, analysing their capabilities is generally easier than ever. Many of these capabilities are portrayed online and through online interaction. They are therefore widely accessible to customers and competitors alike.

Is your company k-ready?

We now come to the third of the 3Cs – your company's capabilities. We have just noted some of the factors needed for a successful k-business – good knowledge capabilities, speed and responsiveness. Knowledge capabilities can be developed as a natural outcome of a knowledge management initiative, as described in Chapter 1. The tools and techniques to create, assess, gather, organize and disseminate knowledge apply equally to building an externally facing knowledge enterprise as they do for internal knowledge management. Other factors that a good k-business needs are a good e-commerce platform and desirable knowledge products, topics also discussed earlier. Your k-business company will need a degree of strength in these key areas, plus an ability to learn rapidly.

A k-business calls for enhanced capabilities over other businesses:

- *Virtual working.* Many activities take place remotely. You have to interact and negotiate with customers online, not in an adjacent meeting room. Many of your suppliers and partners will form virtual teams with your own staff. Virtual working requires specific skills and attitudes amongst the workforce.[11]
- *Wider geographic coverage.* Potential customers can contact you from anywhere in the world. This means that your staff must be *au fait* with international business, your trading policy in different countries and regions, local languages, culture and trading laws.
- *Increased connectivity.* Many more people in your organization can be in direct contact with customers. The positive side of this is that customers can quickly connect to the most appropriate and knowledgeable people. This poses the challenge that everyone who communicates with a customer needs good access to knowledge about that customer. They need their detailed profile, the history of interaction with the company and the customer's status. They also need knowledge of people within the company who can help the customer. Once again, the imperative for good knowledge management and CRM systems is clear.
- *The value of know-how.* Many of your knowledge products will be people-based or hybrids (page 148) enhanced by the personal touch. This human element of value in your products and services is not restricted to the marketing department, nor to the IT department who may well have created your website. This means that a proportion of many people's time should be devoted to product creation and service delivery.
- *Simultaneous production processes.* No longer need production be carried out in sequential steps as in the case of manufacturing physical products. Multiple users can simultaneously access much of a knowledge product's raw material held in information databases. Knowledge can be collated and aggregated from many

different internal and external sources in a time independent manner. Since time-to-market and time-to-deliver are important factors in online product development and marketing, normal times of operations must be collapsed, quite often by factors of ten or more. This calls for new types of production and process management thinking.

- *High responsiveness.* Customer expectations are increased. They demand answers in a timely fashion. This may mean setting standards for speed of response to email queries at hours rather than days. Some companies now achieve an initial 15 minute response at any time of day or night.
- *A cohesive Internet/intranet presence.* Unfortunately, the responsibility for an organization's internal intranet and external Internet often lies in two separate departments. Yet, much of their content is the same. It is therefore better to consider them as a single entity, where different levels of security and detail apply for different groups of users (internal and external).
- *Your website is your shop window.* You need good marketing to attract people to your site. It must convey the right impression and lead visitors quickly to the information that they need to make an informed purchase decision.

What this means is that almost every one of your existing business processes will need to be re-examined and potentially re-engineered to cater for the highly connected, knowledge-intensive and high responsiveness needs of the online environment. For this reason many companies have initiated e-commerce activities as a separate 'green field' initiative. On the other hand, if your organization already has saleable knowledge assets, an innovative culture, an e-commerce infrastructure and fast track business processes that are commensurate with online markets, then this head start is too important to ignore. The danger of a complete hands-off approach

> **Reflect.com – no reflection on its parent**
>
> Reflect.com is an online company that sells makeup and shampoos that are customized using a formulation that matches an individual's skin and hair characteristics. There were worries that this new venture – a concept of executives at Procter & Gamble – might lack the agility of a Web start-up if too close to the traditional business. As a consequence, Reflect.com was spun off as a separate business (with Procter & Gamble retaining a 70 per cent stake), relocated to San Francisco and immersed in the culture of Silicon Valley. Many of the founders had to resign from the parent company and take a pay cut in exchange for stock options.
>
> *Source*: 'P&G gives birth to a Web baby', *Business Week*, p. 85, 27 September 1999

to spawning a knowledge business is that it becomes too detached from the main business. Little knowledge flows between new and old, and the organization fails to enhance its capabilities through mutual learning.

Products: emergent and evolving

We now turn attention to the 4Ps of marketing – product, price, promotion and place. We start by considering product strategies for a k-business. The term product is used in its broader sense of goods *and* services. As discussed in Chapter 5, a knowledge product can vary from standard packages of information to a complex mix of information and human knowledge. The more human and personalized the product, the greater is its variability in delivery from customer to customer. A typical k-business product portfolio will therefore be a mix of standard off-the-shelf knowledge objects that are available for immediate download, alongside services where an appropriate mix of knowledge resources and human talent needs to be assembled on a case-by-case basis. Consider also that different knowledge in the portfolio has different shelf lives, requiring different updating strategies to keep the portfolio refreshed. It becomes clear that the management of a knowledge product portfolio is rather more complex than that of a conventional one.

In product portfolio management the main considerations are how many products to have in the product line, when to introduce and phase out products, and what level of investment to put into each product category or single product. These judgements are based on factors such as technological superiority, potential product profitability, degree of competition and market growth. Marketers commonly use a tool like the market growth–market share matrix to optimize their product portfolio. They will seek a balance of investment in products in high growth markets, while reaping the cash flow benefits from products in markets which are maturing because growth is slowing. The rate of change in knowledge and online environments means that the delineation of a 'market' is continually changing. Consequently, it is difficult to measure reliably market growth and share for knowledge products.

A potentially better approach is to consider the spectrum of knowledge commercialization (Figure 6.4). This depicts the gradual progression from ideas into products. What starts as a large pool of new product ideas is gradually filtered and refined into new product concepts. In turn, some of these are further developed into designs and prototypes. The winners from these are then manufactured and delivered in volume. For highly structured knowledge products, such as information packages, the development process is similar. But the overall time from idea to finished product is much faster. Furthermore, the resultant product may have many variations due to customization.

A more fundamental difference is that knowledge products and services can be easily created at any place along the spectrum. Before knowledge

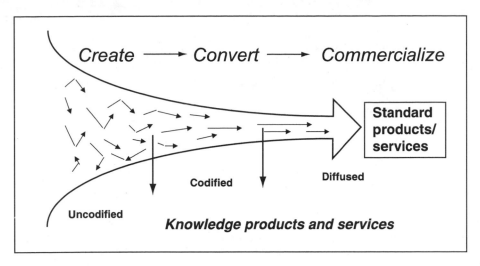

Figure 6.4 The product commercialization process

has been fully codified, the ideas and know-how of the experts involved can be sold as consultancy. After initial codification, the use of the Internet allows the tentative product to be widely diffused and feedback incorporated into a Beta version that is then widely tested before formal release. The knowledge commercialization process is not an end-to-end pipeline but a spectrum of products that emerge with various degrees of codification and packaging. New products and services continually emerge from the supplier's pool of knowledge assets (as well as those of alliance partners). As these knowledge products are used, the knowledge in them can be refined. As long as users feedback these improvements to the developers, the product can be continually enhanced. The development environment is one where knowledge products are continually emerging and evolving from the organization's intellectual capital. It has many similarities to a living organism, where cells (knowledge nodes) replicate and specialize; where successful organisms thrive while others wither away; where there is constant evolution to match the needs of the environment.

In this environment, portfolio management is best viewed as a logical extension of identifying and monitoring an organization's intellectual capital or knowledge inventory – processes described in Chapters 1 and 5. Additional information that helps knowledge exploitation can be kept in the inventory, as part of its metadata. Such information might include reference to the needs served, which customers use it, the pattern and level of usage, their applications and any feedback. Some of this information can be collected automatically if the knowledge product is information

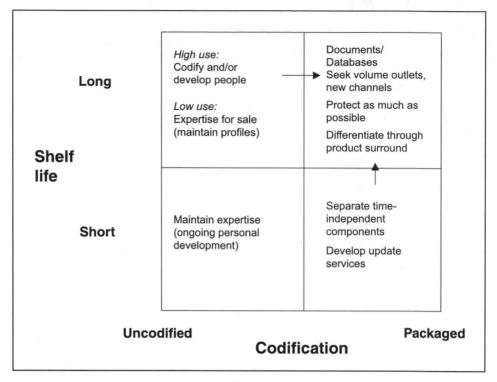

Figure 6.5   Strategies for developing an up to date product portfolio

that is accessed electronically. A more explicit approach is needed where people deliver the knowledge. In this case, information collection needs to be built into the marketing and delivery process.

Another facet of knowledge portfolio management revolves around product shelf life. How often do the individual knowledge components need to be updated? Sometimes this can be judged at product creation time, but frequently it will only become apparent as usage levels drop or as indicated by customer feedback. Figure 6.5 suggests potential upgrading strategies according to shelf life and degree of codification. In general, high usage knowledge should be codified where possible, though if it has limited shelf life, the investment should not be too high. Since many products are constantly evolving, and since delivery of services may be customer-specific, it may be important to keep track of changes and specific deliveries. The question arises whether to do this through formal version releases or not. Detailed delivery tracking can be used to identify opportunities for additional revenues by selling product updates to existing customers whose knowledge is now out of date.

Prices: declining and dynamic

Price is the second element of the traditional marketing mix. For online k-businesses, an unavoidable fact is that prices are in continual decline. Even for physical products, companies are already finding that the wider access to suppliers afforded by the Internet together with lower transaction costs has driven down prices. SmithKline Beecham has found that it is regularly saving up to 25 per cent on its historic prices by posting requirements and having potential suppliers enter a reverse auction to determine the price. This approach is also being used for service contracts.[12] Specific knowledge that might initially command a high price becomes more like a commodity as it diffuses. Even with precautions, such as using legally enforceable contracts, it is inevitable that proprietary knowledge will leak. Even if it does not, there is a high chance that people with similar ideas will develop comparable knowledge. The ability to command premium prices depends on uniqueness, timeliness and all the other value factors outlined in Table 1.1 (page 3). A good product surround that emphasizes level of service, customization and human expertise will certainly help to maintain a relatively high price. However, suppliers must face the inevitable truth that they must continually evolve and package new knowledge into their products to maintain good profit margins.

There are exceptions. Publishers will tell you that whereas it is their new publications that get most of the publicity, it is often titles on their back list that generally bring in the profits. As user knowledge diffuses, good publications receive good reviews and referrals, thus building up longer-term demand. For the publisher, the initial launch costs have been covered, and the profit margins higher, since only distribution costs are incurred, which on the Internet are low. This reinforces the need for product developers to distinguish knowledge content that has a longer shelf life and can be repeatedly sold with minimum additional investment.

In developing a pricing strategy, opportunities must be continually sought to add customer value. Many of these will need relatively little additional investment, yet can significantly increase the value in the eyes of certain customers. Some may prefer email delivery, rather than simply having access to a website. Additional services, such as offering a 24-hour-a-day hot line to human experts could be a premium priced service for other customers. Many of the intangibles in the product surround may also command premium prices – brand name, reputation for quality, reliability, dependability etc. In the fast-changing world of the Internet, the future prospects of your company could be more important than the particular products you offer, especially if customers are looking for an ongoing service and relationship. This will be true if they have integrated your knowledge deliverables into their own processes and products. Such customers will want to do business with a company that will be around in a few years time. They may not want to make their business dependent on a dot.com that is surviving on venture capital funding but is routinely making a loss. They will want to see commitment to ongoing product improvement and development.

A new facet to pricing that online markets make practicable is that of dynamic pricing. The use of auctions with a reasonable number of participants means that prices tend to find their natural level based on supply and demand at a particular time. Knowledge, however, is not necessarily a scarce commodity, nor is it so easily bounded or defined. Only knowledge which is dependent on people being available, such as in a project team, would lend itself to competitive bidding. But as happens now with requests for proposals, many other factors, such as the quality of expertise and track record of supplier often feature more highly than price. Nevertheless, the visibility of competing knowledge products in online environments and competition in online markets means that buyers can more easily make price comparisons. Suppliers can also experiment with price changes for knowledge objects, such as information, that have unlimited supply, and find an optimum position on its price/volume curve to maximize profitability. Although it is possible to do this automatically, rather like financial market trading where computer algorithms adjust the pricing of securities, the pricing of knowledge is likely to remain an art. How will your regular customers feel if they find out that they never seem to buy at the lowest price?

Place: cyberspace

Place in the marketing mix includes all those activities that get products in front of the customer. It includes a range of marketing and distribution channels, such as retailers, dealerships, franchisees and distributors. The Internet radically changes the perspective of place. Paradoxically, potential customers can be remote yet extremely close. They are, after all, only a mouse click away. This makes direct marketing potentially a very attractive option. But to do this successfully requires extensive knowledge of potential customers and how to locate them in cyberspace. As indicated earlier, there are certain locations where different customer segments will tend to congregate. These include specialist portal sites and communities. A channel strategy should therefore take account of where potential customers will seek certain kinds of knowledge and what influences their choice. Are there certain kinds of organization or independent authorities,

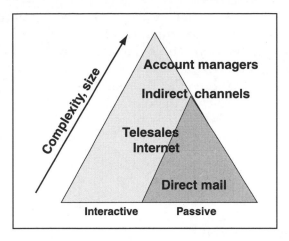

Figure 6.6   Alternative channels to market

whose knowledge of the market place they value above others? Understanding these primary visiting and influencing points is an important
component of on-line channel strategy.

Cyberspace must not be viewed in isolation. It should be just one element of a much broader channel strategy. The choice of best channels
depends on the type and volume of knowledge being sold. Figure 6.6
shows a spectrum of some alternative channels. A complex and large
purchase usually requires extensive interaction and negotiation between
buyer and seller. Hence, such sales favour the direct selling approach.
Large customers will usually have account managers who provide the
primary sales channel. At the other end of the spectrum, straightforward
products such as publications are frequently sold via direct mail. The
Internet acts as a channel that bridges the simple and complex, the passive
and interactive. It can act like direct mail, in that targeted segments can be
emailed or their community websites can host promotional material. In
addition, the Internet can act as a channel for person-to-person dialogue,
via email or online chat. It can also be used in conjunction with other
media. A common variant is to handle an initial sales enquiry via a website
form or via email, but to follow up with direct interaction through the telephone. This has the added advantage that the telemarketer can ascertain
how useful the potential purchaser has found the website in helping
them select products to meet their needs.

An important point to bear in mind is that the higher parts of the channel
triangle do not necessarily reflect higher price. It is increasingly common to
find expensive cars being sold over the Internet, although it may well be
that some direct selling took place in an earlier phase of the sales cycle.
Personal preferences also play an important part in the customer's

choice of channel used for making the purchase decision. An integrated multi-channel strategy is the hallmark of good e-marketing. Too many websites restrict choice. Many still fail to give telephone and email contact details for specific product ranges or applications. Conversely there are many advertisements or direct mail promotions that fail to display email and website addresses. Each of these practices closes one or more channels of communication, even before they have been effectively opened. A good multi-channel strategy will have a range of one-to-one communications channels viz.:

1   Web forms
2   Email
3   Chat
4   VoIP (Voice over Internet)
5   Videoconferencing
6   SMS (short message services) on mobile phones
7   Telephone

Information from all channels should be collated into a single database. Some channels, like chat, VoIP and videoconferencing, are not yet widely used for B2B marketing. However, as the Internet becomes easier to use and the functionality of these methods improves, they will need to be considered as a viable channel to exploit.

> **Talk online at Lands' End**
>
> Consumer clothing website Lands' End encourages visitors to seek help from customer services representatives when they cannot find what they want: 'Can't find an item? Talk to us'. Its 'Ask Us' page invites visitors to click on the Lands' End Live™ button, which shows an image of a friendly face. Visitors have the choice of talking by telephone or using live text chat, which lets them type into a window in their Internet browser.
>
> *Website:* http://www.landsend.com

Promotion: individual and interactive

Promotion on the Internet follows essentially the same phases as in conventional marketing. The prospective customer has to be taken through a set of steps from where they are unaware of your products and services to where they become a committed customer. The main differences are that the Internet provides an additional set of promotional tools, many of them more cost-effective than their off-line counterparts. Figure 6.7 shows such a progression together with suitable Internet tools.

The first stage involves creating awareness among the target population who do not currently know of you or your products. Having informative Web pages is necessary, but not sufficient. Your target audience has to find

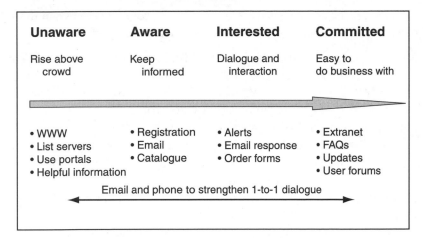

Figure 6.7   Internet marketing tools for different phases of the sales cycle

them! Here are some ways to improve the likelihood of this happening:

*   *Use identifier tags in Web pages*. These include a descriptive title, content and keyword META tags to help them come out higher in search engine results (see page 205).
*   *Use memorable URLs*. Few short words (of less than six letters) are still available for the popular .com domain. Now that there are fewer restrictions on domain name lengths, some easily memorable names are possible using phrases such as www.knowledgeforvets.com or www.ideasintoinsights.com.[13]
*   *Publicize your website in other media*. Include it on business cards, in business stationery and in email signatures. There are many opportunities to associate the Web page with specific information. These don't cost much to implement except thinking time!
*   *Create a web of alliances*. The Web got its name because it is easy to link to related pages. Although independent portals offer links, you may have a group of close business partners who you want to feature in a particular way. Negotiate with them for mutually beneficial links.
*   *Join a Web ring*. This is a sequential list of related sites, usually sequenced by the ring organizer according to the similarity of interests.[14] Users typically get visibility of the five previous and five next entries. You do have to consider, though, whether this might direct your users more easily to your competitors!

> **Personal networks promote Physique**
>
> When Procter & Gamble introduced Physique, a new line of hair products, it identified the 'chatterers', those consumers who were market influencers. They were encouraged to sample free products and refer their friends to the Physique website. This use of personal networks led to over one million referrals in less than six months.
>
> *Sources: Business Week*, p. 74, 28 August 2000; http://www.physique.com

- *Be creative; be different!* There is plenty of scope to be innovative in the Internet environment that goes beyond the above well-developed methods.

There is one technique that has emerged as an important awareness tool. Going under the unfortunate name of 'viral marketing', it is the Internet equivalent of 'word of mouth'. Marketers make it easy and painless for their marketing message to be passed on to others. It taps into individual's motivations and uses the connections that they already have – to friends, business colleagues and online communities. The marketing message ('virus') multiplies and rapidly diffuses into the wider population. Free samples, special offers and relevant information are the basic ingredients. Understanding how to inject these into established networks is the recipe for diffusion.[15]

From dialogue to relationships

The next stage of the sales cycle is that of maintaining awareness and creating interest. You need to get across how your knowledge can help your prospective customers. Product descriptions, samples and application notes are helpful marketing aids. It is at this stage that you move from the invisible visitor to one whom you know, at least to some degree. Over time you will develop a profile of their interests (perhaps from click stream analysis) and use campaign management software to select specific subsets for specific emailings. Regular emails, such as a monthly newsletter, are an effective way of maintaining awareness but can also be used at all stages of the sales cycle.

An important way of generating and maintaining awareness is to make your website 'sticky'. A 'sticky' site is one that users will linger at and repeatedly visit. This will occur if your site is 'essential reading' and keeps adding new and updated material. One way of achieving this is by being an important reference source for your specialist field of knowledge. Your material need not be as comprehensive as that of an aggregator, but it does need to be world-class quality for its specialist knowledge domain. You can provide updated material through a news or analysis service. Perhaps the most powerful way of gaining visitor loyalty is having an active community with several concurrent discussions on specific themes. The community itself will help keep the site interesting and up to date, so that it becomes a homing point for participating members. It is important that active links to the other parts of the site are very visible on the conversation pages, especially where there is material related to the topic of discussion.

At some stage during this period of awareness-building, a website visitor will have a specific need. To be ready for them at that time, you must have a mechanism that moves them into the next phase – that of generating a real interest in your products and services. If you already have some profile of your visitor, then that will help focus ongoing interaction. If you know what pages they visit, or what interests they have registered, then make sure that any updates or changes are sent to them in an email alert. On every information page, there should be a corresponding marketing 'hook'. For example, if you are providing information on a business method, then make sure there are links to related products and services, such as training courses, workbooks and consultancy services. To engender interest you want to encourage some form of dialogue, particularly for more complex knowledge products, since it allows you to guide them better towards the most appropriate product offering that matches their needs. One way of encouraging this interaction is to hold back some essential information from the main Web pages. But you must not do this in a way that annoys your reader. You portray that you have a wealth of knowledge, but that only the tip of the iceberg has been codified and made visible on the website. You might provide a wealth of general information, but hold back on more context specific information, inviting interested readers to contact you with specific queries. You might encourage visitors to go through a short question and answer dialogue on the screen, such that when they make contact with you, they are well prepared. At this stage, you also need to be very responsive. You dialogue and interact, gradually creating a win–win for both parties.

Once a visitor shows a strong interest, you have to make it easy to do business with you. Here a good e-commerce platform is the essential foundation. Good follow up is essential. Confirm any proposals or agreements with email. If the knowledge to be delivered is simple and the contractual arrangements straightforward, let them order immediately online and download the knowledge. If personal interaction is needed as part of the delivery, plan the timing and sequencing of this carefully.

After an order has been processed, you need to maintain and enhance commitment. At all stages maintain regular and focused communication. Too many projects go wrong since participants work on assumptions that have not been made explicit. Every project manager of a consultancy assignment knows the importance of managing expectations. This is more difficult when done remotely, so the occasional telephone call interspersed among the routine flow of emails is important. Many corporations use weekly videoconferencing calls as a way for virtual project teams to maintain regular communications.

Paying customers expect to be well treated and you should be focused on developing and enhancing a long-term relationship. If you deliver satisfaction to them, then you are well placed to be able to offer future products and services as new needs arise. Therefore, have a plan of giving your customers preferential access to your knowledge resources. This may be done through a customized extranet. As a very minimum you should give them access to support information that is kept up to date. You may want to give them special membership to a customer community, such as a users' club, where they can share experiences with fellow customers. Many organizations feel that they lose control of information flows by doing this, but the amount of goodwill engendered more than offsets any potential problems, unless of course you have bad service you want to hide. You might also give customers special access to key experts in their area of interest. There are many such simple ways of opening access into your company. Once you have an identified customer community, you have a highly profiled group whom you can keep updated by using all the promotional elements of the earlier phases of the cycle.

As with channel strategy, offline marketing promotion should not be ignored. Indeed, the best promotional strategy is one that blends the best of online and offline marketing. For business-to-business knowledge products, the preferred offline promotional mix is that which gives potential customers opportunities to sample them. Hence conference presentations, articles in specialist magazines, participation in trade and professional organizations, and highly targeted direct mail are generally preferable to advertising and exhibitions. Each will need to be reviewed against its online equivalents in light of the planned promotional objectives. In common with conventional promotion, online campaigns also need clear promotional objectives, well-defined target audiences and benefit-focused messages.

The knowledge of marketing

Our review of the 3Cs and 4Ps of marketing has primarily focused on how they alter in an Internet commerce environment. To complete this chapter we now consider the contribution of knowledge management to marketing. Table 6.2 indicates the types of knowledge involved in a typical marketing cycle. Several make use of the Internet and an intranet to enhance knowledge flows and improve overall effectiveness of the marketing activities involved. The examples shown mostly had their genesis in a knowledge management programme. As far as Internet commerce initiatives are concerned, many do not initially consider knowledge management as a core activity. It is often only after projects have started that the need for content management becomes abundantly clear. Even then, many projects continue with the detailed process modelling methods associated with IT projects, rather than the use of specialist knowledge

Table 6.2 Knowledge used and generated during the marketing cycle

Phase	Knowledge	Example
Environment analysis	Technology developments; political, economic and social forecasts	Librarians at AstraZeneca routinely gather and disseminate global research and sector knowledge to inform its R&D effort[16]
Market research	Sector trends, customer surveys, buyer behaviours, emergent markets	BG Technology uses Cartia's ThemeScape to identify new market patterns; it alerts staff to new business opportunities and identifies potential business partners[17]
Innovation	Ideas, experts, research consortia, public research programmes	At Shell employees email ideas that are reviewed by 'GameChanger' teams. One idea led to the 'light touch' method which helped discover 30 million barrels of oil[18]
Product development	Development project histories, product characteristics, test results, competitive products	Chrysler's *Engineering Book of Knowledge* is an evolving intranet repository that helps sharing of detailed engineering knowledge across divisions[19]
Marketing	Market research, campaign analysis, marketing programmes, conferences, exhibitions, media	Peapod collects and analyses information from online consumers of its grocery website. It uses this to monitor the effectiveness of its marketing campaigns and also sells some of its research on to its suppliers through its Consumer Directions programme[20]
Selling	Target customers, customer contacts, customer needs	Marriott International tracks customer's likes and dislikes. It uses this to target specific customers with loyalty rewards and customized offers[21]

Table 6.2 Continued

Phase	Knowledge	Example
Service	Solutions to problems, diagnostic strategies	By storing solutions knowledge in a case-based reasoning system, 80 per cent of customer support queries to LucasArts online help-desk are solved without human intervention[22]

management expertise to develop knowledge maps and taxonomies. A k-business initiative needs both IT and KM skills and more besides, not just for managing the marketing knowledge but that of the project as a whole.

Taking a broader view, the marketing function embraces a set of specialist activities, such as market research, product management and marketing promotion, as well as support activities needed in any function (Figure 6.8). In any business, and especially a knowledge business, all these activities can benefit from better knowledge management. Each activity uses information and knowledge generated by others, which it further refines or develops and makes available as a sharable resource to other activities. Thus, knowledge gleaned through service interactions with the customer can be made available to product managers, to help improve existing products and develop new ones to meet customers' changing needs. This is in addition to sharing knowledge within an activity, such as making service

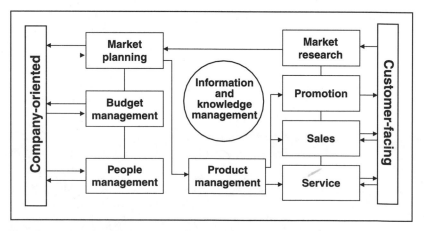

Figure 6.8 Typical activities in the marketing function

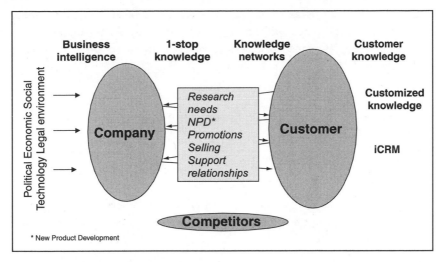

Figure 6.9   KM themes in marketing

knowledge gained through customer interactions available to all service representatives.

The growing importance of knowledge in marketing means that it should be a core activity of every marketing department, as indicated by its central position in Figure 6.8. The practice of KM with a distinctive marketing slant is still in its infancy. Figure 6.9 indicates some of the KM themes in marketing themes that seem to have particular relevance.

In outline, they are:

- *Business intelligence.* Analysis of information collated from many internal and external sources; identification of buying patterns, emerging market segments, changing customer needs, competitor activity etc.
- *1-stop knowledge.* The development of an internal portal that gives marketers a single point of entry to all the information they need to do their job, including embedded applications; another instance is the encapsulation of knowledge into a PC that has all the tools and information needed by a salesperson when visiting a prospective customer.
- *Knowledge networks.* Internal networks or communities of practice that connect marketing staff to sources of knowledge; external forums and 'best practice clubs' where state of the art marketing expertise can be shared.
- *Customer knowledge.* Analysis of customer interactions, e.g. through data mining, but also the sharing of customer knowledge gained by visiting salespeople, customer support lines and other contact points.
- *Customized knowledge.* Using the knowledge of individual customers to personalize the offering.
- *iCRM ('intelligent' customer relationship management).* CRM systems that add analytical and collaborative functions, as well as making inferences about future

customer interactions as opposed to predictions based on past interactions; some of this intelligence will come from computer AI techniques, but much will come from humans, whose knowledge needs to be accessible at the customer interface.

Table 6.3 Main similarities and differences between conventional marketing and Internet marketing

	Similarities	*Differences*
Customers	Customers have needs to satisfy. The selling cycle goes through similar phases	Customers can emerge from anywhere. Significant knowledge about their buying process can be acquired through from click stream analysis
Competitors	In most circumstances, the customer has several choices of supplier	Competition is more intense, with few geographic boundaries, and many new entrants whose unique competence is information and knowledge processing
Company	An assessment of strengths and weaknesses is a pivotal part of determining marketing positioning	Competencies in e-commerce and knowledge management are important determinants of success
Product	Products have intangible product surrounds that can significantly influence in the purchase decision	More product variations are possible, with customization being cost-effective. Many elements of the product can be delivered instantly online
Price	Consumers judge prices on value and alternatives	Prices decline rapidly as knowledge diffuses
Place	There are multiple channels to market, both for influencing the customer and distributing the goods	Cyberspace removes many geographical restrictions
Promotion	Potential customers must be taken through the AIDA cycle – awareness, interest, desire, action	The 'click happy' nature of Web users means that promotional messages must have an immediate impact. Email offers a cost-effective way of maintaining dialogue with potential customers

Over the next few years, more themes will emerge, and new and more powerful computer tools will significantly enhance the use of marketing knowledge. But organizations who do not put knowledge management at the heart of their Internet marketing are likely to miss out on emerging opportunities or suffer from unexpected threats.

Summary

This chapter has explored how Internet marketing differs from conventional marketing using the 3Cs (customer, company, competitors) and the 4Ps (product, price, promotion, place) as factors of comparison. A summary of the main differences is shown in Table 6.3.

Overall, the richness of the Internet environment creates many more possibilities for innovative approaches to marketing. The newness of this environment means that the rules of Internet marketing are still at an embryonic stage compared to the maturity of well-established concepts of traditional marketing. For example, the Porter's five forces model needs re-evaluation. An alternative model more relevant to k-business is proposed.

Success in this dynamic marketing environment calls for better customer knowledge and better management of knowledge in all aspects of marketing. Knowledge management should therefore be a core activity of every marketing function. Several areas where knowledge management has an important contribution to make were suggested. These included business intelligence, a 1-stop knowledge marketing portal and a more intelligent approach to CRM.

Points to ponder

1   Do you know what proportion of your existing customers would prefer to conduct business with your organization via the Web? What additional benefits can you offer them if they do?

2   Do your marketers get regular relevant reports (e.g. via registration forms, Web log analyses) about visitors to your website and how they use it? What further information do you feel would be useful to develop your Internet marketing plans?

3   Has your organization suffered unexpected competition from Internet suppliers? If so, what distinctive advantages do they offer?

4   Look at the bulleted list of k-readiness competences on pages 176–177. Can you think of any more? Rate your capabilities against each factor on a scale of 1 to 10, where 10 represents the best externally.

5   Using Figure 6.4 as a template, map the products and services you currently market over the Internet. Underline those that are also delivered via the Internet. Think of additional products that could readily be added.

6   Compare the pricing of your main products with alternatives available over the Internet. Look at your existing information based products. What would be the repercussions of having to sell them at a third of their current prices?

7   List countries or regions of the world where you would like to increase your market penetration. How could you use the Internet to do so?

8   Put yourself in the position of one of your target customers. Do a search on the Web against the needs they are trying to address. Now repeat for your website. How quickly can they find what they want? How relevant is the information you offer. Now repeat for different customer segments.

9   How do you initiate and maintain a dialogue with your website visitors? Think of a specific customer segment. Use Figure 6.7 as a template for evaluating your promotion effectiveness. Repeat for other segments.

10   How effective is knowledge management within your marketing department. How could it be improved? Use the themes of Figure 6.9 as a guide.

Notes

1   A popular marketing textbook is *The Principles of Marketing* by Philip Kotler *et al.* (different co-authors for different editions e.g. European edition), Prentice Hall. It cites E. Jerome McCarthy (1960) as the originator of the 4Ps of marketing.

2   This is the definition promulgated by the Chartered Institute of Marketing, Cookham, England; http://www.cim.co.uk.

3   At the time of writing (October 2000) the Internet administration body ICANN (Internet Corporation for Assigned Names and Numbers) were evaluating many proposals received for TLD (Top Level Domain) suffixes. Promising ones included .mall (for online shops), .biz (for businesses), .info (for information services) .eu (for European organizations) and .pro (for accredited professionals such as lawyers and doctors); http://www.icann.org.

4   An example of a tool that integrates Web server data from across the enterprise and offers customized reports and graphs in real-time is NetGenesis (http://www.netgenesis.com).

5   An Intelliquest/Zona survey, cited in *Information Age* (June 2000).

6   A good example of a tool that analyses email is KnowledgeMail™ from Tacit Knowledge Systems Inc; http://www.tacit.com.

7   'Weblining', *Business Week e.biz*, p. 17 (3 April 2000).

8   'These days, small manufacturers can play on a level playing field', *Fortune*, p. 156 (20 July 1998).

9   *Competitive Strategy*, Michael E. Porter, Free Press (1980).

10 The purchase of UK's leading Internet bookseller, The Internet Bookshop (http://www.bookshop.co.uk) in 1998 by leading traditional UK bookseller W.H. Smith is one example.

11 See 'The knowledge networker's toolkit' and 'The knowledge team's toolkit', chapters 5 and 6 respectively in *Knowledge Networking: Creating the Collaborative Enterprise*, David J. Skyrme (Butterworth–Heinemann, 1999).

12 'Dynamic pricing', *FT-IT* (1 March 2000).
13 These particular domains were still available in October 2000. Many others such as ideasforsale.com, betterideas.com were not active websites, but the names had been registered by a bulk registration agency, obviously hoping to sell them on for a premium to interested parties.
14 For details see the WebRing site at http://www.webring.org (now a service of Yahoo!).
15 For a good overview of viral marketing see 'The six simple principles of viral marketing', Dr Ralph F. Wilson, *Web Marketing Today*, No. 70 (February 2000); http://www.wilsonweb.com.
16 'Cultural evolution', Michael Robin, *Knowledge Management*, pp. 16–17, Learned Information (May 1999).
17 'Sweating knowledge assets in BG technology', Martin Vasey and Ken Pratt, *Knowledge Summit '99*, Business Intelligence Conference, London (November 1999).
18 Shell GameChanger, cited in 'Reinvent your company', Gary Hamel, *Fortune* (12 June 2000).
19 'Chrysler's new Know-mobiles', Warren Karlenzig, *Knowledge Management*, Freedom Technology Media Group (May 1999).
20 'Streamline leverages customer knowledge', Mary G. Gotshcall, *Knowledge Inc.*, Vol. 4, No. 6 (June 1999).
21 'Web Smart', *Business Week e.biz*, p. 39 (18 September 2000).
22 Inference Corporation press release (3 June 1998). See Yoda's help-desk at http://www.lucasarts.com.

Chapter 7

The 10Ps of Internet marketing

In the digital age the product is very often the knowledge. Marketing that knowledge is the new challenge.

(Gerry McGovern, Founder and CEO, NUA)

In the last chapter we examined how the 4Ps of the traditional marketing mix – product, price, promotion and place – need to be reconsidered in the light of the Internet. Marketing on the Internet is so fundamentally different that a new set of principles is needed. These are the 10Ps of Internet marketing – positioning, packaging, portals, pathways, pages, personalization, progression, payments, processes and performance. Each plays its part in exploiting the Internet as an effective marketing tool.

The 10Ps are introduced roughly in the order in which they are first addressed in a typical Internet initiative. But they are closely inter-related. Therefore, none of them should be considered without exploring the ramification on other elements of the mix. Depending on the specific business context – factors such as market maturity, product complexity, customer segments targeted – some will be more important than others. By explicitly addressing each of the 10Ps for your specific context, the relative importance of each can be gauged, and the appropriate strategies developed. An assessment of each for your own organization and that of competitors provides a benchmark against which to evaluate progress on a regular basis. The section on performance suggests ways to do this. The chapter concludes by indicating which Ps most strongly support each phase of the marketing cycle.

Positioning

A website is a shop window. Within a few seconds of glancing at your home page or one of its main entry points, the reader must clearly understand how they can benefit. Your key pages must position your organization, its products and set of values against those of similar websites vying for their attention. Positioning has three main aims:

1   To claim a distinctive niche in the marketplace. The exception is where you are going for market leadership in a broad segment, but this is will generally require a much larger marketing budget and is the exception rather than the norm for marketing knowledge.
2   To make your website distinctive and memorable. You want your visitors to remember it and keep coming back to it.
3   To support your overall business and marketing business objectives.

How can you achieve these aims in practice? First, you have to have clear in your mind which customer segments you are targeting. You will probably need to develop different positioning strategies for different market segments. For each segment, make sure that you really understand their motivations, how they use the Internet, and what knowledge they seek. These factors then have to be reflected in the way that the website is presented. If you look closely at many websites you will find that they are supplier-centric, rather than user-centric, i.e. the navigation menu points to product lines and organizational divisions rather than the needs of different users. In contrast, the *CIO* magazine website describes its services in user terms (Figure 7.1).

Second, you have to position your product and service portfolio within the overall knowledge value-added system outlined in Chapter 3. How do you add value to your customers' knowledge and business processes? Perhaps you have original content that is useful for helping them analyse their markets. Perhaps you are a knowledge aggregator that offers them a one-stop shop for particular domains of knowledge. Whichever it is, you will need to convey your credentials.

Third, having identified your main contribution to your customer's value system, you need to go further and articulate what makes your offering distinctive or unique. In marketing jargon these are known as differentiators, from which marketers try to identify and exploit a USP (unique selling proposition): a feature or combination of features that competitors cannot match. This USP should address an important need of your target customers. It is often quite effective to encapsulate your USP in a short marketing slogan that can be displayed prominently throughout your website. Examples drawn from the Web include:

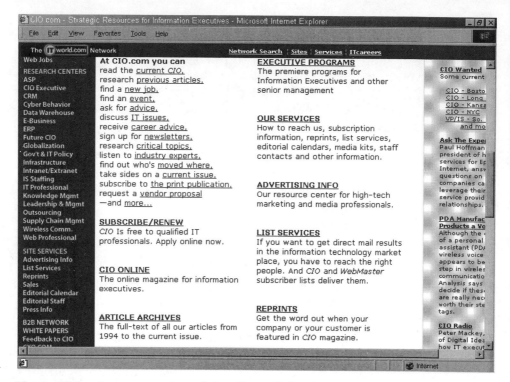

Figure 7.1 A user-centric website. Part of the home page of the CIO website (reproduced with permission)

- ❑ 'Your e-business advisor' (Giga)
- ❑ 'Delivering the world's technical information' (Engineering Information Inc.)
- ❑ 'Setting the business agenda for global electronic commerce' (Commerce-Net)
- ❑ 'World business education' (FT Knowledge)

It is generally better to use metaphors and action oriented phrases. Thus, the phrase 'reducing your financial risk' has more impact than the simpler phrase 'risk management'.

Fourth, your website should support your business and marketing strategy. Are internal stakeholders clear about its purpose and aims? For example, is its primary focus to generate leads, improve customer service or sell products directly from the Web? What partners or business alliances are needed? Have you clear strategies and approaches for involving them?

Consider also whether you need one or more separate Web brands, as in the case of Procter & Gamble whose websites include Reflect.com and Physique.com (see pages 177 and 185). Most large companies will find that they need several domain names (if they are still available!) to reflect different market segments and brands.

Finally, there is a general principle that applies for all of the 10Ps. You must continually monitor how well your strategy is working, and don't be afraid to modify it. The Web is a dynamic marketplace, with constantly changing suppliers and evolving customer expectations. Keep monitoring visitors' use of your site, and their enquiries. Ask them for their opinions. How do they position your site?

> **Don't lose your domain name**
>
> J.P. Morgan is one of several high profile companies who have had their website temporarily 'deactivated' at one time or another. Quite simply, it 'forgot' to pay its $35 annual registration fee to the registrar Network Solutions for jpmorgan.com. In another case, the popular email service Hotmail was unavailable because Microsoft had 'overlooked' its registration payment. A benevolent user paid online using his credit card to keep the service running.

As for any marketing campaign, it is useful to develop a set of metrics that you can monitor before and after any new positioning.

Packaging: open or closed?

Many aspects of packaging have already been covered in Chapter 5. The main aim of packaging knowledge is to make it easier to resell without incurring additional product development or marketing costs. In the context of Internet marketing, two aspects of packaging need careful consideration. The first is how to convey to the prospective buyer the value of knowledge in your product or service. The second is how you can more finely match the knowledge that you have with what the customer wants, yet minimize the extra costs of customization.

Black box knowledge

In most physical products, consumers are generally unaware of the wealth of knowledge that went into it, such as knowledge from research, design expertise, manufacturing and customer knowledge. If the product does the job expected, consumers rarely delve into what knowledge they contain. They view it as a 'black box'. It is often only when things go wrong that knowledge of its inner workings becomes important. As mentioned earlier, knowledge services can be offered that exploit this invisible or untapped knowledge. Advisory services, training and maintenance are examples.

Like black boxes, many knowledge products are based on a wealth of knowledge. But how can customers be sure that the product is really doing what they expect it to? The case of Intel's floating point divide problem with one of its Pentium chips shows that even in the best companies products can have unexpected flaws.[1] Consumers have to exert a high degree of judgement in evaluating a knowledge package. They may receive advice from a consultant, but how good it is will often not become apparent until some time afterwards. Even then, how can they judge whether this was the best advice based on the circumstances and the knowledge available at the time? Depending on how critical the package is to the task in hand, potential customers can make better judgements if they know:

- Its pedigree – what design principles were used; what prior knowledge it is based on?
- The reputation of the supplier – do their products and services generally do what they claim? Will they (like Intel) fix them when problems emerge?
- The sources of inner knowledge – who are the true experts on the packaged knowledge? Are they readily accessible?
- How it works in outline – this will also help them to be better users.
- What temporary 'work-arounds' are there if the product or service fails? While this is generally more critical for a physical product, an online knowledge service without other channels of back up could cause customers considerable difficulties.

Many consumers are too busy to spend much time exploring these questions. They want to evaluate the package quickly and start using it. The package wrapper (see pages 155–156) should therefore offer reassurance of such factors, and give opportunities for potential customers to seek more knowledge about it as and when they need it. This may be in the form of testimonials from customers in similar situations and endorsements from professional or trade associations. However, no amount of 'hype' should try to disguise the basic quality of knowledge on offer. If expectations are unduly raised, then disappointment invariably follows. This can have repercussions on customer satisfaction, and potentially lead to lawsuits for non-conformance. Therefore, another important part of the wrapper concerns validation of quality and procedures for arbitration.

Variety vs. cost

The second main packaging consideration concerns variety. How many variants of a knowledge product should you stock? The answer depends mostly on two factors – the variation in customer needs and the costs of customization. Clearly, greater inherent variety is needed where the

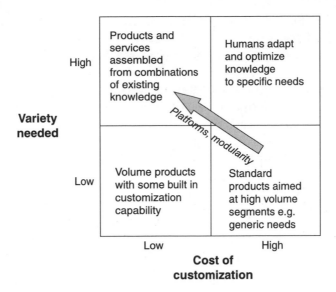

Figure 7.2 Variety vs cost

product addresses several market segments and multiple needs. Figure 7.2 shows the most viable packaging strategies according to the level of variety needed and the cost of customization. Customization to create variety is often not expensive. By using the platform approach described on page 150, many product variants can be created for a small incremental cost. Hence, the top left-hand quadrant of Figure 7.2 becomes a more feasible proposition for packages that initially start in the high-cost quadrants. Variety is further increased when the add-ons include people, albeit at an increased cost. Some of the customization costs can also be passed to the user by allowing them to select the relevant knowledge packages from your portfolio, as in the EIU example on page 144.

There is merit in offering both an *à la carte* and *table d'hôte* approach. The former allows extensive variation, while the latter shows some common combinations for typical customer groups.

Portals: gateways to knowledge

The word 'portal' has arrived on the scene with a vengeance. First, the major search engine sites such as Yahoo!, Excite and Lycos were described as portal sites. Then the term enterprise portal, and other variants, such as enterprise information portal (EIP), came into vogue. The latter is a corporate intranet portal that can be customized by using a set of portal building tools. In 1999, Delphi Group estimated that 55 per cent of Fortune 500 companies had corporate portal projects in progress.[2]

The definition of portal according to *Collins English Dictionary* is 'an entrance, doorway, gateway, especially one that is large and impressive'. Adapt this terminology to the Internet, and a portal should be a gateway to a wealth of knowledge. One equalizing factor on the Internet (or an intranet) is that size is determined by the size of your screen, so 'large' is as large as you can see in one go, although a good portal will naturally have numerous supporting or linked pages. Impressive could be taken as visually stunning, but to most serious knowledge workers, it is how quickly and rapidly they can find what they are seeking.

A good portal will point to information, both internal and external, both structured and unstructured. Many of the top visited websites, such as Yahoo! and MSN, are generic portal sites. For knowledge workers, there are more specialist portal sites. Almost every industry and profession has one or more well-known portals. Examples include WebMD for healthcare professionals, Archnetindia.com for Indian architects, and the more generic Business.com for business information. Increasingly B2B exchanges are assuming specialist portal roles.

> **Healthlinks.net – 1-stop health information**
>
> Healthlinks.net is a comprehensive health portal offering a range of facilities. Its primary resource is its categorized directory that gives qualified links to over 25 000 websites. As well as links to essential information on a range of medical conditions, other topics include alternative medicine, associations, child development, education and employment. There are also chat areas, forums, a newsletter and a classified advertisement section. Its online bookstore offers over 90 000 titles.
>
> *Website:* http://www.healthlinks.net

The features found on a typical portal include:

- *Structured knowledge.* Yahoo! has been the main exemplar of this from day one, with its entries organized in a tree-like structure. Sometimes the higher levels are called channels.
- *Search facilities.* Often there are separate searches for sites in the portal's directory and those on the World Wide Web.
- *Personalization.* Within certain parameters, the user can determine the layout and topics they want to see on their portal entry page.
- *Personal Internet tools.* These include email, email directories and PC search tools.
- *News.* Updates and news on topics of interest, usually filtered and collated from multiple sources by a newsfeed aggregator.
- *Communities.* Topic related libraries and discussion forums.
- *Trading space.* Typically online shops and auctions.

An enterprise portal adds more functionality and company-specific content. It will host company and competitor information and usually an expertise directory as well. It may have embedded applications such as financial analyses. It will make it easy to publish and classify new material. It will also give the ability to set different levels of security for different content and users. A well-designed enterprise portal will address the challenge so eloquently stated by Jakob Nielsen, formerly Sun's expert on usability, who writes: 'most intranets are chaotic collections of documents that cannot be navigated'. He cites the case of Bay Networks that added some order to its chaotic intranet, and so saved an estimated $10 million a year.[3]

Most portals, both on the Internet and within an enterprise, are indeed gateways to knowledge. But how easy is it to find what you want? At first sight, many seem very overloaded with information, but they do contain many links, and familiarity leads the user quickly to their area of interest. But that's where problems often begin for seekers of specialist knowledge. Many business and management topics cannot even be found on generic portal sites. Look for a topic like knowledge management and it is difficult to find. In fact, on most portals it is far quicker to do a search for 'knowledge management', but then you get thousands of hits. The problem is one of classification. Knowledge management sites are variously listed under Computer Science, Management, Consulting, MIS and IT, Quality and Standards. A good classification schema and consistent content tagging, e.g. using keywords or applying XML codes from a controlled vocabulary, are essential for an effective portal.

Another problem with Internet portals is that you do not know how the websites featured have been selected. Does the position in a given listing (when not alphabetical) depend on size, some reciprocal relationship or some level of payment? Today, few generic sites, unlike Magellan (now part of Excite), employ subject specialist reviewers to make quality judgements on the user's behalf. From the marketer's perspective, the generic portals cannot be ignored. They are among the most popularly used pages, and often a starting point for newcomers seeking knowledge in a particular area. However, gaining visibility in these is not necessarily cheap. 1-800-Flowers.com spent tens of millions of dollars in promoting itself on several large portals, but later scaled back its commitments.

The situation is different with specialist portals. Most value their independence and pride themselves on expertise in their subject matter. Specialist portals will feature more prominently in future, and offer marketers an effective way of reaching their target audience more effectively than the large generic portals.[4]

In considering the role of a portal in your marketing strategy, you should address several questions. Are there already established portals for your target markets? If so, what sort of alliances should you develop with portal owners to ensure your visibility? If no such portal exists, does it make sense to create one, either by yourself or with industry partners – some of whom you may regard as competitors? The answers to these questions will depend partly on your overall business model but also on how well the knowledge needs of your target customers are already met.

Pathways

The Web is a vast universe of interlinked resources. In mid-2000 it was estimated that there were 32 million domains, 10 million active websites, and some 5 billion visible Web pages. The proportion that is indexed is estimated at less than 20 per cent and declining, as more pages are generated directly from databases. Your own pages may be hyperlinked from hundreds or even thousands of Web pages elsewhere. A simple way to check this is to type in the search term 'link:mydomain.com' on AltaVista. Visitors can reach you via any one of thousands of interlinked pathways. One of your marketing aims is to open as many pathways to your website as possible.

Your target customers will access certain websites regularly. These will be bookmarked (Netscape) or on their favourites list (Internet Explorer). Usually these include generic and specialist portals, search engines and directories. Your customer research should identify which these sites are. To create pathways to your website, you must make it visible on these attractor sites or others that are directly linked from them.

For portals, this means gaining visibility in the relevant categories. As just indicated, raising your profile may incur heavy advertising or placement costs in generic portals. For specialist portals, much depends on the relative balance of power. Do they need you more than you need them? For their own credibility, specialist portals will want to ensure that all major suppliers are represented and that all relevant domains of expertise are covered. If you already have a well known website, you may be added without your asking, or you may be able to submit a link. Negotiating mutual links is also a common practice. You get visibility in return for linking to the portal. Link2Go exploits its position as a portal by selecting good content sites and awarding certain sites 'recommended' status, for which recipients return the favour by adding a Link2Go icon and link. The Web is full of such reciprocal arrangements.

Raising visibility on search engines is another important aspect of creating pathways to your website. Following a query, most search engines return ranked lists of sites in groups of ten.

Even where hundreds of results are returned, few users venture beyond the third page. It is therefore important to understand the algorithms that are used to determine rankings. Many search engines give extra weight to terms that are in ⟨TITLE⟩ tags, content description and keyword ⟨META⟩ tags in a Web page's header. Some Web page generation programmes will analyse your document and add what it thinks are appropriate ⟨META⟩ tags. However, important words and phrases are best added manually.

Another common way of ranking is by word frequency, while more sophisticated search engines will parse the document and carry out concept analysis. Google looks at the number of links into a Web page. This is another reason for establishing a network of related sites or Web ring, with mutual pointers. Many search engines also filter out pages that try to trick them, for example through

---

How to improve ranking in search engines

The following are some commonly offered tips on improving a websites' ranking in search engines results:

1   Choose relevant keywords.
2   Incorporate these in your title and keyword ⟨META⟩ tags.
3   Optimize your pages so that key words are near the top. Also, ensure that the content reflects the keywords.
4   Submit several representative pages of your website manually to the top search engines.
5   Regularly monitor search engines for your listing and update as necessary.

In addition, remember that many sections of your website will not be indexed – images, frames and dynamic pages generated directly from databases. *Search Engine Watch* gives hints on search engine submission, searching tips, search engine listings, reviews and ratings, resources and a newsletter.

Website: http://www.searchenginewatch.com

---

having repetitive keywords or too many. Since search engines usually display the heading and the first few lines of text in their results, it also helps to put key phrases about the content into the first sentence or so. Although most search engines have automatic spiders that constantly search the Web for new pages, it is usually quicker and more effective to explicitly submit your URL to search engines. With hundreds of search engines now in use, effort is saved by using a submission software program (such as WebPosition or Searchengines.com) or an online submission service (such as Submit-it.com or PositionPro). Even so, most experts recommend manual submission to the most popular search engines.[5]

Directories offer other potential pathways into your site. Like search engines, there are many online Web directories, so selectively is needed. Perhaps the best approach is to visit the relevant specialist portals to see which directories they refer their users to.[6]

You need to understand what else motivates your potential customers to visit certain websites. Influences are usually a mix of offline and online channels including trade and professional associations, specialist magazines, online e-zines, online communities, email discussion lists and conferences. Many of these welcome relevant expert content. Particularly sought after are news analyses, thought leadership papers, case studies, practical guidance and review articles. While obvious sales promotion is usually rejected, this does not mean that they cannot act as marketing tools. You can use your own products and customers as examples. You can ensure that your URL and an email address for enquiries are included. Rather than spend marketing budget on advertising, being featured in highly read magazines and at highly visited websites is much more worthwhile – and free.

Pages: making an impression

Your Web pages must attract and retain attention and guide people easily through your site. Their style must also reinforce your positioning and branding. Despite many facelifts and improvements since the early days of the Web, too many corporate websites are still overloaded with irrelevant graphics at the expense of quality information.

First impressions count! The first few seconds that a user spends on your site are crucial. They will either decide to stay or else they will simply click away to another site. I run a series of Internet marketing workshops in which I ask participants to make notes about the websites that grab and keep their attention. The common consensus is that the best sites have the following characteristics:

- A good clean design – effective layout and good graphics (but not large images).
- Quick to load – often text and menus are visible before all the images are complete.
- Compelling content – relevant to needs; interesting; clear and lucid; key words jump out of the page; perhaps an attention grabber or some 'wow' factor.
- Easy to navigate – have helpful navigation aids such as a site map, index and a search engine.
- Excellent content – in-depth, up-to-date, thoughtful, high quality.
- Some intrigue – another click may uncover yet more valuable knowledge.
- Encourage user interaction – perhaps through use of a drop-down list, or entering some details that are used to guide users through potential pages of interest.

> **Reuters adds wow**
>
> Renowned for its news and information services, aimed mainly at professionals and business people, Reuters wants to make an impression with the younger Internet generation. Through a deal with online magazine Worldpop, it offers pop news and gossip in a more lively way than its traditional offerings. Also planned in this new style are entertainment and fashion news.
>
> *Source*: 'Reuters lightens up for a younger audience', *Financial Times*, 4 September 2000

Look at some corporate websites and see how they match up to these criteria. Last year (mid 1999) I went to the Ford site at http://www.ford.com to look for some basic technical information on a Ford car I own. I was confronted with animated graphics (for which you had to have the relevant ShockWave program loaded into your PC). The website reflected Ford's geographic empires, such that the UK site did not offer a corporate-wide search facility. Needless to say, I could not find the information that I needed. In contrast, the Novartis website has a wide range of information, including in-depth reports from its research laboratories.

What business executives and professionals value most of all on a website is quality information and knowledge. However, that does not mean erring to the other extreme – pages and paragraphs of dense text. Add suitable images and diagrams when they help, and provide an easy-to-follow layout. Make good use of sub-headings, bulleted lists and tables to aid readability. Put yourself in the reader's situation. Guide them through the knowledge they need to solve their problems and answer their questions.

Look 'n' feel

The site should reflect your kind of business. If you are selling professional services, then it must look professional. If you are packaging your knowledge as publications, then you should have sample pages that look familiar. Think in terms of metaphors, such as magazine, loose-leaf binders, file folders, directory or personal adviser to develop a relevant look and feel. If you have multiple lines of business or address both consumer and business markets then you should seriously consider having separate websites, each with a distinctive look. Other features that enhance look and feel include:

- *Context setting.* It should be clear to the user where they are on every page, and where pages fit into the whole. Context-sensitive menus or a hierarchical list of links, such as Marketing > Promotion > Advertising, are ways of doing this.
- *Consistency.* Over time and space. Although there may be variations from page to page, the overall layout should be similar. Don't keep switching formats, styles and colours. Use a few basic templates so that users become familiar with them. If you change your format, as you will from time-to-time, leave your URLs the same and forward people to new pages. If they have changed a lot, offer guidance as to what is different.
- *Gizmo frugality.* Web designers love to show off their use of the latest technical wizardry (Java applets, Javascripts, frames, plug-ins, auto opening windows etc.). These are prone to errors, have unwanted side effects and create security problems. Use them with discretion and make sure that your viewers have alternative ways of reading your pages, or else they may simply not view them.

Remember too that writing for the Web is different than writing for hard copy. Word documents and other electronic content do not easily translate to the Web environment without additional work. Information on the Web is typically divided into smaller sized chunks, has hyperlinks to related pages and is designed to be read in any order, not sequentially (see page 149). Also, do not be afraid of 'white space'. A page frequently leaves a better impression when it is not overcrowded with text, but has plenty of gaps to guide the eye. It also provides room for users to add comments if they print it out!

What visitors notice most

During the 4-year Stanford Poynter project, eyeball movements of visitors to news websites have been analysed. What they look at on each page:

- ❑ Article text – 92 per cent (of pages).
- ❑ Captions – 82 per cent.
- ❑ Photographs – 64 per cent.
- ❑ Banner ads – 45 per cent (spending on average 1 second looking at each).
- ❑ Graphics – 22 per cent.

The researchers recommend that more attention should be given to captions – tantalizing ones do better than bland ones. Also, make sure that graphics and photos make their point quickly.

Website: http://www.pointer.org

Information architecture

Good content management and ease of navigation are important considerations in the design of any website. A good knowledge map that may have been derived from a knowledge audit is often a good start. However, this needs translating into a Web page structure. One way to do this is to create a table of two columns for each audience segment. In the first column write what it is they want to do, e.g. learn more about benchmarking, choose a software application. Then in the right hand column list the knowledge that they need to carry out these activities. Comparison with

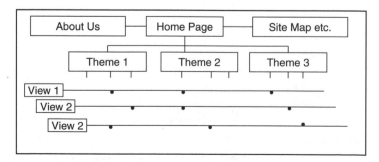

Figure 7.3   Multiple views within a common structure

what's in the knowledge map will indicate how well you serve different needs.

This information then needs to be clustered into logical groups, ideally with a user perspective. However, since this may not tie up with your supply side (the originators) you will then need a translation map from user information needs to supplier and perhaps directory location. Usually a website can have a lot of common low level information (which may be held in a database) that can be organized in several different ways, according to the needs of scalability and ownership. What is important is that there are higher-level 'views' or navigation pages that map this information according to user tasks and needs.

Another consideration is the balance of breadth and depth of information trees. Many sites err too far on providing too many levels for the user to drill down. Humans are quite adept at assimilating 15–20 or more menu items, providing they are logically grouped. Even if you organize your information as a hierarchy, there is no reason why you cannot show parts of more than one level at the same time. Some people believe that today's powerful search engines obviate the need for information hierarchies or views. However, there are many users and many modes of retrieval where the user wants to see the information in context and have an overview of what is available.[7]

A good way of testing your navigation is the 'three click rule'. Can an ordinary user, seeking specific information for the first time, find the first relevant page they are seeking within three mouse clicks? Many intranet and Internet sites fail this simple test!

Ottaker gets personal

UK bookseller Ottaker not only has a corporate website (http://www.ottaker.co.uk) but a set of microsites. Each bookstore has its own website, where staff can share their expertise and feature local authors and topics. The first specialist microsite is Outland, a Sci Fi and Fantasy site. This was created and maintained by enthusiastic staff. Often quirky and individualistic in nature, Ottaker's feels that this approach lets it get away from the 'clinical' nature of many book sites, and also strengthens the links between its physical stores and online audience – a good interplay of 'bricks and clicks'.

Source: 'Online bookshop taps into frontline knowledge', *Knowledge Management*, Learned Information, December 1999/January 2000

Personalization

Constructing different views of your pages for different audiences, as just described, is the first step towards customization. By exploiting the knowledge you have of an individual customer (using the methods described on pages 166–170) you can personalize their experience. You can also serve pages that are relevant to their immediate needs based on their current click patterns. Content management software packages such as BroadVision and Vignette generate Web pages 'on-the-fly' based on visitor information and personalization rules. Personalization is the ultimate in market segmentation. Instead of addressing broad mass markets, or narrower segments with some commonality, it allows true 1-to-1 marketing.

1-to-1 marketing is not new. In large value sales, account managers maintain close contact with an individual account to ensure that the relationship, and the flow of sales, continues smoothly. At another level, telesales techniques are used to contact individuals directly to promote products and services that might interest them. The Internet and customization software now allows personalized interaction to take place more cost effectively for lower value sales. It can be particularly useful when done in an interactive way to guide the buyer to the best choice of product, such as the most relevant knowledge object for the task in hand.

Personalization is very evident at a site like Amazon.com. When you enter its Web store, you are offered recommendations based on your previous purchase patterns. If you select a new title, it suggests other titles as well: 'other readers who bought this book also bought'. Many sites will personalize your interface and give you access to your personal data. For example, Zurich offers customization at My Zurich (http://www.myzurich.com). Customization is also combined with an interesting Risk Cockpit metaphor at its risk engineering site http://www.risk-engineering.com (Figure 7.4).

Personalization must be seen in its wider context. It is part of developing and sustaining an ongoing win–win relationship between your organization and its customers, as well as other stakeholders, such as business partners, suppliers and the wider community. Ongoing relationships are important. Gaining repeat sales from existing customers is much easier than creating new ones. Marketers have a rule of thumb that says regaining a lost customer costs ten times more than keeping an existing one. Sustained relationships between organizations are built on personal relations, where openness, integrity and trust are important. For people-intensive knowledge products, such as consultancy, developing a relationship, even before the initial sale, requires the development of one or more personal relationships between the relevant individuals in both organizations. Personalizing Web pages is often just a small part of the relationship-building process. It needs to be supplemented by person-to-person interaction. The strength of the Internet is that it allows such interaction over a distance. Email allows dialogue without incurring the problems of telephone tag. If greater richness is required, then synchronous communication using VoIP (Voice over Internet Protocol) or videoconferencing are further options. Each adds to the exchange of knowledge and when conducted

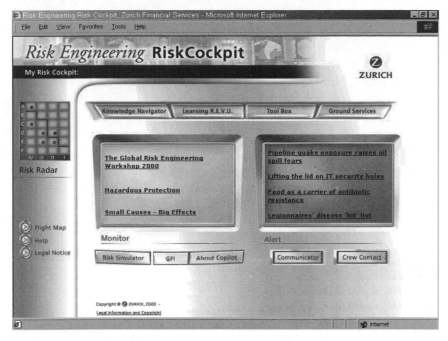

Figure 7.4 The personalized Risk Cockpit offered by Zurich

effectively helps build a relationship. Not to be overlooked is how such knowledge exchange is captured for subsequent reuse, perhaps when the individual representatives of each organization have moved on.

This raises an important question relevant to all aspects of personalization. How much should individual person-to-person knowledge exchange be recorded in computer systems and shared with others? A delicate balance needs to be drawn between making customer information available for the benefit of the organization against protecting the privacy and interests of individuals. The use of cookies to personalize Web pages is popular, and with clear privacy policies and assurances about use, most

---

Five principles of privacy

The Online Privacy Alliance is an association of 90 organizations that promote privacy self-regulation. Its members must agree to the following five guidelines:

1 Adoption and implementation of a privacy policy.
2 The policy must be easy for website visitors to find, read and understand and explain what information is being collected and how it is used.
3 Choice and consent. Users must be allowed to exercise choice of how information is to be used.
4 Data security. Measures must be taken to protect individual information from loss, misuse or alteration.
5 Data quality and access. Reasonable steps must be taken to ensure that personal information is accurate, complete and timely for the purposes for which it is used.

Website: http://www.privacyalliance.org

users are not too concerned. They do get concerned when they do not know about it, or they think it will open the door to unjustified 'snooping'. The Internet makes snooping easier, since traffic can be analysed at key points, such as mail servers, or intercepted while it travels through the connecting networks. Only recently has the public become aware of the Echelon system, operated by US intelligence, that intercepts Internet traffic and sifts it for certain phrases.[8] The interest of marketers in finding out as much as possible about users through click stream analysis and other mechanisms is fuelling the debate about where to draw the line on privacy. From the perspective of a firm, it makes good sense for employees website visitors to know what policy and guidelines are being followed, and what safeguards are in place to protect individual rights.

Progression: from free to fee

While it is relatively easy to sell standard products directly from a Web page, things get difficult when selling more expensive items and knowledge. The art of progression is to lead the user, step by step, from being a casual visitor to a valued customer. If you are selling high priced and complex knowledge products or services, such as an expensive software package or consultancy, it is highly unlikely that the first time visitor will readily click the 'buy' button. To aid progression you need products in your portfolio that represent small low risk steps for the potential customer (Figure 7.5). Consider what you can offer for free, for $10, for $100, $1000 and so on. For example, many of today's popular software

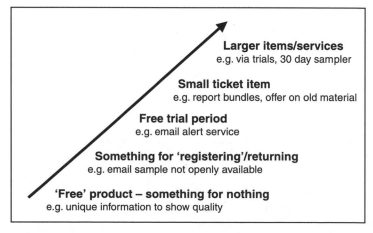

Figure 7.5 Progression

packages are offered in free 'lite' versions, usually with limited functionality. Users then become familiar with the product, and many will want to progress to the paid versions that offer more functionality.

Each stage of progression offers the customer value for money and gives them knowledge and the confidence to progress to your higher priced offerings. Here is a good progression for a knowledge business:

- A free sample or 'taster' product, e.g. last year's analysis, a summary of a report.
- Something in return for disclosing information about themselves, e.g. a special offer or email newsletter for registering their interests.
- A low cost item, e.g. a magazine subscription, briefing paper or short report. At this stage some form of efficient online payment mechanism is needed.
- Higher value items, e.g. in-depth reports, advice lines. Here you must help the user be confident that they will get value for money; engage in email dialogue, offer some form of guarantee.
- Premium items, e.g. consultancy. Most will require some amount of individual selling, perhaps via telephone.

At each stage of progression, the user should receive offers that make it attractive to progress further. For example, you may allow them to deduct the purchase price of a low-ticket item as a credit against any higher priced item ordered within a given time frame. You will need to keep enticing the user to return to your site and deepen the relationship. Regularly updated content, limited time offers, customization, email alerts, are all ways that good Internet businesses do this.

Payments: a virtual necessity

In theory, online payments should be one of the easiest of the 10Ps to incorporate into the marketing mix. There are, as discussed in Chapter 2, many payment service providers who handle the technical details of conducting secure transactions and processing payments with the buyer's and seller's bank. It seems that all you have to do as a seller is offer and price your goods, take orders, deliver them and receive payment. This is a typical trading transaction that most of us carry out routinely with a wide range of goods. Simple? In theory, yes. In practice no!

The Internet adds several complications. Often there is no prior relationship between buyer and seller and so brand loyalty or mutual trust has not been developed (hence the importance of progression). There are more practical considerations:

- What is the point of sale for legal and tax purposes?
- In what currency should the transaction take place?

- How much will foreign exchange transactions cost?
- How much more will a credit card transaction cost since the cardholder is not present to give a signature?
- How do I authenticate the identity of the other party?
- How secure are online transactions?

Technologists have solutions to many of these problems – built-in security functions in browsers (SSL – Secure Sockets Layer), digital certificates (e.g. Verisign http://www.verisign.com) and PGP (Pretty Good Privacy – http://www.pgp.com). But, as in many other aspects of online working, it is not the technology that will determine outcomes but the policies and practices of everyone in the supply chain – buyers, sellers, and banks. One of the problems has been the lack of a critical mass of the major players to back particular systems. For example, a few years ago, there were several promising developments on the payments front, but many have not matured as quickly as anticipated:

- SET – Secure Electronic Transaction – a more secure way of sending transaction information than SSL.
- Digital cash – the ability to send cash via software over the net from a digital wallet in your computer. An early pioneer, Digicash, went bankrupt (though its technologies have survived in eCash Technologies[9]), while Cybercash is phasing out its first cybercoin system.
- Micropayments – where each trader authenticates software scrips, i.e. pieces of millicash. Millicent, an early micropayments system developed by Digital, allows individual transactions as low as 1/10th of a cent. Although several years in gestation, Millicent faces the practical problem of 'potentially unmanageable numbers of issuers of scrips and the difficulty in matching a spent scrip with its issuers could again raise costs'.[10]

Another interesting innovation is Beenz: 'It's like money but better!'. You earn currency units called Beenz by visiting certain sites and spend it at other sites. They can also be redeemed at some offline retail outlets. There are several more conventional loyalty schemes, such as MyPoints, where points can be accumulated by clicking on advertisements, completing surveys or buying certain products. InstaBuy is another scheme whereby you can register your credit card details once and shop at many sites without having to re-enter your details. The success of all of these payment methods depends on a sufficient number of suppliers and buyers adopting the same schemes, although the emergence of 'online currency' exchanges may help.[11]

Irrespective of the types of payment that your online store accepts, the golden rule of online payment is to make sure that you are easy to do business with. Offer a range of payment mechanisms, and reduce the risk for the buyer. Make your terms of trading and which laws and taxes apply clear. Above all, honour your price and delivery commitments.

Processes

It may seem slightly odd to put process as a part of the Internet marketing mix. After all, aren't business processes part of the general fabric of the business, whereas marketing primarily involves dealing with the customer interface? Yes, and that's the point. For a k-business, knowledge is likely to be sourced and delivered from many parts of an organization, particularly where specific expertise is required. Bob Buckman of Buckman Laboratories recounts that 85 per cent of its staff now has regular dealings with customers. A customer orientation should be an integral part of every business process, yet frequently it is not.

As examples of broken processes – both computerized and human – here's some online experiences that I encountered during a two week period while writing this book:

- A website whose home page had a message that started 'Microsoft OLE DB Provider for ODBC Drivers error 80004005'.
- A bad link (404 error) on the home page.
- No phone number to contact for product information.
- A magazine subscription made online that vanished, yet while two customer service representatives (one by phone, one by email) were convincing me it had not been processed and that I should pay again, the magazine started arriving!
- A promise of a 2–3 day delivery for a product, which two weeks later had still not arrived.
- Emails to several customer support departments that took more than 3 days to receive replies, and in one case no reply was received at all.
- A website that rejected my registration since it did not recognize my (valid) postcode.
- Several sites that gave unrecoverable Javascript errors.

I could go on, but these examples are symptomatic of the general problems that abound. And they are not from small businesses just starting on the net. They are from large companies, supposedly Web-savvy, many of them household names. The point is that a Web store is only as good as the processes that support it. And these involve the whole of the organization, not just the customer-facing parts.

The conventional approach to solving such problems is to define rigorous business processes and check their interdependencies through process modelling. But as any process modeller will tell you, once a process has been created it is nearly always obsolete, overtaken by events and by the fact that smart people have found better ways to do things. Processes that are viewed as proscribed procedures, to be followed to the letter (or computer program), will fall into disrepute. The knowledge perspective of a business process is different. Processes are merely the codification of best practice knowledge into a form that lends itself to automation and reuse at lower cost. Think of business processes in terms of knowledge flows and knowledge repositories. More routinized processes will have stable repositories with well-defined methods and predictable flows. Other processes, those that often arise as a result of internal innovation or customer requirements, are more fluid and subject to change. When considering each process, map the flows of information and knowledge to and from the customer. If it takes more than two or three steps of internal processing, then the chances are that your organization is limiting its use and exploitation of knowledge at the customer interface.

Since dealing with the customer interface takes time, it is important to factor this into the activities of each person involved. If staff are measured purely on their productivity for the core process for which they are responsible, then they may consider time spent with customers as a non-essential activity. However, if they are measured on the increase of intellectual capital derived from the customer interface, then they will spend time doing that. Five internal process managers spending 20 per cent of their time in this activity could create more value for an organization than one dedicated customer representative, who would probably still have to access specialists and use some of their time anyway. Rethinking process in terms of knowledge flows and stocks is a distinguishing feature of a truly integrated k-business.

Performance: the bottom line

Performance is the last of the 10Ps of Internet marketing. All of the previous nine contribute to this, perhaps the most important P of them all – performance for the customer in terms of online experience and satisfaction; performance for the provider in terms of business results. The world of e-commerce is littered with a litany of poor performers. Orders, processed after a couple of mouse clicks, arrive late or never at all. A heavily promoted site keels over with the volume of traffic generated by its promotion. A new website fails to generate the level of business expected. All are indicators of poor performance.

The focal point of performance improvement is a performance measurement and management system. With such a system in place, you can track levels of customer service, the impact of changes in your strategies and marketing mix, and have some measures that can be used as a focus for management efforts and objective setting. Performance measurement systems (such as the Balanced Business Scorecard or the European Foundation for Quality Management model) are increasingly used to track the progress of businesses. But are they suitable for relatively new e-businesses and k-businesses? Some of the main differences are:

- K-businesses have more intangibles (e.g. intellectual capital).
- The rate of change in the Internet environment is such that any long-term track-ing of changes may be difficult.
- There are so many unknowns that the link between cause and effect is not clear.
- Managers need to understand a new set of indicators which may not be familiar to them.
- New methods of data collection are possible (e.g. online surveys and statistics).
- Performance at the customer interface is dependent on the performance level of many others in the supply chain, e.g. ISPs, PTTs, software suppliers.

These are differences in detail rather than fundamental. In common with conventional businesses the general approach to setting in place a perfor-mance system is the same – clarify objectives, develop indicators and measures, introduce the system into the organization's routine, collect and analyse data. Let's look briefly at each.

Clarify objectives

Many websites were initially created as a reactive move to external devel-opments: 'we have to have one'. Over time, particularly as your organiza-tion's Internet presence matures, you will need to ensure that the website continues to support your overall business plan and objectives. What is its primary objective? Is it to create awareness, while still using conventional sales channels? Is it to sell low cost items directly 'off-the-page'? Is it for reputation building? Is it to reduce the cost of telephone support? Usually there is a hierarchy and network of objectives. Having these explicitly agreed and prioritized (not an easy task when many senior managers have different perspectives) will at least give you a head start in develop-ing suitable performance measures.

Illuminating indicators

The selection of indicators should be based on your objectives and should be balanced across customers, internal processes, intellectual capital etc. A useful tip is to make sure that you distinguish inputs, output and out-comes. Here are some potential indicators for a k-business:

- *Inputs:* number and quality of knowledge sources used; time and resources to generate new material; cost of Web page publishing.

- *Outputs:* number of unique Web pages; number of visitors; number of queries answered; speed of response; percentage of visitors converted into customers (for a k-business this last one is probably the most important of all website performance indicators).
- *Outcomes:* website visitor satisfaction; impact on your business bottom line; impact on their business.

Usually the input indicators are the easiest to measure, while the outputs and outcomes are the most important. That's why it is essential to work back from customers' needs. Listen to them carefully, and observe their online actions. Then consider how they can benefit from your service and develop some customer measures around these. The measures will be a mix of 'hard' and 'soft', more and less precise. But in the difficult world of measuring intangible knowledge, it's better to be roughly right than precisely wrong!

Initiating the system

Good practice follows that of any other new system introduction. It requires involvement of all stakeholders, understanding how a new system interrelates with existing practice and measurement systems, and not – as frequently happens – underestimating the need for training and for time for the new system to become embedded (many months if not a year or more in a large organization). The new system must be woven into the management decision-making fabric of the organization. If it isn't, your Internet presence is a 'bolt-on' or a 'side-show'. If marketers, operations managers, new product developers and others do not act on the results and just use 'top of the head' – or worse – 'seat of the pants' decision making, then why bother at all with a more systematic approach?

Data collection and analysis

As described in the previous chapter, various Web analysis packages offer an effective way of gathering hard information on website usage. Other hard data can be obtained through online forms and emails that are generated by your pages, provided that you track and log their content. You may also get hard data from your service provider or in-house MIS department on server availability and response times.[12]

You might think that online surveys would provide useful hard data. Often they do not. The reason is that the respondents are self-selecting and you miss the added information that might be revealed in a face-to-face or telephone interview. Often more interesting are the views of those who are not accessing your website. For these, you will need to use conventional market research techniques, such as focus groups (discussed below).

With such abundance of hard data, it is easy to dismiss soft data. However, soft data usually reveal more qualitative information about what users are thinking and what their needs are. Conventional soft methods include customer visits, telephone conversations, use of feedback forms etc. Much of this will be ad-hoc and therefore you will need to be alert for patterns. More effective sources of useful insights are observation and focus groups. These can be combined in an online focus group. Have a small group of users, e.g. your customers or potential customers, come together to review your website. Give them each a terminal and ask them to carry out a typical task. You can structure their review to some extent or pose questions to which you seek answers, e.g. 'does this help you make better buying decisions'? Encourage participants to talk and comment while they are browsing. They will also prompt each other with things they like and don't like and point out competitor sites that do things better.

Another thing that is relatively easy to do is to act as if you were a customer. Conduct random tests on your website. See how well it measures up to customer expectations in areas such as ease-of-use, responsiveness to queries, order fulfilment. Such blind tests, carried out by independent market researchers are a common method in the consumer marketplace. In view of some of the personal experiences cited at the beginning of this section, they should become established practice in online markets.

The bottom line

The process does not, of course, end there. The real test of the usefulness of a performance measurement system is that it will guide you in making change and improving your k-business. Performance is about the bottom line. This means attracting customers (using portals and pathways), packaging what they need, positioning your company, showing pages that attract them, personalizing their experience, helping them progress from a mere visitor to a valued customer, processing payments, and reorienting your business processes to support the marketing effort. All these Ps, properly implemented, will make a major contribution to the performance of your Internet presence and k-business strategy.

The marketing cycle revisited

In the previous chapter we introduced a sales cycle where your prospective customer is led through four stages: unaware – aware – interested – committed. This is reproduced in Figure 7.6, but with the addition of the 10Ps to the parts of the cycle in which they are mostly applicable. They

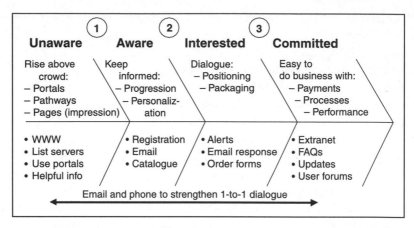

Figure 7.6   The Internet sales cycle showing transition points and the 10Ps

are used to help move your prospective customer through three transitions as follows.

Transition 1: From unaware to aware   Make your site known through using portals and pathways. Be active in relevant online forums and steer potential customers to helpful pages on your site. Also use conventional marketing methods to publicize your website, such as free publicity through articles and conference presentations. If potential customers don't know you exist, you have not even reached the first rung of the marketing ladder.

Transition 2: From aware to interested   You have to grab people's attention within the first few seconds and make them want to read more, hence the importance of positioning and page impressions. Provide plenty of relevant and useful content. Be user-focused. Help visitors with problem solving, product selection and frequently asked questions, rather than merely promoting your products. Encourage them to register their interest through a simple form. Keep them informed of developments and personalize offers via targeted email (not spam!). Keep key pages fresh with interesting and updated content, so that users return and eventually progress through the next transition.

Transition 3: From interested to committed   To make this transition you have to make it easy to do business with you. This means answering their detailed questions as they are on the point of deciding. So think of what they might ask and have ready answers. Provide obvious contact points, e.g. an email contact for knowledgeable and responsive answers (not just links to your Webmaster). If you are serious about Internet marketing you will view your email response system in the same way as a telephone call handling system. Then make it easy to buy – an appropriate e-commerce solution with shopping basket and choice of payment mechanisms.

Finally, maintain an ongoing commitment and relationship. Ensure that your business processes support your customer through the complete sales cycle, and deliver quality knowledge products and services. For all phases,

Table 7.1 Summary of the 10Ps of Internet marketing

Factor	Overview
Positioning	Making clear the role of the website and how visitors can benefit. Often helped by a memorable 'strap line'
Packaging	Packaging knowledge in different formats and with appropriate levels of customization. Providing wrapper information to allow potential buyers to judge its quality
Portals	Creating entry points for knowledge. A website must either act like a portal or be referenced by existing portal sites in the same field
Pathways	Making a website easy to find in search engines, directories and other places which potential visitors frequent
Pages	Having good content, a crisp design and a website that is easy to navigate. A good information architecture and content management processes are essential
Personalization	Giving visitors pages that are personalized to their preferences and click patterns. This typically involves the use of 'cookies' and registration information but concerns about privacy need to be addressed
Progression	Providing a smooth path from free information to expensive knowledge products and services. Free and low-cost information attracts interest and helps convey the quality of premium-priced products
Payments	Making available a range of payments options for customers. Real-time credit card processing is the most common option currently, although micropayment and digital wallet systems may emerge in the future
Processes	Ensuring that all the business processes that support the customer experience work well together, especially order fulfilment. Providing an error-free website is the start
Performance	Developing a performance measurement system that monitors overall website performance and customer satisfaction. A mix of hard and soft metrics are used, some collected online, others using more classical techniques such as focus groups

develop and use performance measures to ensure that your Internet marketing mix is effective.

Summary

This chapter has described the 10Ps of Internet marketing, a summary of which are provided in Table 7.1. Appendix C is a website evaluation template that incorporates the 10Ps.

Points to ponder

1   Find a website that you feel is a competitor of yours. Evaluate it using the website evaluation template (Appendix C).
2   Now complete the template for your own website (or relevant part of it).
3   Consider in what way the 10Ps relate to the 4Ps of conventional marketing.
4   Review your e-business or website strategy. To what extent have the 10Ps been addressed?
5   For your k-business (or any other line of business), rank the 10Ps in order of importance for a specific customer segment. Repeat for others as necessary.
6   How do your product wrappers change as you move along the progression from fee to free?
7   Review your privacy policy. List its benefits in two columns, the first for your customers, and the second for your organization. How would you know if it has been violated?
8   How much does it cost you to process an order worth $1 on your website? How could it be reduced?
9   How well does your current performance measurement system address (a) knowledge assets and their exploitation; (b) your Internet presence?
10 What other Ps can you think of that are also important for improving your online k-business?

Notes

1   This situation was one where under a specific set of circumstances, arithmetic calculation produced the wrong results. The details of how the knowledge about this flaw diffused and how Intel responded are explained in *Creating the Digital Future: The Secrets of Consistent Innovation at Intel*, Albert Yu (Free Press, 1998).
2   http://www.delphigroup.com.
3   You will find a good summary of a Delphi study on portals by David Orenstein at the *Computer World* website http://www.computerworld.com/home/features.nsf/all/990628qs which also has a resources section. Nielsen's comments are taken from Alertbox No. 4 (April 1999) at http://www.useit.com/alertbox/990404.html, while one description of the Bay Networks case is

described in 'You think tomaytoes, I think tomahtoes', Peter Fabris, *CIO* (1 April 1999).

4   There are several broad-based medium sized portals, but Forrester Research predicts that by 2004 the big three (Yahoo!, MSN and AOL) and niche sites will account for 64 per cent of all Web traffic and 72 per cent of advertising revenues. Portals that are 'stuck in the middle' will account for just 1 per cent of Web traffic ('The great portal purge', *Business Week Online*, 26 June 2000; http://www.businessweek.com.)

5   For more information on search engines and how to get the most out them see Search Engine Watch http://www.searchenginewatch.com.

6   A 'directory of directories' can be found at http://www.directoryguide.com.

7   A hyperbolic visualization tool such as InXight (http://www.inxight.com) gives the user another perspective of a website's content. They see the connections and can select items of interest and drag them to the centre of their screen and so bring other items that were 'over the horizon' into view.

8   Similar issues of balance surround the use of encryption in email and e-commerce transactions, and the right of public authorities to have access to the keys. There is an interesting discussion of these issues in 'Pretty Good Privacy', Chapter 7 of *The Code Book*, Simon Singh (Fourth Estate, 1999).

9   http://www.digicash.com.

10 Millicent was reported as operational in Japan, with releases for Europe and North America 'coming soon' (October 2000), http://www.millicent.com.

11 Websites for these schemes are http://www.beenz.com, http://www. mypoints.com and http://www.instabuy.com respectively. RocketCash (http://www.rocketcash.com) is an online currency exchange for Beenz and similar units.

12 In the UK, the performance of 130 different ISPs is regularly monitored by *Internet* magazine. It reports on availability (up time) and throughput (time to download a typical mix of web pages). Various providers do checks on corporate websites from different locations to check overall performance. The Novartis website (http://www.novartis.com) encourages visitors to check performance through its home page menu item: 'Test the Server'. This gives it an ongoing record from actual visitors from around the world.

Chapter 8

Developing a successful k-business

The secret of success is constancy of purpose.

(Benjamin Disraeli)

In many respects, developing a k-business is no different from developing any other business. You need a good business idea, a viable business plan and the right resources to implement it. But there are additional considerations where the product is knowledge and where the Internet is used for marketing and delivery. One consideration is time-to-market. A new k-business must be created in months not years, if it is not to be overtaken by events. Additionally, dependence on human talent means that more attention must be given to attracting and retaining the right talent.

This chapter looks at the main factors to address when planning and building a sustainable k-business. After introducing a generic k-business framework, the rest of the chapter is based on the acronym kbiz.com.[1] K is for knowledge, the primary asset of a k-business. B is for business concept, the idea and business model that lay the foundations for revenue generation and profitability. I is for incubation, the process of nurturing the idea from concept to reality. Z is the Z-factor, derived from the German *zusammen* – together. It is the process of integrating the many different facets of implementation, including the content, technology and organizational elements. C stands for customer experience: how you add extra value as well as meeting customers' general expectations. O is for operational excellence, an area where many fast-growing businesses, especially dot.coms, have fallen down badly. Finally, M is for momentum. In today's fast-changing business and Internet environment, every business needs to continuously adapt and evolve.

What makes a successful k-business?

Success is in the eyes of the beholder. In the dot.com world, many might view success as making the transition from idea to IPO (initial public offering). Entrepreneurs have succeeded in turning their visionary concepts into a valuable business, at least on paper. But as we saw in Chapter 2, many dot.coms will disappear before their businesses become viable. A better notion of success is one where every stakeholder benefits, in the long term as well as the short term. This involves delivering useful products and services to customers, exploiting knowledge for the benefits of the wider community, motivating and rewarding employees and partners, and delivering ongoing and increasing value to shareholders. In short, it is about developing a sustainable business.

What contributes most to success when measured in these terms? In a nutshell, it is having a good idea that is effectively commercialized. It depends on the effective execution of many of the concepts discussed in earlier chapters. Chapter 1 covered the concepts of identifying knowledge assets and exploiting them externally, while Chapter 5 suggested how these assets might be packaged into products and services. Chapter 2 and subsequent chapters have reiterated the role of the Internet as a way of enhancing marketing and delivery. Chapters 6 and 7 specifically considered the perspectives of customers and how to market in the online environment. These considerations are summarized in the business framework of Figure 8.1.

Creating a new business calls for clear thinking, bringing together the right knowledge and skills, and a systematic approach to business development. But this is not all. Every new business needs inspirational leadership and entrepreneurship. Organizations must create the right conditions where innovation can flourish. If, as happens in many established organizations, too much time is spent analysing business plans and conforming to corporate processes and constraints, then it will be difficult to get new businesses off the ground in a timely fashion. If, on the other hand, a separate new start-up business is created, then there is the danger that over-optimism and enthusiasm will overshadow management experience and realism.

Aspiring k-businesses need an optimum blend of both. Several large organizations have done this by investing in start-ups or incubator companies, and making available some of their management expertise. For

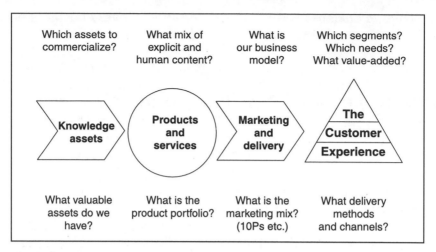

Figure 8.1   An overall knowledge business framework

example, Cable & Wireless has invested in Gorilla Park, a European incubator and venture capitalist company. Taking an alternative tack, Procter & Gamble created Reflect.com as a semi-autonomous company in Silicon Valley, into which it placed some of its younger executives and created alliances with the region's entrepreneurial organizations. Arthur Andersen has done a bit of both. It has successfully evolved some of its existing businesses into the online environment. At the same time it has created an e-commerce incubator, which its own staff can use to commercialize their ideas and take a stake in the companies that they help start.

Analysis of successful knowledge businesses and Internet ventures suggests seven critical success factors. These are summarized by the acronym kbiz.com (Figure 8.2). Kbiz.com is also chosen to indicate a dot.com knowledge business (kbiz for short). In summary, the seven factors represented by the letters in kbiz.com are:

1   *Knowledge assets.* These represent the intellectual capital that is to be
    commercialized. They include information assets, such as databases or
    publications. Human expertise will also loom large.

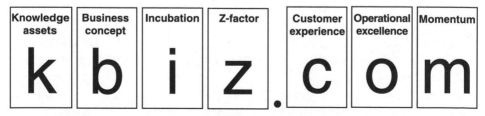

Figure 8.2   An acronym for successful k-business creation and growth

2 *Business concept.* This is the core idea behind the business. It may be expressed as a vision statement or slogan, such as Ernst & Young's 'From Thought to Finish'™. It will be backed up by a viable business model.

3 *Incubation.* A suitable environment, either inside or outside the company, is needed to incubate the business concept from idea into a tested business model. External business incubators provide a range of advice and services to help e-commerce start-ups. These including business planning, office services, legal advice and access to sources of funding.

4 *The Z-factor.* An integrated and scalable business architecture. Each strand of activity – asset packaging, Web development, organizational development and so on – must be developed in a coherent fashion, while being capable of coping with fast growth.

5 *Customer experience.* The factors that create an enhanced customer experience are grouped into a three-layer model – the foundations, the customer-centred differentiators and the value-added enhancements.

6 *Operational excellence.* All business processes, especially the order fulfilment cycle, must be efficiently managed to deliver excellent service and value to customers.

7 *Momentum.* In the fast evolving knowledge economy and Internet environment, the need to continually reassess, and if necessary, reinvent your business, is an essential activity.

Let's now consider each of these factors in turn.

Exploitable knowledge assets

The starting point for a k-business is to consider what knowledge assets to commercialize. For established organizations, the process of conducting a knowledge inventory or audit, as outlined in Chapter 1, will give a good indication of which existing knowledge can potentially be converted into products and services. The inventory should give due attention to human competencies. It is also important to view the inventory from the perspective of potential customers. How might this knowledge be delivered? How will they use it? What benefits can customers gain by getting rapid access to your knowledge? Look at the benefits for knowledge management described on page 3 and ascertain which ones apply to each potential product and product use. The final choice of which knowledge assets to use as the core of your k-business will also depend on the customers' perception of value and the cost of productizing. The section on value in Chapter 1, and on packaging in Chapter 5, will guide you in making this choice.

For new businesses, the primary knowledge assets are the initial ideas and the knowledge of the founders. Care should be taken to protect these assets until they can be nurtured and leveraged to grow the business. Some form of legal protection may be necessary. Business secrets and proprietary information can be protected by confidentiality agreements. Employee knowledge can be protected by employee agreements and incentives such as stock options that motivate them and limit damage in the event of their leaving. The use of the patent system, though popular in larger companies, may prove to be too much of a distraction for a start-up. The benefits of protection must be put against the costs and effort involved.

For all k-businesses, it is good practice to apply the disciplines of knowledge management from the start. Capture the learning that comes as the business grows. Early on, put in place early mechanisms to capture customer knowledge. Consider carefully what knowledge is being accumulated that will (a) help the business and (b) provide potential knowledge assets for future products and services.

A good business concept

A good business concept is one where knowledge products and services can be sold profitably. This is most likely where the knowledge product or its surround has some uniqueness, so that that a premium price can be charged. Operational efficiency gained through exploiting the cost-effectiveness of the Internet can also contribute.

Novel methods that exploit the special characteristics of the Internet can lead to some excellent business concepts. Examples include online advice lines and business-to-business exchanges. The problem with most new concepts is that unless they are patented they are easily copied. Businesses that follow in the footsteps of the pioneers have less risk. They will know whether the original business concept proved successful or not. Because of the multiplicity of ways in which buyers and sellers can connect and engage with each other, there is plenty of scope for the invention of new methods.

Carving a profitable niche

For most companies, the business concepts with the most potential are likely to be those that use or adapt an existing method, and combine it with a unique knowledge offering targeted at a specific group of customers. This leads to the selection of a specific niche. Examples of the type of niche that can be developed include the following:

- *Customer segment.* A good niche is a target group whose information and knowledge needs are currently not well served. An example of this is Youreable.com, a UK website targeting the specific information needs of the disabled. It gives information about facilities for the disabled at hotels, the accessibility of specific buildings, and details of travel restrictions on public services. Although an obvious niche in hindsight, this target group of some 5 million people with some degree of disability had previously been completely ignored.[2]
- *Specific knowledge domain.* As the volume of knowledge expands, there are more opportunities for sub-dividing domains of knowledge into more specialist areas. Pharma-outsourcing.com provides information to the pharmaceutical industry on outsourcing strategies, with a particular focus on Japan.
- *Capability niche.* This is the provision of a specific type of expertise, primarily delivered by people. The Internet is used predominantly as a marketing tool. The consulting and workshop side of my own business is an example, where many leads initially come via the Internet.
- *Knowledge processing niche.* Value is added by pre-processing knowledge to make it more immediately usable for the customer. An example is Reuters 3000 XTRA service. Financial information is customized for its users, and made available in the form that can be quickly integrated into customized spreadsheets.
- *Service niche.* This is an example of part of the product surround being used to differentiate a generic knowledge product. Gigaweb's online research service gives clients access to Gigaweb's network of external experts.
- *Enhanced user experience.* This combines the previous two niches by providing higher levels of service based on customization. A personal adviser would be one example. Subscribers to Teltech.com can talk directly to knowledge analysts to get additional help in finding solutions to their problems. Another example is the provision of supported Linux packages. Essentially a free operating system, many Linux customers are happy to pay for it in order to receive additional services and support offered by Linux experts.
- *Geographic location.* In many fields, the location of knowledge sources is becoming irrelevant. However, there remain many activities where location is a key parameter. Conducting business in a given country, visiting a specific town or city, and searching for natural resources are examples where location-specific knowledge is important. In the delivery of people-based services, the availability of experts local to the customer can give a distinct service and cost advantage where face-to-face delivery is required.

The options available for picking a particular combination of knowledge domain, customer segment, method of processing and additional services, mean that a large number of potential unfilled niches exist. A niche is only likely to prove profitable if the potential customer base is of sufficient size to make the investment in product development and marketing worthwhile. Most niches are therefore based on only one or two of the above variants.

Developing a viable business model

Having selected a niche, the other main element of a good business concept is a viable business model. Different types of model were discussed in Chapter 3. For most embryonic knowledge businesses, there is insufficient knowledge of how realistic its business model will prove for their chosen niche. Estimates can be made of market size and potential level of demand. Business plans may have rows and rows of carefully considered costs. But profitability can be very sensitive to many assumptions, two of the most crucial of which are customer acceptance and the level of demand they place on resources. For example, one company offering unlimited free Internet access in the UK based its business model on a core assumption about the length of time each consumer would spend online. In the event, they spent much longer than envisaged. The ISP's offer had to be withdrawn since its line usage payments to telecommunications companies increased beyond the point at which it could make a profit. As often happens, customers don't always behave as planned! What starts as a promising business concept might not stand the test of market reality.

Business planners must plan for the downside risk. A good way to do this is to have a 'light' business model, with minimal fixed costs. Knowledge products lend themselves to low inventory costs. Equipment can be rented rather than bought. It may be possible to defer payments until revenue streams are guaranteed. The best way to minimize risk is through knowledge. The business concept must be researched and tested. Are there similar concepts already being used? What does market research say about consumer acceptance? Focus groups and user observation are particularly effective ways of gauging consumer reaction to online services. Knowledge efforts should be focused on gathering and assessing knowledge and

> **Validating the concept – Branson-style**
>
> The concept behind Virgin record stores in the early 1970s was one of having a store that was fun to go into, where music could be heard in a sociable atmosphere and with plenty of soft seating. The records too were cheaper than traditional stores. Richard Branson and his colleagues would walk up Britain's high streets at the cheaper end of town and talk to young people, gathering informal knowledge about their shifting musical tastes and where best to locate a store. To minimize downside risk, Branson was adamant that no property would be rented without the owner agreeing to a 3 month free rental period.
>
> *Source: Losing my Virginity*, Richard Branson (Virgin Publishing, 1998)

performance indicators that give early proof (or otherwise) of the assumptions behind the core business concept.

Incubation: nurturing the idea

In many corporate environments, good business ideas are stifled at birth. They fall foul of corporate bureaucracy, which insists on detailed business planning, applies full corporate overheads onto a newly fledged venture, and adds layers of burdensome administration. In areas where business innovation thrives, such as the Silicon Valley area of California or the Austin area of Texas, the environment encourages and supports innovation. Budding entrepreneurs are helped by multiple business networks. They get access to financial capital, not just venture capitalists but individual investors. They can tap into a network of legal and business advice, often by people who have deep knowledge of the particular kinds of business which they are trying to create.

A particular channel through which all of this support is funnelled is that of a business incubator. Incubators are not new. Many of the earlier ones were started as non-profit ventures in science parks adjacent to universities. The highly successful Austin Technology Incubator (ATI) was created in 1989 as a joint venture of several partners in the locality, including the city government and the University of Texas at Austin. It provides office space, shared office facilities, access to expertise and links into venture capital networks. It has spawned over 50 high-technology companies, many in computer software. A more recent phenomenon is that of incubators dedicated to

> **Equityengine.com – a virtual incubator**
>
> With backing from Hewlett–Packard, Equityengine.com promotes itself as the world's first automated virtual incubator. As an online marketplace, it provides mechanisms for visionaries, entrepreneurs, resource providers and investors to incubate start-up businesses. Equityengine.com provides the processes, infrastructure and support.
>
> *Website:* http://www.equityengine.com

e-commerce and Internet ventures. Most are private ventures that take stakes in the firms they incubate. An early example is idealab!, founded by Bill Gross, which has some 30 ventures incubating at any one time. The well known retailer eToys started as one of idealab!'s start-ups. By mid-2000 there were over 150 incubators specializing in e-business.[3]

How can a large company create an innovative environment where new business start-ups get a similar boost to that provided by an incubator? Many invest in new start-ups or incubators themselves. But this often a hands-off arrangement with little transfer of knowledge between the firm and the start-up, and it certainly does not create the same innovative 'buzz' within the large firm. To nurture an entrepreneurial climate within big business needs a rethink on how new initiatives are funded. Even ideas that get initial funding are likely to get chopped in any reversal of fortune or when any setback in business puts pressure on budgets. Innate conservatism in larger companies often means that only projects with near certainty of success are backed. Venture capitalists, on the other hand, are quite happy to bet on people with ideas and commitment, even if their ventures may appear more risky. They view investments as options, only some of which will succeed. Typically, for every ten companies in their portfolio, five will fail, three will progress steadily, one will double their money, while the star investment may become another Yahoo!, more than compensating for their failures. Look at how closely your own organization emulates Silicon Valley. Does it have an investment arm specifically for new ventures, rather than simple extensions of existing businesses? Are employees allowed to make unsolicited applications for corporate funds directly, without going through their normal management channels? If their in-house investment funders say 'no', are they supported by the firm to take the idea outside to find another backer? Some large corporations have now created this kind of environment (see below).

Hotbeds of innovation

Enron

Enron has done much to model its innovation processes on Silicon Valley. Its culture encourages innovation from the bottom up. Individuals are given a high degree of autonomy and freedom to take their ideas forward and to move around the organization to pursue new opportunities. It also rewards employees in ways not dissimilar to start-ups. Each new business has its own customized reward plan that gives the start-up team stakes in business. It is not unusual for them to receive Enron stock options worth $1 million or more. Once a medium-sized gas-pipeline company, Enron has branched out into other energy utilities and is now the largest gas and power trader in Europe. Other new ventures include innovative trading operations in paper, coal, plastics and Internet bandwidth. Its track record in innovation has helped it top the rankings four times in a row for innovation in *Fortune's* annual survey of Most Admired Companies in America. This is reflected in its financial returns to shareholders, which at 58 per cent in 1999 were eight times higher than its peer group and three times that of the S&P 500. Its 1999 annual report explains: 'We are clearly a knowledge-based company, and the skills and resources we have used to transform the energy business are proving to be equally valuable in other businesses.'

GameChanger at Shell

Started in late 1996, GameChanger is a process introduced in the Exploration & Production Division of Shell. Any employee can prepare an outline plan and propose their idea in a short session with a review panel – a 10-minute presentation followed by 15 minutes of questions and answers. Ideas with potential are then reviewed by relevant experts. Typically, successful applicants will receive an initial grant of $100 000 to take the idea to proof-of-concept, after which they are often further developed within an existing business initiative. Four out of five of Shell's major growth initiatives in 1999 started as GameChanger submissions. GameChanger had a slow start, though, with very few ideas in its early days. An entrepreneur's workshop was needed to coach budding entrepreneurs in the ways of Silicon Valley, rule-breaking behaviours and how to anticipate and exploit discontinuities. Seventy-two people attended this initial workshop, and generated 240 business ideas, 12 of which were given seed funding.

Sources: 'Reinvent your company', Gary Hamel, *Fortune* (12 June 2000); Enron Annual Report 1999 (http://www.enron.com)

Innovative companies create marketplaces for ideas, supported by a well-funded and timely knowledge commercialization process. Ideas can enter the incubation phase quickly, with the selection being based more on the criterion of 'what happens if this turns out to be a missed Yahoo!' rather than 'will it succeed?' And, unlike Silicon Valley, the failed entrepreneur usually still has a job.

The Z-factor: putting it all together

Z stands for the German *zusammen* – together. The implementation of a knowledge business requires the integration of several strands of activity – the creation of the product, the design and development of a website and supporting applications, the creation or restructuring of business processes, the development of the marketing plan, and the development of the k-business knowledge base. For a k-business, the website is the focal point that pulls together these strands of activity (Figure 8.3).

Many of the activities to create and market knowledge products have already been discussed in earlier chapters. The task of implementation is to draw these together into a coherent project plan, with some clear milestones on the way. The ideal milestones are to release versions of the website, at sufficiently aggressive timescales, e.g.:

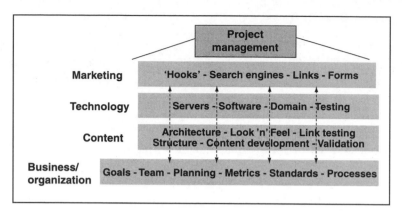

Figure 8.3   Integrating the activities needed to build a k-business

- *15 days: concept release.* A skeleton of how the finished site might look and feel, with navigation aids; some draft pages for each main section and samples of detailed pages of each type.
- *45 days: pre-release version (Alpha release).* Completion of all main pages; core applications in prototype form, a substantial amount of content, but gaps to be filled.
- *75 days: test version (Beta release).* Applications are fully functional and virtually all content is online; testing for usability, coherence of content, robustness under different conditions of use; real customers are involved.
- *100 days: full release version.* Available on the Web to all comers.

The 100-day figure is important. In many situations where a Web project is taken on by an IT team, the formal processes of a traditional IT project are used. Requirements specifications are spelt out in great detail, incomprehensible process flow diagrams are drawn, and the final product is promised for 1–2 years into the future. This is wholly unacceptable in the fast moving world of the Internet, and in businesses where it is difficult for business managers to fully articulate what they want. Much preferable is an iterative development approach where the IT developers are challenged by asking them: 'what can you deliver in 100 days?'. Even then, business managers should be aggressive and stretch the goals slightly beyond reasonable limits. They must also realize that many non-IT staff will need to commit time to deliver content to the Web development team.

A website is organic and must be developed in an organic way. Rather than specify too much in detail on paper, develop the product iteratively, gradually refining it into a released version. Designing websites is now a fairly well developed discipline. Many organizations, including in-house project teams, offer a comprehensive set of Web development services.

Appendix D gives a checklist of activities for a typical website development project. However, several aspects of development are commonly not addressed properly. These are now considered in the sections that follow.

Roles and responsibilities

First, it is important to remember that a Web project is a business project, not a technical one. The primary focus should be on the knowledge product and its information content. As a result some very clear roles emerge. These may be full-time or part-time; the responsibility of one individual or shared among several; carried out by in-house people or external consultants and contractors (Table 8.1). Depending on the level of business and technical complexity there may be additional roles. Each project will need to develop its own set of roles, but be very clear as to who owns them. Role managers must also be supported by people with the requisite skills.

Product and content management

The way that content is organized on a website has significant impact on user acceptance and perception of value. Developing a coherent information architecture is a good starting point (see pages 208–9). The development of content within this architecture requires a well-defined set of content management processes. This includes content creation, content tagging (adding metadata), content workflow, Web authoring processes, approval procedures, and version control. A growing body of content management software tools, such as Interwoven, will help in these tasks, but there will still be a high reliance on content owners to identify sources, adapt content to the users' context, and to classify it appropriately. In many organizations these tasks fall to the Webmaster by default, leading to bottlenecks in content publishing. This problem can be overcome by providing content owners with templates or database forms to specify sources of content, add wrapper information and provide status information for each unit of content, e.g. its stage of development and review.

One attribute of content is its level of richness (see page 146). Added richness increases development effort but enhances the user experience. A careful judgement has to be made to determine the right balance. A content database that reports content attributes and status is a prerequisite for overseeing content development in a large Web project. Another important process is that of collecting and collating user feedback so that content quality and currency can be maintained. Another aspect that needs careful handling is that of product updating. A publication has a specific release date and all references to information are valid at that date. But Web pages are easy to update; conversely they can be left to get out of date. If updating takes place regularly, will you regard the page as an active

Table 8.1 Roles and responsibilities in a Web development project

Role	Responsibilities
Steering committee	Sets the business goals of the project. Reviews progress (e.g. at milestones) and implications for business, initiating changes in business policies or processes if necessary
Management team	Oversees the project progress on a regular basis (e.g. weekly meetings). Resolves disputes and makes decisions
Project leader	Responsible for day-to-day running of the project. Prioritizes activities, allocates resources and coordinates activities
Product manager	Defines the nature of the knowledge product and service. Responsible for the main elements of the marketing mix, e.g. product functionality, packaging, pricing, promotion
Information architect	Designs the knowledge map for positioning content, and identifies relationships between content items. Classifies different content into categories and sets templates and quality standards. Develops alternative views and navigation aids. Ensure cohesiveness across different content
Editorial board	Sets general principles and procedures for content authorization and review. May review individual content, but usually just samples to check adherence to policy
Content and service owners	Responsible for contributing, validating and maintaining specific content to agreed quality levels. Generate links to related content. Define levels of interaction and the nature of the customer experience
Knowledge refiners	Regularly review content, generate summaries, synthesize key knowledge from multiple pages into new content
Process owners	Design and manage business processes, ensuring that online and offline elements work together seamlessly, e.g. ensuring that processes are in place for responding to enquiries generated online
Graphic designers	Create the site's look and feel, and set layout criteria and guidelines. Select, create and optimize images and multimedia. Provide templates for page producers

Table 8.1 Continued

Role	Responsibilities
Page producers	Convert content into Web-ready format (e.g. HTML) optimized for speed and usability. Often this will be handled semi-automatically by content management or Web editing software
Webmaster	Ensuring the integrity and reliability of the site, e.g. through a systematic updating and back-up procedures. Handles fault reports, generates usage statistics
Users and customers (selected individuals)	Test and critically review the website for practical applications. Provide feedback on product features, quality and the usefulness of the website and supporting services. Identify usability problems and suggest product and website improvements

continually changing object, or will you treat each update as a separate version? What are your policies regarding updating existing customers, and will you track which version they downloaded? Will you spend the extra effort needed to ensure that all related pages are similarly updated? The alternative approach is to update at specific release dates. Will this be guided by a specific timetable or when a sufficient number of changes are needed that makes a new release worthwhile? There is no simple answer to these questions, but they must be considered and a good updating and recording process established.

Usability

The most common complaint about websites is their poor usability. Despite a wealth of established knowledge in human–computer interaction (HCI), many website developers have either ignored it or are not aware of its existence.[4] Confused and multiple layouts, poor colour combinations, incomplete information and inadequate navigation aids proliferate, even at the websites of major corporations. A few techniques widely applied can make a big difference to overall usability.

- Use of common layouts across sets of pages, so that users gain familiarity of the overall layout.
- Good use of headings and subheadings, preferably with content-specific headlines rather than generic ones. Thus, 'Usability is the top concern of users' is generally a more helpful heading than simply 'Survey results'.
- Context specific navigation aids, either in a sidebar or at the top of a page.

- Good context setting. Explain at the beginning the purpose of the page and what the reader will find.
- Make key text display before images. Images should not be right at the top of page, and they should load quickly, achieved by reducing the size of images (e.g. to thumbnails) or use interlacing techniques.
- Good writing style – clear and concise.
- Hyperlinks to referenced material and related concepts; use hyperlinks within a page when it is large.
- Suitable selection of fonts – a good rule is to use no more than two typefaces and three font sizes on a given page.
- Make good use of the information the user has already supplied, e.g. use registration information to customize pages.
- Easy backtracking and error correction. For example, users should be able to review and edit order forms before confirming a sale.
- Make it quick and easy for the user to achieve what they want.

This last point sounds obvious and trite, but it is frequently ignored. A common complaint amongst reviewers is that users have to type in passwords or unnecessary registration information, even if they just want to browse the website to find what's there. To overcome this, many sites offer rapid search facilities and display information about content (e.g. wrapper information), even though additional details may be requested to view the content or to make a purchase.

The obvious way to test for usability is by observing users. Large software corporations have usability laboratories where controlled experiments are carried out with groups of users. Less elaborate, but equally adequate for most websites, is observation of users by developers during prototyping and testing. Added insights are gained using focus groups (see page 219).

Technical considerations

Developers must be conscious of the variation in users' computer equipment. Many users do not have the latest browsers or all the plug-ins that a website developer might wish. They may also have slow modems or monitors that can display only a limited range of colours, typically 256. Such variations must be accommodated or explicitly excluded. It may be quite reasonable to display a message that 'this site can only be read with a frames capable browser' since fewer than 3 per cent of all Internet users have version 2 or earlier of Netscape or Internet Explorer which do not support frames.[5] On the other hand, it may be unwise to rely on HTML version 4 features that are only partially supported by today's browsers. Different browsers support different features, and have different effects on the way that pages are displayed.

It is essential to develop a set of standards that developers and testers will follow, so that the widest range of all possible user variations are accommodated. Standards should also cover software and application packages. Will developers be allowed to use Java applets? While they may offer additional functions, they may be disabled by customers because of the security implications of potentially malicious applets. Another area that needs attention is that of quality of service. What availability and response times can users expect? Will this be validated by tests from different locations around the world on a regular testing programme? It may be desirable to use mirror websites, which replicate content on Web servers in different locations.

Other areas where standards or guidelines should be developed include:

- *Databases*. How will Web pages be generated from databases? Will they be carried out by Microsoft's ASP (Active Server Pages) or by some other tool like Cold Fusion? Who validates the database entries?
- *Directory structures and access*. Who will allocate directories and set up authority to update content? How will updating and version control be managed from a technical perspective?
- *Security*. How will the site be protected from unauthorized hackers, or from other threats such as 'denial of service' attacks? What processes are there to archive and back-up customer transactions?
- *Architecture*. How will Web and application functions be distributed? Many organizations opt for a multi-layered architecture where applications, a Web front-end and databases are held on different servers and communicate via some form of 'middleware'.
- *Scalability*. How will capacity be expanded, both from a hardware and software perspective?

Testing

In the rush to get online quickly – which is a natural desire in the dynamic world of the Internet – too many website launches finish up as marketing disasters. In the space of just one month, two of Britain's largest banks, the Halifax and Abbey National, had serious problems with new website launches. On its first day, Abbey National's Cahoot site collapsed under the volume of users and had to be temporarily taken off air. Partly to blame was the high publicity for this new Internet banking service and an offer of interest-free credit cards for the first 25 000 subscribers. Halifax, in planning its new IF (Intelligent Finance) service, had carried out computer simulations that revealed no problems. However, when the system was tested by human testers, it could not cope. Being prudent, and having witnessed their competitor's misfortune, the launch was delayed for several months.

There are some important lessons to be learnt from these and similar examples. Anticipating demand in new markets is hazardous guesswork. Further, however rigorous your testing regime, it is almost impossible to test every conceivable pattern of use or traffic load before launch. A marketing strategy of gradual emergence might be more prudent rather going for a highly publicized 'big bang' launch. There is also the paradox that the more popular your website, the more problems you may potentially have. The bottom line is that contingency plans need to be in place to cope with the unexpected.

Testing is not an activity that should be carried out as the last in a line of development tasks, but should start early in the cycle. A study by The Newport Group showed that where applications had scalability problems, 60 per cent of them had never been tested before going live, and 34 per cent were only tested at the later stages of development. In comparison, of those that scaled up as expected, 96 per cent were tested throughout the development process.[6] There are some simple but effective toolsets for testing website basics, such as browser compatibility, loading performance, dead links and search engine readiness.[7]

The customer experience

Many websites fail to deliver a satisfactory customer experience. A useful e-commerce service model has been described by Chris Voss.[8] It consists of three levels of service – the foundation, customer-centred and value-added. An adaptation of this model is shown in Figure 8.4, using terminology for particular elements used earlier in this chapter.

Foundation level   Customers expect a website that is responsive, easy to use, meets their needs and delivers what is promised. Responsiveness includes the speed at which pages download, and the speed with which users can find answers to queries. This is determined by having relevant content that is easy to find as well as providing fast turnaround to email enquiries. Voss reports on comparable studies conducted in the UK and US that showed that only 47 per cent and 35 per cent of enquiries (in the US and UK respectively) were answered within a day, while around 30 per cent received no response at all. Also important are the elements of usability described earlier, including intuitive navigation, consistency and guidance for specific user segments. In meeting customers' needs consideration must be given to the various quality attributes of information, such as being accurate and up-to-date. Once a transaction has been completed, customers expect to receive the products within the promised delivery period. For

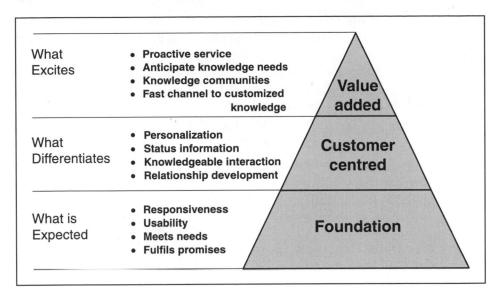

Figure 8.4   The customer experience

knowledge that is downloadable, this must be easy to do; to overcome download problems, there should be a suitable alternative, such as forwarding material by email.

Customer-centred service   This higher level of service goes beyond the basics and helps to create a competitive edge. Elements of this layer include some of the 10Ps, such as personalization of the Web experience to match the customer's specific interests and giving them access to account information, such as a record of their orders. The process of cementing the longer-term customer relationship is another aim at this level. Suppliers can give access to unique expertise that forms part of the product surround. Interaction by email or phone can be encouraged, so that the product offering can be closely matched with the customer's needs. Such dialogues, done in an effective way, make good inroads into establishing a successful customer relationship.

Value added service   Here the customer receives a level of service that delights them. This requires the provider to be proactive. If the customer is at one of the earlier phases of the sales cycle (see Figure 7.6), this involves alerting them with new information or contacting them occasionally to check if there is anything further that they need. If they have placed an order and are waiting for delivery of a customized service, then ongoing person-to-person dialogue should be used to help them with preparatory planning and inform them of current status and any changes. Added extras, such as community participation and customized newsletters, all add to a positive experience. Revisit the elements of the product surround and marketing cycle of Chapter 6 (page 157).

Over time, customers' expectations increase. Therefore, what is regarded as a customer-centred service today may well become the expected minimum of tomorrow. Defining standards of service at these different levels for different groups and classes of customer should be incorporated into your performance measurement system (page 216).

Operational excellence

Operational excellence is closely related to customer experience. Almost every aspect of the latter relies on an operational process. Such a process may be embedded into the Internet application, or it may be a back office process using other systems and resources. The different parts of the operational system have to work in harmony and respond efficiently to requests for action. Unfortunately, too often they do not. Several studies have shown that many customers are not receiving even the basic levels of service they should expect (the foundation layer in Figure 8.4). One UK study found that 58 per cent of e-commerce shoppers were dissatisfied with their experiences. Long download times, lack of response to emails, no phone numbers, bad web design and poor fulfilment were all cited as major irritants.[9]

Poor performance is not uncommon in new and fast growth industries. Many customers of mobile network operators have found their networks often congested, billing systems that creak and customer service representatives that never seem to call back. Where investment costs are high, where monopolies or quasi-monopolies exist (such as found in regulated utility and telecommunications markets), and where the customer has few alternatives or high switching costs, suppliers can often get by with inadequate operational performance. Knowledge businesses are inherently different. Consumers have choice. Similarly, the Internet is a highly competitive market where switching suppliers is generally quick and inexpensive. However, do not underestimate the cost to the customer of gaining familiarity with a new supplier's products and processes. Good service and added value are often key elements in the consumer's choice. Even though Amazon.com now has many emulators in the book marketplace, it has a loyal following of customers who like the usability of the site and value the level of service, even though competitors may boast lower prices. To remain sustainable long term, a k-business needs to build its operations to support its customer service through all phases of the sales cycle and to develop long-term relationships.

Designing knowledge processes

In mass production, material flows sequentially from one process to the next. Analysis and modelling allows systems designers to apply the optimum level of resources and skills at each stage and identify potential bottleneck and interfacing problems. Operations to support knowledge products and processes are rather more complex. Some knowledge will flow from computer system to computer system, but much knowledge delivery will need human intervention. Designing such a delivery system combines workflow analysis with that of resource and skills planning. An additional complication is that the level of demand for specific types of knowledge may fluctuate. If the knowledge has been codified and is accessible from the computer, this is unlikely to be a problem if computer capacity planning has been well done. If it is human knowledge, and particularly the scarce knowledge of just one or two people, then they are potential operational bottlenecks.

Handling the disposition of human talent is something that many people-intensive organizations do routinely. Service organizations, design consultancies and legal practices, all have in place systems to estimate the scope and size of a job and to assign resources. Their methods use a combination of computer-based systems and human talent. Computers can help optimize the allocation of resources and design work schedules. But it is the talented planner or dispatcher, who knows the capabilities of their people, who juggles around resources to optimize client satisfaction or to cope with unexpected delays or demands. The extra speed and volatility of the Internet environment makes this more challenging. But knowledge management can come to the rescue.

Systematic analysis of incoming demands for knowledge can indicate which operations currently carried out by humans would benefit from codification and automation. An example is the creation of FAQs (Frequently Asked Questions) to reduce the demands of handling customer queries. Having in place a performance measurement system, where information is automatically updated can help identify pressure points. Carrying out an investigation in these areas can indicate problems in process design or gaps in knowledge and knowledge flows. Moreover, if knowledge management is being properly applied throughout the operational arena, then the knowledge that is derived from all these operations will be continually updated and appropriate lessons learned. Where performance is better in some areas than others, then best practices can be developed. Specialists can share experiences and learn from each other as part of a knowledge community.

Maintaining momentum

A k-business must never stand still. The creation of a k-business with a new website is just the beginning. Many companies relaunch their Internet sites at regular intervals as their strategies evolve, as new services are launched, as new customer groups are addressed, and as they gain insights into what improvements are needed. A k-business, whose product is knowledge, has additional characteristics that put additional pressure on maintaining momentum. First, as the core knowledge in its products becomes more widely diffused, it loses value (see Figure 1.3, page 23). Second, its customers generate application knowledge that can be used to enhance the product. In addition, much of the knowledge in the product line needs regular updating to maintain its currency.

Evolutionary adaptation must be built into the product development process and the organization's operations and marketing. The key to both these is the continual gathering, refining and packaging and exploitation of knowledge, i.e. repeatedly going around the knowledge management cycle (see page 10). The evolutionary approach to the first of these cycles, that of product development, has already been discussed in Chapter 5 (page 160). That of the organization's operations is similar, but with added attention being given to the organizational support structure. The structure that most lends itself to adaptation is that of a knowledge network (Figure 8.5). A knowledge network consists of nodes of activity interlinked by knowledge flows and work processes. The network is

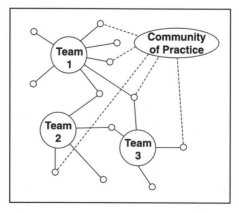

Figure 8.5   A knowledge network

continually evolving, with teams growing and waning as the demands on their activities change. The teams can be specialist teams, such as product development, or cross-functional teams, like a customer service team that has all the skills needed to deal with particular groups of customers.

The networked organization is not a new concept, but in most organizations is often suppressed by much stronger hierarchical and functional arrangements. However, organizations that are project based, such as consultancies, tend to mirror networks more closely. Tetrapak Converting Technologies, which designs product packaging, is almost wholly organized by project teams. In part, management consultancies provide a good model of a knowledge network in that they are continually creating and restructuring project teams as their client work changes. However, many of them have also built up large functional and support teams that are relatively stable. If teams get too large they lose their edge and should be subdivided. Virgin follows this model assiduously. When Virgin records started to look too complacent, Branson created a new business in new premises headed by the deputies of the sales, marketing and managing directors of the original team. This released creativity and new business models that helped make Virgin the largest independent record company.[10] Stability in an organization has the advantage that important knowledge can be embedded into its structures and processes. But it also has the disadvantage that systems and procedures may ossify and become resistant to change. A company's annual budgeting process, personnel, policies and similar cultural baggage reinforce these characteristics.

The 100-day cycle is a good one to follow. This is the product development time in many fast-moving industries. It is, as indicated earlier, the time limit that one should put on creating a new website. Therefore, every k-business should reinvent itself every 100 days. To reinforce this time cycle, you should budget and re-budget quarterly. Rather than spend tremendous effort in an annual budgeting ritual, where reality often overtakes events, why not make the main organizational planning processes work on a quarterly rolling cycle? To ease the blips of activity that fall on the specialist support teams such as analysts and planners, each part of the business could start its process in a different month. Financial reporting systems these days are flexible enough to do real time reporting, and that is the way that companies like Cisco now operate. It's a way of rethinking the business in terms of shorter planning and review cycles where everything is up for grabs. Every assumption (which is hopefully being recorded as part of the knowledge base in the planning process) is critically re-examined. Every budget holder is asked to do zero-based budgeting. Possession of resources in one time period should not guarantee continuance into the next. That does not mean that the baby should be thrown out with the bathwater. A good knowledge management system should retain organizational memory and keep track of what works well and what does not. If, at a later date, old activities need to be restarted, then the knowledge is there to enable a rapid resumption.

Each planning cycle can be organized as a knowledge market. After all, knowledge is likely to be a more critical resource to budget than finance. The knowledge for sale is that of knowledge products and knowledge talent. In each period a third comes up for sale or renegotiation. A team leader can argue that a cohesive team is worth more than the individuals within it. Rather than pitching their proposals to line managers or a corporate management team they offer their products and services to buyers. The buyers are two main groups – representatives of the customer (the marketers), and those developing future businesses (this could be the organization's top strategists as well as existing development teams). The challenge for the management of the company is to develop a few simple rules that make this open market process work well.

In summary, the things that should drive the activities and structure of the network are:

- Customer knowledge and service (what do they want now and in the future?)
- The knowledge product portfolio – what is currently offered and how can it be improved?
- Intellectual capital – how is it growing and which parts of it can be exploited?

Summary

This chapter has considered some of the implementation issues of creating a k-business. It has reviewed the main activities over a business life cycle based on the acronym kbiz.com – knowledge assets, business concept, incubation, integration (the Z-factor), the customer experience, operational excellence and maintaining momentum.

Two important themes are relevant in all these activities – speed and knowledge. Knowledge products must be developed quickly. Websites must be built fast. Plans and actions must be modified in real-time. The methods and approaches usually associated with large projects must give way to more pragmatic and flexible approaches. The key to this is knowledge management. In every business development activity and every operational area, systems are needed to ensure that pertinent knowledge is easily captured, lessons are quickly learnt and operational knowledge is widely diffused. Flexible organizations built around knowledge networks provide the most suitable structures for building a k-business.

At this point in the book we have come full circle. In the first chapter we talked about the role of knowledge management in identifying knowledge assets that could be commercialized for the external market. In the intervening chapters we have described how to create knowledge products and market them over the Internet. In this chapter we have described the key factors that need addressing to build a successful k-business. This k-business, whether a start-up business or a line of business in an established company, creates new knowledge as part of its core processes. Harnessing and managing this knowledge presents opportunities for creating new k-businesses. And so the cycle repeats itself. That's why, once the k-business formula becomes established as part of an organization's genetic code, then new k-business opportunities will continue to spawn, as they do at companies like Amazon.com, Enron and Virgin.

Points to ponder

1 Consider a k-business in your industry. What factors, not captured in the kbiz.com acronym, are important and need addressing?
2 What knowledge assets are under-exploited in your business? (Review your answers to question 2 at the end of Chapter 1).
3 Find three to five websites of start-up companies that operate in a business similar to yours. How easy is it to deduce their business concept and business model? Critique them for long-term viability.
4 How are new initiatives encouraged in your organization? What are the opportunities and barriers for an individual to progress an idea? Compare your own organization's processes with those of Enron and Shell's GameChanger.
5 Find out about the organizational responsibilities for maintaining and enhancing your corporate Internet website (or one of its associated sites). Complete a table similar to that of Table 8.1. How do they compare? Are any role changes needed?
6 Consider the content management processes for creating and maintaining your website. How streamlined are they? What procedures are in place to collect metadata, validate content and ensure that it is kept up to date? How could they be improved?
7 Develop criteria for how you would gauge the usability of a website. Now select three to five websites (such as your own or those used in question 3) and review them according to your criteria? Having reviewed them, should other criteria be added?
8 Select one or more target customer segments. For each segment, develop a chart similar to Figure 8.4 depicting the elements that constitute an excellent customer experience. Are these elements built into your performance measurement system?
9 Review your operational processes. To what extent are you (a) capturing operational performance information; (b) analysing this and comparing it with targets; (c) sharing knowledge on how to improve performance?
10 What plans are in place for the next major revision of your website within 100 days?

Notes

1 For the record, kbiz.com happens to be a registered domain name, which at the time of writing was 'up for sale to any sensible offers' by a Korean businessman (the K in this case standing for Korea). Many other unused domain

names are bought speculatively by companies who make bulk registrations of names, in the hope of selling these knowledge assets on at high prices to businesses that do want to use them for active websites. This practice of 'cybersquatting' has led to companies paying very high prices for particularly desirable names. In other cases, companies and celebrities have gone to court to recover domain names that represent their trademarks or their personal name.

2   Youreable.com was one of the winners of the TV show *E-millionaire* on UK's Channel 4 (http://www.channel4.co.uk/emillionaireshow/). The show, transmitted in summer 2000, was the culmination of a process of sifting through 7000 applicants for a prize of, £1 million in venture capital and business start-up support. 15 finalists presented their business ideas on five consecutive nights – three presentations per show. Many of these ideas were based around some kind of unmet knowledge need or new access to markets. Examples included 'walk around' images of hotels and resorts aimed at holiday makers; finding the best deal for various rentals; guiding householders through the options and contract negotiation with builders; helping composers compose new music and find buyers for their compositions.

3   In the US, the National Business Incubator Association (http://www.nbia.org) provides a good source of information about incubators. Like their dot.com residents, the change of market sentiment in spring 2000 meant that many e-business incubators found it tough to attract new funds. A planned IPO for idealab! was deferred and had still not occurred at the time of writing.

4   An overview of the concepts was published in *A Guide to Usability*, Department of Trade and Industry (London, 1990). Software usability is the subject of international standard ISO 9241 that defines it in terms of efficiency, effectiveness and user satisfaction. For Web page design and usability, a useful resource is that of Jakob Nielsen's *Alertbox*, a regular newsletter on usability issues. Popular topics have included 'Is navigation useful?', 'Do interface standards stifle design creativity?', 'Disabled accessibility' and 'The top ten mistakes of Web design' (http://www.useit.com/alertbox).

5   The Internet statistics site http://www.statmarket.com gives continuously updated statistics on browser usage, and the most popular plug-ins.

6   Cited in 'Crash test dummies', *Information Age*, pp. 46–47 (June 2000).

7   Two popular services are the Web Site Garage (http://websitegarage.netscape.com) and Net Mechanic (http://www.netmechanic.com).

8   'Developing an eService strategy', Chris Voss, *Business Strategy Review*, pp. 21–33 (Spring 2000).

9   Survey by firstdirect.com cited in 'Service continues to let down e-commerce', *IT-Analysis.com* (9 June 2000); http://www.it-analysis.com.

10 'Rule 9: Make like a cell – divide and divide', from 'Reinvent your company', Gary Hamel, *Fortune* (12 June 2000).

Chapter 9

Directions and dilemmas

Opportunities multiply as they are seized.

(Sun Tzu)

The knowledge economy is still in its infancy – online knowledge trading even more so. This book has focused on knowledge as a driver of wealth and e-business as an enabler of new business methods. Developments in knowledge products, online knowledge businesses and knowledge markets are seen as pivotal in the twenty-first century economy. This book has given indications of how they might develop in future. Yet, as we know from the short history of the commercial Internet – less than a decade – developments often unfold in unexpected ways. Napster, a service in which a small but important piece of computer code allowed millions of people to share their music files, much to the consternation of the established music industry, is but one example of the kind of collective power unleashed by the Internet. We cannot predict precisely what other phenomena like Napster will occur. But it isn't just new technologies and applications that alter the shape of the knowledge business landscape. It's a wide range of interdependent factors, among which political, economic and social developments loom large. For instance, the collective behaviour of individuals acting in unison globally can potentially have more impact on the future course of events than major corporations or governments.

This final chapter looks at some of these factors both at the level of the enterprise and at the broader societal level. All in some way involve the relationship between knowledge and those who own it and use it. At both levels are challenges of innovation and entrepreneurship, balancing the needs and rights of the individual against those of organizations and society at large, institutions and the wider issues of knowledge ownership and governance. We address most of these issues in terms of dilemmas, the pull between two opposing forces. The art of resolving these dilemmas is to think creatively in 'both–and' rather than 'either–or' terms, and to strive for a 'win–win' outcome for all stakeholders, rather than a divisive 'win–lose' situation. Shared knowledge is the key to creating an optimum approach. The final theme of the chapter draws these strands together into the ultimate 'win–win': that of building a sustainable knowledge economy for the benefit of all.

Innovation unleashed

Innovation lies at the heart of every sustainable k-business, more so if the business starts from a truly novel idea. The process of innovation has been discussed in earlier chapters. Not to be confused with creativity, innovation is the process that converts ideas and knowledge into saleable products and services. Therein lies a dilemma. How do you balance the flow of new ideas with the effort of commercializing them? Ideas abound, yet only a few are commercialized. Does that mean you stop creating new ideas? In the traditional economy the scarce factors of production were land, labour and capital. In the knowledge economy, land is insignificant, financial capital readily available, and more often than not, labour (human capital) and knowledge (the new fourth factor of production) are not scarce. An apparent abundance, yet still not enough to commercialize every idea.

Behind this dilemma are two crucial factors: knowledge of how to innovate in a specific context; and time. Add these in as distinct factors of production, and the dilemma can be addressed by applying meta-knowledge – knowledge of the quality of ideas, judgements as to their ease of conversion into products and their market potential, knowledge of who is best able to put them into practice. How well do organizations manage this meta-knowledge? One can infer from the writings of economist Paul Strassmann, who has developed metrics for knowledge-based firms, that managers are the key to this meta-knowledge.[1] The crucial investment decision, he therefore argues, is that of return on management investment. While true to a point, I would argue that managers have no monopoly over such meta-knowledge. However, in the typical organization, they do often have a monopoly over allocation of funding for new ventures (although as noted on page 233, companies like Shell are changing that). Does this arrangement result in the optimum innovation performance and wealth creation? I doubt it.

What, however, if an organization operates a true knowledge market – at all stages of the knowledge innovation conversion cycle? Ideas, as in the Schlumberger case, are routinely captured and stored in an idea bank. Other people refine and add meta-knowledge to these ideas, for example by suggesting potential applications or proposing refinements. These contributors will have invested additional knowledge, potential product enhancements in a way. Now make all of these knowledge objects tradable items that can be bought and sold – some restricted to sale within the company, but others made available externally. In Chapter 4 we saw that such markets already exist for intellectual property. An active organizational knowledge market simply extends this notion to less formalized, but equally valuable forms of knowledge.

The upside-down enterprise

Many enterprises are in a state of flux. If the Internet has not already caused a major rethink of business strategy, then it soon should. As we have seen in Chapter 3, many old business models are breaking down while innovative online marketing models are attracting attention. How should businesses respond? Do they treat e-business as just another project or should they view it as a wholesale reinvention of their business? If they face start-up dot.com competitors, do they downplay the threat – after all, many of them are predicted to go bankrupt – or do they embark on a crash programme to capture the online market? For every company that is complacent, another has invested heavily and often ineffectively into territory that is new and uncharted for them. Getting the right balance between these two extremes is another challenge facing many organizations.

Here again, knowledge is key. Organizations need to learn from their environment – their customers, competitors and business partners – and from their own initiatives. But they are often too focused on the job in hand, such that the process of extracting and exploiting this business development knowledge is overlooked. Much can also be learned from knowledge entrepreneurs. These are individuals who have created successful e-businesses or knowledge initiatives. Many, having made their mark in established corporations, have joined dot.com companies or started their own. Many more budding k-business creators lurk inside large organizations, their entrepreneurial abilities waiting to be unleashed. But do they get the chance? Most organizations need to learn from the likes of Enron and Virgin, encouraging bottom-up initiatives as well as deciding top-down.

Artificial or human intelligence?

This book has repeatedly emphasized the need to address both explicit and tacit knowledge. It has shown how a k-business will benefit from exploiting both object-based knowledge and people-based knowledge and how human factors must be central considerations when implementing computer solutions. Many exciting developments are taking place in the field of Internet and knowledge technologies. Glimpses were given of some current developments in Chapter 2. However, it will not be too many years before the Internet becomes ubiquitous, pervading every aspect of daily life. Information and knowledge will be continuously streamed to our personal devices ready for immediate use. If we want to know something, then a single click or push of a button could get us the knowledge we need. Even easier, we may only need to speak to our personal digital assistant.

With so much knowledge and so much technology, the challenge then becomes one of making everything work well together and delivering the best knowledge in the most appropriate way. Will our technology 'know' that at this moment in time and for this knowledge, I need an alert delivered through a mobile videoconferencing call, while at another time, I simply want one of my knowledge bases updated in background mode? Artificial intelligence will make many things possible, but it may be several years before we get to a truly adaptive and intelligent knowledge companion. And when we get that far, we may prefer to enter the realm of virtual knowledge worlds where we explore knowledge databases through visual and other stimuli. Imagine weaving your way effortless through rooms of knowledge artefacts playing different mood music as you navigate your way through knowledge space. Imagine sitting in a knowledge cockpit and making critical business decisions by moving a joystick and pressing a button.

Even before such virtual worlds are commonplace, which may happen sooner than we think, there arises the issue of trust. Do we, as human beings, trust this knowledge, once technology has removed it so far from its human origins? Incidents like the nuclear accident at the Three Mile Island power station in 1979 illustrate the problems humans have of coping with unexpected information and information overload. The film *The Matrix* shows that the dividing line between real and virtual worlds may become harder to discern in future. When technology suggests one course of action and your instincts another, which do you choose? The pace of technology suggests that much more attention must be given to the human issues that arise because of the different knowledge processing capabilities of people and machines.[2] K-businesses will need to enhance their understanding of the relationships between human and machine-based knowledge and exploit the relationships symbiotically. The personal touch will remain an important factor in knowledge businesses for many years to come.

How do we value knowledge?

The difficulties of measuring the value of knowledge have already been mentioned (page 17). What is valuable to one person in one context may have little relevance or value in another. Clearly, financial accounting systems and financial balance sheets are becoming increasingly irrelevant in terms of assigning values to companies. But since there is little agreement on valuation methods for knowledge assets, does that mean that organizations should not even attempt to value their knowledge? What is the right balance to strike between spending on financial systems versus spending on intangible asset accounting systems? Knowledge accounting is another dilemma where there are no clear-cut answers, other than that today's answers are clearly wrong!

Commercializing knowledge is a central theme of this book. Much has been said about packaging knowledge assets and making them available for sale. To some readers my stance may seem somewhat mechanistic and mercenary. This is not wholly my intention. I recall the time while selling minicomputers in the 1970s that my company started charging for software (until then it had been provided free with the hardware). 'Immoral', shouted one professor. Yet, our company's investment in software research and development had surpassed that for hardware development. Charging for software therefore seemed legitimate and fair, also giving customers who wanted to install independent software lower prices for their hardware. A similar situation faces us with knowledge today. We share knowledge in many conversations, but how are the donors of knowledge rewarded? Purchasers of expensive equipment might legitimately expect to ask questions of the supplier's experts and receive answers as part of their ongoing relationship. But there comes a time when the volume of free advice becomes costly for the supplier. As a consultant, I am very well aware of prospective customers who call meetings, ostensibly to discuss a project, but where it quickly becomes apparent that all they want to do is to 'pick my brains'.

The dilemma for most knowledge providers is where to draw the line between free and fee. Relationships can count for a lot, but if you are spending all your day answering telephone and email queries, or being helpful to people who seek your advice in social settings, then you will not have time to exploit your knowledge for those who pay for your time. If you work for a large organization they may have policies about the extent to which individual may offer free advice, or have ways of shielding knowledgeable people from an overwhelming number of knowledge seekers, but if you work for yourself you will need to be fair but firm as to where to draw the line. Pay-as-you-go knowledge is becoming more acceptable, especially if it can be done in a painless way. Many PC support lines, once free, now use premium-rate telephone numbers to recover their costs. The popular phrase 'a penny for your thoughts' obviously has some logic about it. As international micropayment mechanisms become established, and it becomes easier to transfer advice in small packets, then perhaps the saying will become reality.

Knowledge value is tied up in value systems. Your individual and organizational values may be such that you will willingly impart your knowledge freely to certain kinds of knowledge consumers and in certain circumstances. The same knowledge that you charge thousands of dollars for to a large corporation, you might give freely to charities. But if you do place a value on your knowledge and on how it is used, then at least you have a basis to decide when and how much you charge for it, in a more transparent and fair manner.

Whose knowledge is it anyway?

An issue related to value is that of ownership. Much knowledge is the result of amalgamating other pieces of knowledge from many different sources. Knowledge evolves with many individuals making their contributions. Frequently, many of those whose knowledge contributes to the resultant product or service may not be known. What then happens if this knowledge is then sold commercially? Within a firm, things are generally clear. The firm owns it. But what about an inter-organizational community of practice, where a new knowledge asset is created, but where initially contributors did not realize what the outcome might be? Often, in informal collaborative activities, and sometimes even in more formal collaborative ventures, the issue of the ownership of knowledge only arises where there is clear evidence of value that one of the contributors wishes to exploit. In more formal collaborations, such as in European Union R&D development projects, clear rights and obligations are built into collaboration contracts for what is called background knowledge (that which consortium members contribute to the project) and foreground knowledge (that which is generated during the course of the project).

Knowledge ownership issues also arise when people leave companies and move elsewhere. Whilst most organizations have legal agreements making sure that knowledge generated during the course of a person's employment belongs to the organization, where do you draw the line? What about that idea that an employee had in their spare time? What about their knowledge based on a lifetime of experience, not attributable to any specific period of employment? It is inevitable that a company's proprietary knowledge will leak. The best firms strike a fair deal between the interests of the individual and that of the firm. They also motivate and reward the individual such that the temptation to take their knowledge elsewhere is diminished. Many organizations that have bought dot.com or other entrepreneurial start-ups have given insufficient attention to sustaining the entrepreneurial culture of the company they bought and as a result have found the value of their acquired dot.com haemorrhaging as the original people leave.

Another area of concern surrounds the patenting process. Take the growing practice of granting patents on Internet methods. Patenting of business methods has been allowed in the US since 1998 and gives the patent holder rights to prevent copying or to seek royalties. Amazon.com has been vigorous in defending its patents for its 1-Click^{SM} ordering, in which a pre-registered customer needs make only one mouse click to place an order. In another situation relating to intellectual property, UK telecommunications company BT announced in early 2000 that it held the patent for hyperlinking, a fundamental feature used on virtually every Web page. Although its European patent had expired, its US patent had not. It therefore expressed its intent to extract royalty payments from US ISPs. Are such inventions too fundamental that the notion of monopoly rights is inappropriate in this day and age?

A more important question surrounds the ownership of scientific knowledge that is for the public good. There has much concern about the patenting of human genes by large corporations. Whereas the publicly funded Human Genome Project has published and made freely available basic DNA sequences, many companies have filed for patents based on what genes do. Often the full effect of a gene is not known, and therefore advocates of public ownership accuse companies of going on 'fishing expeditions', filing gene sequences that may one day prove exceptionally valuable. Patenting medicinal cures based on centuries of third world knowledge of remedies that work is also criticized as 'bio-exploitation'.[3] These and similar situations raise some very real ethical issues. The cost of drugs to treat AIDS is proportionally higher in the third world than in the developed world. Much of the price is for the intellectual property (protected by patents), with suppliers citing the need to gain a fair return on their R&D, otherwise they may not find it attractive to develop new drugs in future. In the case of AIDS moves are afoot to make special concessions to third world countries. But what if an effective cure for cancer is invented and the developer insists on making unreasonable profits? What if an organization has the solution to an intractable problem affecting a country, but refuses to divulge the knowledge without an extortionate fee? These are the kinds of dilemma we will see more of, highlighting the need to develop equitable systems for the sharing and rewarding of knowledge.

Do we need a WKO?

As the use of the Internet and sales of knowledge grow, anomalies in legislation and taxation become more apparent. Naturally, governments are anxious to tap potentially new sources of tax revenue or to insist on regulating them in some way. The problem is that these new businesses crisscross national boundaries, and therefore uncoordinated policies between different governments lead to conflicting taxation and regulatory regimes.

Here are a few examples of what's happening. The European Union has proposed that US companies larger than a certain size selling to EU customers must register for Value Added Tax (VAT) in a European Community country and collect and pay this tax. In other examples various states in the US have proposed various Internet taxes including one proposal in Texas for a bit tax on Internet traffic passing through the state. The French government has tried to stop Yahoo! publicizing certain sites that while they may be illegal in France are legal elsewhere. Letsbuyit.com, a website that aggregates consumer purchases for a better price deal, has found that its pooled buying methods are illegal in Germany. If a k-business has to adjust content and business terms for every country in which it trades, this places unnecessary burdens on it.

There are many other areas where new and changing legislation affects k-business – intellectual property rights, privacy laws, the right of employers to read employee's emails, digital signatures, consumer's rights etc. The days of *laissez-faire* by governments, allowing the Internet to develop unhindered, are rapidly passing. Internet legal and taxation issues are now an essential consideration for every e-business. In fact, one lawyer I know has had no problems in coming up with an A–Z of different legislation that website developers need to be aware of. With a growing litigious society, this makes the development of a website more than the informal casual affair that it was a few years ago.

While k-businesses, like every other business, should pay their fair share of taxes, and accept a necessary degree of regulation to safeguard consumer and other rights, the global nature of knowledge and the world's interdependent economy needs a more timely and harmonious approach than is currently apparent. International organizations, like the OECD (Organization for Economic Cooperation and Development), WTO (World Trade Organization) and WIPO (World Intellectual Property Organization), have started to address some of these issues. Some have also looked at particular issues surrounding knowledge based products and services. Some general principles have merged, such as taxation at the point of use. Even so, whose responsibility is it to collect taxes for a piece of digital content created in one country, packaged in another, hosted at several mirror sites and downloaded by a person visiting one country but resident in another? The intangible nature of knowledge and the fact the same knowledge can have different manifestations (e.g. a database entry, a printed document, imparted by a telephone conversation) can lead to vastly different legal protections and taxation approaches. As knowledge markets and exchanges take hold, the situation can only get worse. Several regulatory bodies, for example, are reviewing B2B exchanges to see how anti-competitive they might be. Will the different authorities reach the same conclusion?

The current inconsistencies and slow pace of regulatory reform suggest the need for a body focusing on knowledge trading, especially if complex knowledge derivates are invented (see below). If we truly are entering a knowledge economy, as suggested below, and the pace of innovation is high, then surely there is a need for regulation to get ahead of the game for once. The dilemma is whether we rely on existing international organizations or create an entirely new WKO – World Knowledge Organization – where global knowledge experts develop a regulatory framework for the future not the past.

For the present, k-businesses have to balance regulatory compliance with a pragmatic approach. If innovation is not to be stifled, they will have to make a careful business judgement of how much time and expense they invest in trying to be as compliant as possible with all the uncertain and conflicting rules, against using their energies to build the business. As a minimum, they will need to keep abreast of the most relevant developments. Naturally, the legal profession is taking this opportunity to develop its own k-businesses, in the form of online advice or publications to fill this need.

The meta-knowledge economy?

There is strong evidence that knowledge is at the heart of wealth creation in all economies. The World Bank's Annual Development Report of 1999,

Knowledge for Development, highlighted many ways in which knowledge can increase national and individual prosperity. Even in predominantly agricultural economies, applied knowledge brings new methods, disease-resistant seeds and increasing productivity. Indeed, many people argue that some of this knowledge is misapplied by using genetically modified seed and striving for maximum productivity at the expense of good husbandry and sound organic methods. But we do have choices, and better knowledge allows individuals and organizations to make these choices.

In more developed economies, knowledge is a key factor behind successful products and services. As we saw in Chapter 1, using the best available knowledge and applying the techniques of knowledge management can significantly enhance the development and delivery of products and services. We have also seen the emergence of new businesses based almost entirely on knowledge – computer software, biotechnology, management consultancy and financial derivatives are examples. The last industry also highlights some of the potential pitfalls. By developing complex financial products that few people understand, buyers can be misled, markets can be volatile, and what seemed like safe hedging funds or companies that are bastions of stability (such as Barings Bank), can lose their value overnight. The same kinds of things can happen as knowledge markets develop. Not only will packaged knowledge be sold, but also we might see the development of innovative knowledge derivatives, where buyers are sold knowledge futures and complex options, ostensibly to safeguard future access to knowledge or minimize risk, but which may, like many 'junk bonds' in financial markets prove not to be quite what they seem.

History has shown us time and time again, that where new products and markets emerge, organizations and individuals will find innovative ways to exploit these markets, some legal and some not. Opportunists will missell products and services to ill-informed and less knowledgeable buyers. Once again, knowledge can come to the rescue. Just as an advanced manufacturing economy adds new knowledge roles to make it work effectively, a well-developed knowledge economy will see the emergence of knowledge advisory roles. Knowledge advisors will counsel buyers on which knowledge products and services best serve their individual needs. To some extent, this role is currently performed by various independent organizations, such as some research consultancies, consumer or professional associations and independent reviewers. Where there is a growth in knowledge, there needs to be meta-knowledge and sometimes even meta-meta-knowledge, such as directories of directories, or reviews of reviews. As the knowledge economy grows, we can expect to see these supporting knowledge businesses grow as well.

Sustaining the networked knowledge economy

Inevitably, as the importance of knowledge grows in the economy and society at large, we must expect governments and international agencies to take a more pivotal role in furthering its development and wealth creation opportunities. Many governments now have knowledge economy or knowledge society programmes as well as initiatives to stimulate the uptake of e-business. Some of these can prove a useful boost to k-businesses in terms of support with R&D, development of a supportive infrastructure, and the growth of the necessary skills through special training and education initiatives. In the UK, for example, the government's professed aim is to be the best place in the world to develop an e-business. A recently launched programme *UK Online* will help businesses get online through local advice centres and a central call centre and Web-based advisory service (a government-led k-business!). However, one recent UK law, the RIP Act (Regulation of Investigatory Powers) has led to some ISPs planning to go 'offshore' to another country because of the powers it gives the UK government to intercept Internet traffic. Governments too, have to strike the right balance between stimulating new knowledge businesses and scaring them away. Unlike major manufacturing investments, knowledge businesses can migrate quickly to the most favourable locations.

Governments can only do so much, and what they do may well prove ineffective unless done in an internationally coordinated way or unless it meets the needs of individuals. In the networked knowledge economy, power lies increasingly in the collective knowledge and will of individuals. Smart campaigns by pressure groups sharing knowledge internationally can have an effect way beyond the number of people involved. More sinisterly, concerted campaigns by hackers or anti-establishment groups can cause damage to international infrastructures. If the complacent majority do not orchestrate their collective knowledge and will when necessary, the world could lurch from one crisis to another. On the other hand, there are global initiatives in sustainable development, digital cities, education, environmental monitoring and many other fields, where collective knowledge is creating many individual and societal benefits. Many of these initiatives succeed primarily through the effort of individuals, networks, communities and loose federations rather than through more formal organizations and governments.

These societal knowledge networking initiatives, more than the development of commercial knowledge products and services, perhaps represent the true wealth creation opportunities of capitalizing on knowledge.

Notes

1 A selection of articles can be found at the Strassmann Inc. website http://
   www.strassmann.com. See for example 'The value of computers, information
   and knowledge' (January 1996).
2 Interestingly, in one technology establishment I was at recently, over the past
   two decades the original emphasis on research in physical sciences shifted
   first to information and communications, while now the fasting growing
   area of research is in behavioural science.
3 See for example, 'Dealing in DNA', Tim McGirk, *Time*, pp. 58–64 (30 November
   1998) and 'Battle pending', J. Madelaine Nash, *Time*, p. 67 (17 April 2000).

K-business readiness assessment

This short assessment gives you an indication of your readiness to launch a k-business. It considers five factors – knowledge management maturity, e-business capabilities, customer and market knowledge, knowledge asset potential, and marketing innovativeness. The questions can be considered from the perspective of an organization as a whole or from that of an individual unit. Column headings represent scores from 1 to 4. Make a judgement as to how far along the scoring scale you are, guided by the response shown in the respective columns. If you haven't even started to address a question, then score 0! Compare and contrast your ratings with those of your colleagues.

Score interpretations are given for each factor at the end of each set of questions. These interpretations suggest areas for attention. Combine the scores from each of the five sections to give a general k-business assessment (out of 100). The overall score can be broadly interpreted as follows:

- **<20:** Your organization may have dabbled here and there, but needs to take a more serious look at the knowledge agenda and the Internet if it wants to prosper in the knowledge economy. Embark on a general programme of education and awareness.
- **21–40:** There are likely to be pockets of excellence in some of the core activities needed for a k-business, but they are mostly addressed in an ad-hoc manner. Consider combining some of the disparate effort into a new initiative that can attract senior management support. A more coherent and systematic approach should help.

- **41–60:** Some activities are performed more systematically than others. Look to identify the areas of experimentation and best practice, and put in place mechanisms to share this experience more widely throughout your organization.
- **61–80:** Your organization has a lot of practical experience. Make sure that this is not lost and is continually built upon. Strengthen the links and knowledge flows with customers, in order to keep moving forward. If you scored lower in Section 5 than in most of the other sections, you may need to be more adventurous and throw out some of your more bureaucratic procedures.
- **>80:** You are well on the way to creating one or more successful k-businesses. Work on some of your weaker areas as identified from your scoring, but spend most effort in exploiting your strengths. You may need to consider spinning out some of your k-business initiatives to give them freedom to grow.

Section 1: Knowledge management maturity

Question	1	2	3	4	Score
1 Does your organization have a formal knowledge programme?	No program but a few ad-hoc knowledge initiatives.	There are many knowledge activities around the organization, but most are done in an ad-hoc manner.	There are some formal initiatives in different parts of the organization, but they are not coherent.	There is a formal corporate programme, with strong support from business divisions and a significant budget.	
2 How well does your organization share best practices?	Some are documented but people stumble across them by accident.	Some attempts have been made at creating a database of best practices or creating best practice forums.	There are active forums for sharing best practices and a best practices database.	Every department is formally required to share best practices and the mechanisms to do so are well established.	
3 How pervasive is knowledge management?	Some KM practices are used, but in a very ad-hoc way.	Knowledge management is talked about a lot, but few departments take it seriously.	Over 50 per cent of organizational units have people assigned for KM responsibilities.	KM is formally integrated into most organizational and management processes.	
4 How thriving are your communities of practice (CoPs)?	There are a few, but they are seen as a peripheral activity.	There are quite a few CoPs, but the level of participation is only small or moderate.	Most functional specialisms have communities of practice, but only some are active.	Virtually every function has one or more CoPs which are active and encouraged.	

Section 1: Continued

Question	1	2	3	4	Score
5 Are benefits of knowledge management evaluated and measured?	There is no formal evaluation of knowledge management activities, though some project managers carry out their own evaluations.	Some work has been done at comparing our KM activities with those of other organizations or on articulating the business benefits.	Benefits realization is an explicit part of every knowledge initiative. Individuals are measured on their knowledge contributions.	The organization has a full programme of benefits measurement and has also embarked on IC accounting.	
				Total score	

Score interpretation:

<5: Your organization has barely started to take knowledge management seriously.

5–10: Your organization is familiar with KM, has taken some important steps but needs to adopt a more systematic approach.

11–15: Your organization is familiar with knowledge management, and does some things well. However, it probably lacks corporate-wide coherence. The appointment of a Chief Knowledge Officer may help.

>15: Your organization has integrated KM into its normal activities, but it will need to maintain momentum and learn from its experiences.

Section 2: E-business capabilities

Question	1	2	3	4	Score
6 How important is the Internet to your business?	Our organization's website is used mostly for PR or promotional purposes.	Most business lines have up to date information on the website. There are useful information resources and a search engine.	Most inter-organizational communications now take place by email. Email requests to our website are responded to within 2 days.	Over 50 per cent of our business is now transacted over the Internet. Our business would be seriously impacted if our website was inaccessible for more than 4 hours.	
7 How well developed is e-commerce on your website?	There are no facilities to place and pay for orders at our website, but we do have facilities that allow potential customers to contact us by email.	A potential buyer can access our full product catalogue and place an order, but cannot yet pay online.	Order processing online is fully automated. We can handle all parts of the sales transaction without recourse to other media.	Orders taken online are automatically integrated into our order fulfilment and customer information systems.	
8 Do you personalize your offers according to users' preferences and click patterns?	'Cookies' are used to the extent that we recognize a returning visitor.	Web pages are personalized based on interests expressed in registration forms or other pages that have been viewed.	Users can choose personalization preferences and customize their screens.	Both pages and offers are personalized. Microsegment analysis is used. Customers can access their account history and status.	

Section 2: Continued

Question	1	2	3	4	Score
9 How closely are your e-commerce activities integrated into other organizational processes?	E-business is viewed as a separate activity.	There is a formal e-business initiative within our organization.	Every business manager has to consider the impact of e-business and address it within their planning and budgeting.	Information from all our processes, external sources and internal systems is fully integrated whatever the source – telephone, email, website.	
10 What is your involvement with e-business software and service suppliers?	We deal almost exclusively with our main IT suppliers or business consultants.	We maintain awareness of new developments in e-business and Internet software and solutions.	We have access to a knowledge base of e-business solution suppliers and their product features.	We have formal partnership agreements with specialist e-business and Internet solution providers and have opportunities to Beta test their new software.	

Total score

Score interpretation: <5: Your organization has a website, but most employees have little exposure to e-business.
                       5–10: Your organization has some e-business experience, but it needs significant development.
                      11–15: Your organization is using e-business extensively, but is not maximizing its potential.
                       >15: Your organization is well along the road to becoming a fully integrated e-business.

Section 3: Customer and market knowledge

Question	1	2	3	4	Score
11 Do you analyse customer transaction data for new insights and knowledge?	Some standard analysis reports are produced on a routine basis.	Conventional query and reporting tools are used by marketers to analyse data and to make ad-hoc queries.	Data mining and other analytical tools are used to identify new patterns.	A full range of analytical tools is used extensively throughout the organization.	
12 Is market and customer information readily available throughout your organization?	Only sales and marketing people can access customer information.	Access to this information is available throughout the organization's intranet. It is reasonably well organized.	When a phone call is received from a customer, all the relevant information can be aggregated into a customizable screen.	When significant new customer information is obtained, email alerts are automatically sent to those people who are interested in these developments.	
13 Do you have effective CRM systems?	We are considering implementing a CRM system.	We have implemented a CRM system, but it does not tell us all that we want to know.	We make extensive use of a CRM system to understand and anticipate customer needs and to plan campaigns.	CRM systems are central to our product and market planning. They are used extensively to personalize offers.	
14 Do you have detailed analyses of website visitors?	Monthly log analyses are produced.	Customized analyses of website statistics can be produced at any time.	Information about website visitors can be correlated with some other soruces, but not easily.	Information about website visitors is automatically correlated with customer information from external and internal sources.	

Section 3: Continued

Question	1	2	3	4	Score
15 Do you use customer panels or focus groups on a regular basis?	Customers act as reviewers when we introduce new website or e-commerce enhancements.	We have used focus groups or user panels when the website was first launched, but not since.	We incorporate customer review mechanisms into every aspect of e-business development.	We have customer panels that are engaged on an ongoing basis to carry out a programme of evaluation and feedback.	
				Total score	

Score interpretation:
- <5: Your organization is mostly ignorant about its customers.
- 5–10: Your organization collects some useful customer information, but some vital information is lacking.
- 11–15: Your organization has a significant amount of customer knowledge, but it could use it more effectively.
- >15: Your organization applies customer knowledge well and goes a long way to anticipating their future needs.

Section 4: Knowledge asset potential

Question	1	2	3	4	Score
16 Does your organization carry out regular knowledge audits or maintain a knowledge inventory?	A sample audit has been carried out, but it is not up to date.	A comprehensive information audit has been carried out.	A comprehensive knowledge inventory and map are maintained. It identifies knowledge assets, owners and users.	The knowledge inventory is regularly evaluated for the exploitation potential of the knowledge assets that are recorded.	
17 Do you have a valuable intellectual property portfolio that you actively manage?	We leave intellectual property issues to our legal department.	We maintain good records of intellectual property and give it similar attention to our physical assets.	Intellectual property is treated the same way as other knowledge. There is an active programme of review and exploitation.	Individual managers are responsible for maintaining and enhancing intellectual property. Significant revenues are generated from licensing and other avenues of exploitation.	
18 Do you already offer advisory and consultancy services?	Advice and consultancy is offered on an ad-hoc basis when requested by customers.	Advisory services and consultancy are promoted as part of our products and service offerings.	Consultancy services are an integral part of every new product launch. Consultancy services are actively marketed as a service in their own right.	Consultancy and advisory services are the major contributor to revenue and profit.	

Section 4: Continued

Question	1	2	3	4	Score
19. Do you have a system to monitor and develop your human expertise?	Individual competencies are recorded in HR systems but are not widely used.	Competency profiles are widely used. An expertise directory is also available.	The expertise directory is a widely used tool in the organization and actively maintained.	Business managers regularly review expertise profiles and instigate development activities to increase the organization's competencies.	
20. Do you already have a portfolio of knowledge products (other than consultancy services)?	Some information products are sold as an add-on to existing products and services.	There has been a focused effort to create more knowledge products.	There is a broad portfolio of knowledge products including publications, databases, and other intellectual assets, which is actively developed.	The development of new knowledge products is a core activity of every business line.	
				Total score	

Score interpretation: <5: Your organization has a few knowledge products, but this is more by accident than design.
                        5–10: Your organization has put in place some essential groundwork on which to develop a knowledge product portfolio.
                       11–15: Your organization has some knowledge products, but has not fully exploited the possibilities.
                        >15: Your organization is generating revenues from knowledge products, and has established itself as a knowledge business or is well on the way to becoming one.

Section 5: Marketing innovativeness

Question	1	2	3	4	Score
21 How well known are you for your Internet marketing?	A few customers have commented favourably on it.	Our Internet presence is always near the top of features that customers value in general market and customer surveys.	Our efforts have received recognition in the press or through an award. We have been used as a case study for our industry.	Our Internet activities are regularly cited in major business magazines like *Fortune* and *Business Week*.	
22 How well does your organization exploit online communities?	A couple of divisions have experimented with discussion groups on their website.	A good proportion of the business uses them regularly. Some have hosted their own at their website.	Most lines of business use them regularly and exploit them as a marketing tool.	Virtually no new product is announced without a corresponding discussion group or online community.	
23 How much have you experimented with new online marketing models?	We stick to B2B or B2C marketing.	We have tried out banner advertisements and affiliate programmes.	We have experimented with a wide range of marketing models, such as sponsorship, loyalty schemes and auctions.	We have experimented with some more novel approaches, such as dynamic pricing. We have a body of accumulated knowledge about our experience with a wide range of models.	

Section 5: Continued

Question	1	2	3	4	Score
24 Does your organization participate in business exchanges or online marketplaces?	We have considered them but rejected them.	We continue to study them carefully, but have only experimented with a few of them.	We are participating in several of them (perhaps anonymously) in order to develop a better understanding of their impact and potential.	We are enthusiastic followers of them. This may mean participating in them openly or simply closely monitoring them to identify new opportunities and threats.	
25 What support do you give to the development of new e-businesses?	They have to go through the business development planning process like any other initiative.	New business ideas are encouraged from anyone, anywhere in the business. Aspiring e-businesses are given help with developing business plans.	We are quite liberal in giving individuals, wherever they are in the business, some seed funding to develop 'proof of concept'.	We support an e-business incubator. Our employees are encouraged to develop new e-businesses, in which both the organization and they take equity stakes.	
				Total score	

Score interpretation: <5:   Your organization is very conventional – it needs shaking up if it is to prosper in the knowledge economy.

                         5–10:   Your organization knows what to do, but seems inhibited at getting too deeply involved.

                         11–15:   Your organization is an active experimenter, but could probably benefit from some more publicity.

                         >15:   Your organization is a hotbed of potential new e-businesses. Just be careful not to spread into too many new directions at once.

Online market evaluation template

Use the following checklist to review knowledge marketplaces and other B2B exchanges. Section A deals with some common factors of interest to both buyers and sellers. Sections B and C cover some specific topics primarily of interest to buyers and sellers respectively. Score each section out of 10. Compare your evaluations with those of your colleagues. Compare the various markets in which you are planning to participate and draw some conclusions.

Name of marketplace: . . . . URL: . . . .

Date reviewed: . . . . Reviewer: . . . .

A: Factors for buyers and sellers

Factor	Considerations	Score	Comments
Easily locatable	Would seekers find this marketplace readily on search engines and related portals? Is it well publicized in the communities that it serves?		
Critical mass	Are there sufficient buyers and sellers in the part of the market space in which you are interested in participating? Does it attract those of whom you might not otherwise be aware?		
Well presented	Are the different zones immediately clear? Is it easy to hone in on that part of the marketplace relevant to your immediate needs? Are the offers and wants properly and accurately classified?		
Good descriptions	Are the items on sale well described, conveying the distinctive features of the product or service and providing ways for the buyer to make an accurate assessment of its content and quality?		

Factor	Considerations	Score	Comments
Fair and transparent pricing	Are prices set and monitored in a fair way? Are there mechanisms for buyers and sellers to adjust pricing easily in light of changing circumstances? Are there any hidden charges?		
Simple and easy payment mechanisms	Is it easy for the buyer to make payments? Do they have a wide choice of methods? Are they still economic for low value items?		
Effective reward mechanisms	Does the market owner offer incentives for introducing new buyers and sellers to the marketplace? Are there any loyalty schemes for regular users?		
Sharing knowledge	Are there mechanisms to share knowledge with other buyers and sellers? Can this also be done in closed communities?		
Sense of community	Does this marketplace have a sense of community? Does it provide a platform for enhancing the development of the market sector as a whole?		

Factor	Considerations	Score	Comments
Reasonable fees	Are the fees reasonable for the type of facilities available in the marketplace? Are they offset by the reduced costs of searching for buyers or sellers?		
	Section score (out of 100)		

B: Specific factors for buyers

Factor	Considerations	Score	Comments
Sampling (try before buy)	Can you sample products before you buy? Does the market allow you to contact sellers directly with questions before proceeding with the sale?		
Validation of supplier	Does the market owner pre-qualify sellers? Are there independent ratings of sellers' performance? Does the market have a code of practice and trading standards that are enforced?		
Validation of product quality	Are there independent reviews of products? Can users give product satisfaction ratings together with explanations? Can you contact them for additional clarification?		

Factor	Considerations	Score	Comments
Guarantee of satisfaction	Is there helpful guidance on how to get the best out of this marketplace? What sort of guarantee does the market give if you are unsatisfied with the purchase?		
Influence	Are there mechanisms for buyers to pool needs or to collaborate privately? Are there mechanisms for the collective voice of buyers to shape the operation of the marketplace?		
	Section score (out of 50)		
	Total score (out of 150)		

C: Specific factors for sellers

Factor	Considerations	Score	Comments
Positioning	Is participation in this marketplace commensurate with your overall image and brand positioning? Are you able to present your products and services in the way that you like?		
Promotion	Can you pay extra for premium positioning or for advertisements? Does the market owner provide affiliate or other fees for encouraging newcomers to the marketplace?		

Factor	Considerations	Score	Comments
Payments	Are payments passed through from buyers with minimal delays? Does the market owner guarantee buyers' payments (e.g. through an insurance policy or by absorbing the risk as part of their fee)?		
Competition	Is competition fair and regulated? Does this marketplace offer any unique advantages for you over your competitors?		
Influence	Are there mechanisms for the collective voice of buyers to shape the operation of the marketplace?		
	Section score (out of 50)		
	Total score (out of 200)		

Website
evaluation
template

Use the following checklist to review websites for their potential impact. Score each section out of 10. Compare your evaluations with those of your colleagues. Derive lessons from what you have seen and apply them to your own website.

Name of site:........................ URL: ....

Date reviewed: .... Reviewer: ....

A: General

Factor	Considerations	Score	Comments
User orientation	Is it user-centric? Does it have material relevant to your needs? Is the intended audience and usage clear?		
Content	Is there 'compelling' content? Is it relevant, timely, well written and of good quality? Is it unique?		
Usability	Can you quickly find what you want? Is the design good? Are there good navigation aids – site map, search, menu etc. Is it free of annoying gimmicks and unnecessarily elaborate graphics?		
	Section score (out of 30)		

B: 10Ps of marketing

Factor	Considerations	Score	Comments
Positioning	What kind of site is it? How clear is its purpose? In what way is it distinctive from related sites?		
Packaging	What products and services are sold? Is it all the range? Are there special Internet products and packages? Are there special offers and pricing for Internet users? What value-added services are there?		
Portals	Does this site purport to be a portal site? Does it link to other portals or portal-like features, e.g. news, articles, resources, links, jobs? Does it provide facilities for communities of interest?		
Pathways	How easy is it to find from general, specialist portal sites? Does it have relevant titles and META tags?		
Pages	What do you like/dislike about the site, e.g. content, look, navigation? Would you 'bookmark' it or visit it again? How up to date is it?		

Factor	Considerations	Score	Comments
Personalization	Are the pages customizable to your personal preferences? Do offers and pages displayed reflect your interests as defined in your registration details or interactive choices? Are there clear and acceptable policies on privacy and use of 'cookies'?		
Progression	What does it offer that is free? What does it do to entice you to visit again, or to get you more involved? What marketing 'hooks' are there? What ongoing benefits or relationship does it offer?		
Payments	How easy is it to pay for goods online? Would you buy online from this site? Are terms and conditions clear? Is it clear what taxes are levied and which laws are applicable?		
Processes	Are there clear and multiple ways of contacting page owners or relevant experts? Did you receive a helpful and timely response to your enquiries?		

Factor	Considerations	Score	Comments
Performance	Is it error-free? How fast do the pages load? How good is follow through and order fulfilment?		
	Section score (out of 100)		
	Total score (out of 130)		

C: Overall

Factor	Consideration	Comments
Strengths	What are the main strengths of this site?	
Weaknesses	What are the site's main weaknesses and how could they be overcome?	

Website project plan checklist

This checklist provides a useful summary of activities needed for planning and developing a website.

A: Preparation and planning

1 Briefing
2 Appraisal of existing website, IT systems and capabilities
3 Appraisal of competitor websites
4 User research
5 Confirmation of corporate and marketing objectives
6 Budget and resource indication
7 Roles and responsibilities
8 Selection of pilot or trial
9 Initial development plan – timetable, resources. milestones, deliverables
10 First draft Web marketing plan

B: Content development

1 Overall look 'n' feel
2 Standards and templates
3 Information architecture
4 Static vs. dynamic pages
5 Overall site navigation – sitemap, search, menu bars
6 Navigation paths within areas
7 Assembling existing content
8 Writing new content, external acquisition to plug gaps
9 Page markup
10 Other special content

C: Content enrichment

1 Multimedia content
2 Interaction (drop down boxes etc.)
3 Other processing/scripts (e.g. Javascript)
4 Database interaction
5 External feeds, e.g. news
6 Special tagging (META tags, XML tags etc.)
7 Response forms
8 Discussion groups, chat – formats, rules
9 Any special applications development
10 Integration with other applications and systems

D: Technical

1 Server/provider selection
2 Mirror sites – if applicable
3 Server software
4 Domain registration
5 Applications development
6 Transaction and payment systems development, e.g. catalogues, shopping baskets
7 Development systems
8 Uploading and updating processes – static vs. dynamic pages
9 Management and support processes – back-up, continuity, problem escalation
10 Technical standards – supported browsers, features

E: Testing and going live

1 Page quality check, validation, independent review
2 Link testing – internal, external
3 Coherence and consistency checking
4 Security testing – password access etc.
5 Application testing
6 Transaction testing including payment system
7 Complete testing off-line
8 User testing
9 Site uploading
10 Retesting at live site

F: Marketing

1 Marketing model – ads, referrals etc.
2 The 10Ps – how are these addressed?
3 Link negotiation

4   Marketing 'hooks' in each relevant page
5   Response mechanisms
6   Entries in search engines
7   Off-line promotion
8   Research and feedback
9   Data collection and analysis, e.g. log statistics, click stream analysis, user registrations
10 Revised marketing plan

G: Sustenance

1   Webmaster activities
2   Responding to visitors
3   Ongoing page maintenance – correcting errors
4   Collating feedback
5   Content updating programme
6   Commissioning new content
7   Supporting new facilities, e.g. video streaming
8   Link maintenance
9   Periodic reviews of look and feel
10 Update release planning

H: Management processes

1   Overall project management – progress vs. plan
2   User liaison
3   Legal and contractual, e.g. copyrights
4   Release/change tracking and control
5   Performance measurement system
6   Budgeting and resourcing – ongoing roles and responsibilities
7   Process descriptions
8   Documentation, e.g. process maps, content owners' manual, layout standards
9   Extracting lessons
10 Periodic strategic audits and reviews

Each element may include lower level elements. A project plan should be drawn up with milestones, resources and dates. Development of the information architecture and agreeing quantity and quality of content are crucial elements in determining resources needed. A master plan may well include list of all pages and owners with dates for completion and independent testing. Developing a Web presence or Web-based services is not an ad-hoc activity, but needs careful planning and good project management. It also needs an ongoing commitment. Therefore do not neglect resources for sustenance (point G).

Glossary

3G. Third generation. Refers to the next generation of mobile telephony. The first generation was analogue, the second digital. The third generation provides much higher bandwidths and many additional services, such as Internet services, using protocols such as UMTS (q.v.).

404 'Not Found' error. One of the most common error messages seen by users of Web browsers because of a bad link. The error message is generated by a Web server to indicate that the requested file was not found. The HTTP protocol defines a set of status codes, of which other examples are 403 'Forbidden' and 500 'Internal Server Error'.

AAR. After Action Review (q.v.).

ADSL (Asymmetric Digital Subscriber Line). The most common form of DSL (q.v.). It is asymmetric since download speeds can be up to 8 Mbps, whereas upload speeds are much lower (up to 640 Kbps).

Affiliate model. An Internet marketing and business model, where a supplier pays affiliate fees to Web page owners that route visitors to their website, and which result in sales. Contrast with an advertising model, where fees are paid simply for referrals.

After Action Review (AAR). A systematic process to extract the learning from an event or activity. The process addresses the questions: What should have happened? What did happen? What can be learned for the future?

Aggregator. An organization that aggregates information or knowledge from many different sources and owners.

Answernet. A service provided by a network of experts who answer questions posed online.

Applet. *See* Java-based applet.

Artificial Intelligence (AI). A set of computer techniques that makes computers appear to act with a degree of human intelligence. AI techniques are used in neural networks, intelligent agents and expert systems.

ASP (Applications Service Provider). A supplier of application software, which is accessed over a network, such as the Internet. Users do not have to buy and install the application onto their own computers but access it remotely, typically paying by level of use.

B2B (Business-to-Business). A direct relationship between business suppliers and their business customers.

B2B Exchange. An online trading exchange that connects multiple business buyers with multiple sellers.

B2C (Business-to-Consumer). Trading between a business and the end consumer. Contrast with B2B (q.v.).

B2X. Another set of initials to denote a business-to-business exchange.

Banner advertisement. An advertisement displayed as a banner across a Web page, usually at the top. The term is often used more generally to include any type of advertisement displayed in a rectangular advertising slot, although there are more precise terms and standards, such as half banner, button, micro button (see page 95).

Benchmarking. A systematic process for comparing the performance of an activity or process across a range of organizations or departments.

Best practice. The distillation of accumulated wisdom about the most effective way to carry out a business activity or process.

Broker. *See* Network broker or Knowledge broker

Bulletin board. An online area where messages can be exchanged and viewed by a workgroup or community. Many bulletin boards show the messages grouped into topics and replies as threaded discussions. Many bulletin boards were created independently of the Internet (using bulletin board systems which were dialled into directly), but most have migrated to the Internet, where they are more commonly known as message boards.

Caves and commons. Denotes two main types of physical working area – a cave is a private area for concentrated thinking; commons are open areas for socialization and meeting rooms for team discussions.

Chat. An Internet facility in which users type messages into a window that is simultaneously viewed by other participants in that chat room or area.

Chief Knowledge Officer (CKO). A senior manager, often at board level, responsible for setting an organization's knowledge agenda, introducing good knowledge management practice and overseeing major knowledge initiatives.

cHTML. Compact HTML. The slimmed down version of HTML used in DoCoMo's i-mode devices.

CKO. Chief Knowledge Officer (q.v.).

Click stream. The sequence of mouse clicks as a Web user surfs from one Web page to another.

Codification. *See* Knowledge codification

Commercialization. *See* Knowledge commercialization

Community of practice (CoP). A group of people who share their knowledge in pursuit of a common purpose or task, even though they do not work in the same department.

Community of interest. A group of people who share knowledge and experience around a common interest.

Community. An online community of interest or practice. The focus of a community is usually part of a website that typically provides message boards and other conversational facilities (such as discussion lists and chat) as well as a library of online resources.

Computer conferencing. The use of shared computer facilities to exchange messages on a subject and its various topics. Unlike email, in which new messages are sent to every member, a computer conference stores messages on a central server, which users browse or search by topic headings. Today, most computer conferencing is Web-based (Web conferencing q.v.).

Concept analysis. Analysis of text into its key concepts. This technique is used to generate document keywords and improve text search and retrieval.

Concept mapping. A visual representation of core concepts showing the relationship between them. A typical concept map comprises a set of bubbles (the concepts) with arrowed links between them (the causal relationships).

CoP. Community of practice (q.v.).

CPM. An advertising term used to describe the advertising fee in cost per thousand (Roman M) units (e.g. circulation for hard-copy material, page impressions for websites).

CRM. Customer Relationship Management (q.v.).

CTR. Click through rate. The percentage of page impressions (q.v.) that result in a click on an advertisement.

Customer capital. The component of intellectual capital represented by customer assets – customer relationships, loyalty, brands etc. Other components of intellectual capital are human capital and structural capital.

Customer Relationship Management (CRM). An approach that gathers and uses knowledge of customers' buying habits and preferences in order to strengthen the ongoing relationship for mutual benefit.

Customization. Tailoring a product, service or online experience for a particular user and user need.

Cyberspace. The world behind the computer screen, e.g. the Internet. The prefix cyber- refers to cybernetics – the science of control and communications systems, both biological and machine-based.

Data mining. A computer technique using artificial intelligence methods to discern patterns and hence derive new knowledge and insights from large amounts of transaction data. Contrast with text mining (q.v.).

Decision diary. A diary in which decisions are recorded, together with the assumptions and reasoning behind them. They are used to derive lessons and to help future decision-making.

Desktop conferencing. Videoconferencing used on a desktop PC. A small camera is usually mounted on top of the user's display screen.

Digital rights. The rights and conditions of use for a piece of digital content. These rights may be part of the product's wrapper, or may be embedded in the product as part of a watermark to reduce illegal copying.

Digital signature. A digital code attached to an Internet message, such as an email or Web-based form, that authenticates the originator. A signature is encrypted by using two 'keys', one a public key, and one usually held by a trusted third party (q.v.).

Digital subscriber line. *See* DSL

Digital watermark. A piece of hidden code embedded into a digital product, especially images and music, that is used to indicate authenticity, to trace tampering or to prevent illegal copying.

DoCoMo i-mode. A mobile telephone service developed by NTT in Japan. It provides an always-on connection and allows high-speed transfer of images and other information using cHTML. Contrast with WAP (q.v.).

Document management system. Computer-based system for storing and retrieving documents held in a variety of formats. Many provide version control management and audit trails of changes and usage.

Domain name. The text-based name of an Internet domain that appears after 'http://www.' or after the '@' in an email address. Under the IPv4 protocol, Internet domains are referenced by a string of numbers e.g. 194.205.225.1. A Domain Name Server (DNS) translates the text name into the matching numeric string for transmission of data through the network.

Dot.com. This refers to a company that trades predominantly over the Internet. The .com is the high level Internet domain suffix meaning a 'commercial' organization, as opposed to .edu (education), .gov (government) etc.

DSL. Digital Subscriber Line. An ordinary telephone line, consisting of a twisted-pair of copper wires, that is used to send digital data at high speeds. The most common variant of DSL is ASDL (asymmetric DSL) (q.v.), but there are a growing number of other variants, e.g. SDSL (symmetric), HDSL (high data rate), VDSL (very high data rate).

Dynamic pricing. Changing the pricing of a product or service in real-time. This may be done in response to demand, to reward loyal customers or to adjust to perceived value based on other variables, such as the age of the asset or time of day.

E-business. Electronic business. An organization where the majority of its activities are enhanced through online working. Wider in scope than e-commerce.

E-commerce. Electronic commerce. Carrying out commercial sales transactions online, either via the Internet or private electronic networks.

E-journal. Electronic journal. Usually refers to a journal that is published exclusively online and does not have a hard-copy version. *See also* E-zine.

E-learning. Electronic learning. The provision of online learning material that ranges from small and specific learning resources to the provision of complete courses that include online tuition and conferencing.

E-marketplace. An online marketplace. Knowledge markets and B2B exchanges are specific examples.

E-zine. Electronic magazine. An online magazine, generally without a hard-copy counterpart. *See also* E-journal.

eCRM (electronic Customer Relationship Management). A CRM system oriented to e-business. It gathers information about the online actions of customers (e.g. through click stream analysis) and can integrate this information with that from conventional sources.

EDI. *See* Electronic Data Interchange

EIP (Enterprise Information Portal). A personalized starting page on an organization's intranet that offers a single point of access to enterprise information, wherever it is held. *See also* Portal, K-portal, Vertical portal.

Electronic commerce. *See* E-commerce

Electronic Data Interchange (EDI). A method of transferring structured information in a business transaction, such as a sales order, between two computers. EDI transactions have traditionally been carried out over private networks but are increasingly being replaced by Web-based transactions using XML (q.v.).

Email discussion list. An online community whose members share information and knowledge using a single email address to communicate to all members of a given list. Typically all messages generated during one day are grouped together and sent as a single email in a 'digest'.

Encryption. The conversion of information into code. On the Internet, most encryption methods rely on the fact that an encryption 'key' can easily be generated by multiplying two large prime numbers, but that the reverse process is almost impossible without extensive computing resources and time.

Enterprise Resource Planning (ERP). An integrated set of computer applications used for planning and managing the core processes and resources of a firm, such as manufacturing processes and human resources.

ERP. Enterprise Resource Planning (q.v.).

Expertise directory. A database of personnel and their skills that allows users to search for people with specific skills.

Expertise profiling. The identification and classification of personal knowledge and skills. Typically the input for an expertise directory (q.v.).

Expert system. A computer system that emulates the responses of a human expert. It is created by encapsulating the knowledge of a human expert into a set of rules. The system can then be interrogated by people who are not as knowledgeable for guidance in solving problems and making decisions.

Expertnet. Expertise held in a computer (expert system) that is available over a network. For example, a user makes an enquiry that is routed by artificial intelligence techniques to the best source of answers – human or computer.

Explicit knowledge. Knowledge that is codified and documented, for example in databases and documents. Contrast with tacit knowledge (q.v.).

Extensible Markup Language. *See* XML

Extranet. A portion of an organization's intranet that is opened up for external Internet access on a selective basis, e.g. for customers to access specific areas following input of a password.

FAQs. Frequently Asked Questions. A list of questions that are most frequently asked or are anticipated by website or bulletin board visitors, along with the answers. Information providers use this technique to minimize the number of recurring queries and calls. Some organizations use the term AAQs – actually asked questions – since many writers of FAQs anticipate what might be asked or what questions their content answers.

FTP (File Transfer Protocol). An Internet protocol for transferring files between computers. Since a separate FTP program is needed in the user's computer, it has generally been replaced by HTTP transfer for downloading files from Web servers. However, because of its greater efficiency (speed), FTP is commonly used to upload files from a development system to a website's server.

Groupware. Computer software tools that support collaborative working. Lotus Notes was the archetypal groupware software, but many groupware facilities are now provided on the Internet, e.g. bulletin boards, discussion forums, chat.

Hit. A request made to a Web server for a file. The display of a single Web page may require the serving of several files, since each image is separately requested. *See also* Page impressions.

HTML (Hypertext Markup Language). The format in which Web pages are stored. Information content is surrounded by tags, enclosed in ⟨ ⟩ brackets, that denote page structure and formatting, such as paragraphs and bulleted lists.

HTTP (HyperText Transfer Protocol). The protocol for transmitting information over the Internet between Web servers and clients that are running browsers.

Human capital. The component of intellectual capital represented by people – their skills, expertise and know-how etc. Other components of intellectual capital are structural capital and customer capital.

Hyperlink. Part of a Web page, usually a word or phrase, that is highlighted and contains a link to another Web page (that may reside on another server). When selected with a mouse click, the page that the link refers to is downloaded. Hyperlinking is a fundamental feature of the Web.

Hypertext Markup Language. *See* HTML

i-mode. *See* DoCoMo i-mode

IAM. *See* Intangible Assets Monitor or Intellectual asset management

IC. *See* Intellectual capital

Implicit knowledge. Knowledge that is not explicitly identified but can be inferred from its context or packaging. An example is the knowledge held in software that can be deduced by reverse engineering.

Impression. A term used in Web advertising to mean the display of an advertisement on a Web page. *See also* Page impression.

Incubator. An environment to help the development of start-up businesses. The incubator may include office facilities (although some incubators operate virtually), but more importantly it offers access to sources of advice, finance and other resources.

Information audit. A systematic assessment of an organization's information and needs and assets. Strictly slightly narrower in scope than a knowledge audit (q.v.), although the terms are often used interchangeably alongside side that of a knowledge inventory (q.v.).

Information block. A discrete unit of information, typically a paragraph, a list or a table.

Information management. The processes of identifying, classifying and managing information throughout its life cycle. Uses the techniques and skills of library science.

Innovation. The process of converting ideas into new products and services, or new organizational methods and processes.

Intangible assets. Non-physical assets, such as brands, knowledge, patents and customer loyalty.

Intangible Assets Monitor (IAM). A method of intellectual capital accounting developed by Karl Erik Sveiby.

Intellectual assets. A subset of intangible assets related to knowledge, primarily intellectual property but may include human expertise.

Intellectual asset management (IAM). A systematic process for the identification and exploitation of intellectual assets.

Intellectual Capital (IC). The value of a company represented by its intangible assets. A close approximation is the difference between the market and book value of a company.

Intellectual capital accounting. The process of identifying, measuring and reporting on the components of intellectual capital within an organization.

Intellectual property. Intangible assets that are protectable by law. It includes copyrights, designs, trademarks and patents.

Intellectual Property Rights (IPR). The rights associated with intellectual property, e.g. the right to a monopoly with a patent; the right to prevent unauthorized copying of documents. Rights to use an owner's intellectual property are usually granted through licensing.

Intelligent agent. A piece of computer software that acts autonomously and learns from its actions. Typically, agents are used to roam the Internet in order to find and gather new content that matches its owner's interests, to do comparison shopping, and to filter incoming emails for relevant information.

Intelligent publication. An online publication that has some built-in intelligence, such as customization of content and presentation, an interactive document, or links to human experts. *See also* Expertnet.

Internet. A global computer network that uses an agreed set of transmission protocols and standards, such that individual computers can easily share information.

Internet commerce. Electronic trading over the Internet. The most prevalent form of e-commerce, which is a broader term that also includes trading over private networks.

Internet Service Provider (ISP). A supplier who provides end-user access to the Internet infrastructure, such as home-based consumers. The primary means of access is usually through a dial-up telephone line and modem, although most ISPs will allow ISDN (q.v.) access as well.

Intranet. An enterprise-wide computer network based on Internet technology.

Intrinsic value. The value inherent in an asset by itself. Contrast with utility value (q.v.).

IP (Internet Protocol). The basic protocol for defining the format of data packets on the Internet. The current version is IPv4 (version 4), which limits the number of unique domain addresses to 2^{32} (around 4 billion). The practical limit is much less, since some domain space is more crowded than others. To remove these restrictions and to cope with millions of appliances that might be connected to the Internet in the near future, a new version, IPv6, with an address capacity of 2^{64} has been developed, but it is likely to be a few years before it becomes widely adopted by all software and service providers (e.g. ISPs).

IPO (Initial Public Offering). The first offering of shares in a company on a public stockmarket, used to raise capital. Until then, the company is private, with capital being provided by its investors, often venture capitalists.

IPR. *See* Intellectual Property Rights

ISDN (Integrated Services Digital Network). Digital services provided through telephone lines, with a typical speed of 64 Kbps per channel. Most commonly used for high-speed Internet access, although can be used by ISDN devices such as Class 4 fax machines.

ISP. *See* Internet Service Provider

Java-based applet. A small piece of computer code written in the machine-independent Java language. Applets are downloaded by PC browsers from Web servers and executed within the user's PC. Because they execute autonomously, they pose a potential security hazard. Contrast with Javascript (q.v.).

Javascript. A scripting language used in Internet browsers to produce responses to events. Events such as keyboard or mouse inputs can result in highlighting, pop-up windows, or the processing associated with an online shopping basket. Because Javascript operates within the browser, it does not pose the same security threat as a Java-based applet (q.v.).

K-aggregator. A knowledge aggregator. An organization that aggregates knowledge from many different sources and owners.

K-business. A knowledge business that markets and sells over the Internet.

K-community. An online community whose focus is the development and possibly the commercialization of knowledge. More specific than a general online community.

K-mediary. Knowledge intermediary. A business that acts as an interface between knowledge creators and knowledge consumers. Intermediaries include aggregators, brokers and analysts.

K-portal. Knowledge portal. A gateway to a wide range of knowledge resources.

K-refiner. Knowledge refiner. An organization whose core business is knowledge refining (q.v.).

Kbps. Kilobits per second. A bit is a binary digit (0 or 1). The K refers to the binary number $2^{10} = 1024$. The speed of modems and other communications equipment is expressed in this way.

KM. *See* Knowledge management

Know-bot. Knowledge robot. An intelligent agent that gathers or exchanges knowledge from other agents or computer systems.

Knowledge analyst. A person or business that interprets the needs of a knowledge seeker and finds the most suitable sources. May also act as a knowledge broker (q.v.).

Knowledge archaeology. The process of rediscovering an organization's historical knowledge that has become lost.

Knowledge asset. An identifiable piece of knowledge that has some intrinsic or extrinsic value.

Knowledge audit. The systematic analysis of an organization's knowledge needs, sources, users and uses. Includes people-based knowledge resources as well as information. The term is often used interchangeably with information audit and knowledge inventory.

Knowledge-based product. A product in which knowledge is a major component. Contrast with a knowledge product, which is wholly knowledge.

Knowledge broker. An intermediary that connects knowledge seekers to knowledge providers. It may involve brokering a deal and retaining anonymity between buyer and seller until a suitable stage of negotiation. Some overlap with a knowledge analyst.

Knowledge business. A business whose primary outputs are knowledge products and services.

Knowledge café. Informal meeting area for the exchange of knowledge. Cafés can be virtual meeting rooms as well as real ones.

Knowledge centre. A central function for managing knowledge resources. Often developed around a corporate library, a typical knowledge centre will manage both physical and virtual resources – documents, databases, intranet content, expertise directories etc.

Knowledge codification. The process of articulating knowledge in a more structured way. It typically involves eliciting tacit knowledge from an expert, making it explicit and putting it into a template and format that aids dissemination and understanding. High levels of codification are found in computer software and mathematical formulae.

Knowledge commercialization. The process of creating tradable goods and services from a body of knowledge.

Knowledge cycle. A sequence of core knowledge processes that results in new knowledge. There are two main cycles – the innovation cycle and the knowledge sharing cycle.

Knowledge economy. An economy in which knowledge is one of the main factors of production and constitutes the major component of economic output. This may occur directly through knowledge products and services or indirectly where knowledge is an added-value part of other products and services. Contrast with agricultural and industrial economies.

Knowledge elicitation. The process of eliciting knowledge from a human expert in order to codify it into some form of explicit knowledge base or rule based computer system (expert system).

Knowledge inventory. A list of knowledge entities – its sources, users and uses. May be the result of conducting an information audit (q.v.).

Knowledge management (KM). The explicit and systematic management of vital knowledge and its associated processes of creating, gathering, organizing, diffusion, use and exploitation in pursuit of organizational objectives.

Knowledge mapping. The process of identifying core knowledge and the relationship between knowledge elements. A map may be portrayed in many visual formats, such as a hierarchical tree or a node and link diagram.

Knowledge market. A marketplace for the buying and selling of knowledge. Online knowledge markets are sometimes referred to as knowledge e-marketplaces. They commonly allow the posting of knowledge needs and knowledge offers, and may conduct sales by auction.

Knowledge networking. The process of sharing and developing knowledge through human and computer networks.

Knowledge object. A piece of knowledge held in a well-defined and structured format, such that it is easy to replicate and disseminate. Although predominantly in the form of explicit knowledge, it may contain some element of human knowledge.

Knowledge practice. A specific method or technique used to manage or process knowledge. Several methods may be used within a knowledge process.

Knowledge process. A broad knowledge activity often performed at an aggregated level. Examples are knowledge gathering, sharing and dissemination. Knowledge moves from one process to another as part of a knowledge cycle (q.v.).

Knowledge product. A product that consists almost entirely of information or knowledge.

Knowledge refining. The process of filtering, aggregating and summarizing knowledge drawn from a wide range of resources.

Knowledge repository. A store of knowledge. While the term typically refers to explicit forms of knowledge, such as documents and databases, it can also refer to human-held knowledge.

Knowledge wrapper. Information associated with a knowledge object that accurately describes the contents within. Forming part of the product surround (q.v.), it holds metadata in a standard format.

Learning network. A network of individuals who share knowledge for the primary purpose of personal development and learning.

Log file. A file that holds a record of all requests made to a Web server. To make sense of this large stream of data, a log file analysis programme is used to summarize the data and generate statistical reports.

M-commerce. Mobile commerce. Trading over electronic networks using mobile phones and other portable wireless devices.

Marketing hook. A small piece of promotional material in what is otherwise a straightforward piece of content. The idea is to hook the reader, so that they respond to the message, for example by clicking to read details of a related product or service.

Market segment. A group of potential customers that share similar characteristics in terms of their response to marketing stimuli. Industries, needs, buying patterns and applications are common dimensions of segmentation.

Mbps. Megabits per second. The Mega is a binary million $2^{20} = 1\,048\,576$. *See also* Kbps.

Message board. An area on the Web where messages can be exchanged and viewed by a workgroup or community. Sometimes referred to as a bulletin board (q.v.). The conversational interaction via the Web is sometimes called Web conferencing.

META tag. One of the tags in the header of an HTML file. It contains metadata (q.v.) and may be considered as part of the knowledge wrapper. There are several different types of META tags, such as author, content description, keywords. They are used by search engines and other applications.

Metadata. Data about data. A structured piece of data that describes the contents of a database record. One common metadata format is that of the Dublin core (page 155), which defines metadata fields for bibliographic databases. *See also* Knowledge wrapper.

Meta-knowledge. Knowledge about knowledge. Knowledge inventories, knowledge maps and directories are examples of meta-knowledge.

Micropayments. Small payments that can include fractions of a cent. Such payments are only economic if the transaction costs are extremely low, which is the promise held out by digital wallets and other software means of encoding payment transfers into Internet communications.

Micro-segmentation. Dividing the potential customer base into much smaller segments than is done in traditional marketing (where a business may typically have a handful or a few tens of segments at most). Micro-segmentation is possible because CRM systems allow more customization of marketing promotion and offers. The ultimate micro-segment is the 'segment-of-one', in which offers are personalized for an individual.

Mind mapping. A visual method of organizing ideas. In most mind mapping systems the ideas branch out from a central point. In turn, each branch can have additional branches or links to other mind maps. A specific form of concept mapping (q.v.).

Multimedia. Enhancement of raw text information through the use of images, audio, video and animation.

Network broker. An intermediary that connects participants in a network. This may be to form a virtual organization to carry out a specific project, or to connect buyers and sellers in an online marketplace.

Object-based knowledge. Knowledge that is held in discrete entities (knowledge objects).

Online community. A community of interest or practice that uses groupware facilities, such as bulletin boards, email lists and chat, to share knowledge.

Organizational memory. The core knowledge of an organization's past, including project histories, important decisions and their rationale, key documents and customer relationships.

Page impression. The serving of a request made on a Web server for a Web page. It may involve the serving of several items, such as images, to complete the request. *See also* Hit.

Pay-as-you-go, pay-per-view. Ways of paying for content according to what is actually needed at the time that it is used. Contrast this with a subscription service where payment is made ahead of time and covers unlimited usage (within limits).

Payment service provider. A provider of online payment services, in which credit card payments made at a supplier's website are validated and processed.

PDA (Personal Data Assistant). A portable information device, such as a palm-held PC. The latest generation of PDAs also includes mobile communications facilities.

PDF (Portable Data Format). A document format that allows them to be displayed in their original format and layout, i.e. as images of pages.

Contrast with HTML (q.v.), in which the browser determines how the document will look on the user's screen.

People-based knowledge. Knowledge which is held in people's minds and needs the holders to deliver it.

PGP (Pretty Good Privacy). A method for encrypting messages so that they can be sent securely via email. It relies on the sender knowing the public key of the recipient.

Platform. A product base onto which a variety of different modules can be added to create a wide variety of products. Most commonly refers to a computer platform, such as a PC running Windows, or an Apple Mac, onto which applications software is added.

Pop-up window. A small window that pops up on a PC user's display screen as the result of performing an action. It comes up on top or alongside the main window in which they are working. On the Internet, it is commonly used for advertisements or to draw user's attention to some important details.

Portal. A single point of entry on the Web or an intranet to a wide range of information and knowledge resources and personal tools (contrast common definition of 'gateway'). *See also* EIP, K-portal, Vertical portal.

Product surround. Attributes and services associated with a product that enhance its value. Many elements of the product surround are intangible, such as quality, brand and warranty. In a digital knowledge product, the surround may include a knowledge wrapper (q.v.) and digital rights information (q.v.).

Productization. The process of developing products and services that can be reproduced for selling commercially.

Project history. The main activities and decisions taken during a project, recorded in a way that aids knowledge sharing and derives lessons for similar projects in the future.

PTT. Postal, Telephone and Telegraph. The abbreviation given to organizations that traditionally combine postal and telephone services and are government owned. Many have now been split up into distinct businesses (post and telecommunications) and privatized (to a lesser or greater extent).

RDF. Resource Description Framework (q.v.).

Reach. The extent to which knowledge is accessible in various locations. The Internet extends reach, as does the use of portable computers and mobile telephones.

Resource Description Framework (RDF). A framework developed by W3C (q.v.) for developing metadata standards for WWW resources. It brings together in one place metadata activities for resources such as sitemaps, content ratings, search engine data collection and digital library collections. The resource descriptions use XML as the interchange language.

Richness. The depth of knowledge, such as contextual knowledge, that enhances a piece of core knowledge. Multimedia also adds richness by giving the viewer more visual information and cues.

Search engine. A piece of software or a service that indexes pages from the Web and lists those that match or closely match a user's search terms. Results are ranked by relevance or other factors and include items from sources all over the Web.

Segment. *See* Market segment

SET (Secure Electronic Transaction). A specification jointly developed by Visa and MasterCard in 1996 to enable more secure online credit card transactions than the conventional method of transferring data using SSL. It is a broader system that also includes the use of digital certificates to authenticate sellers. It has yet to become widely used.

SGML (Standard Generalized Markup Language). A language used to define the structure of documents. It uses tags to delineate blocks of text and handle formatting for printed output. HTML is a newer derivative of SGML geared to marking up Web pages.

Share fair. An event especially constructed to encourage the interchange of knowledge. Typically organized as an exhibition with booths.

SMS (Short Message Service). A standard service on digital cellular networks, that allows short messages (up to 160 characters long) to be sent to a mobile telephone handset.

SSL (Secure Sockets Layer). A software protocol that creates a secure communications connection between an Internet client (e.g. PC using a browser) and server. It uses encryption techniques with key lengths that are typically 128 bits long. The US government restricts export of browsers that handle key lengths of more than 64 bits (more than 40 bits until early 2000). Most browsers signal a secure connection by displaying a closed padlock in the status bar. Web pages that use SSL connections normally have URLs that start with https:// (http secure) rather than http://.

Stickiness (of a website). A website that encourages visitors to spend significant time there and return repeatedly. Generic portal sites and search engines are very 'sticky'.

Storytelling. The use of stories in the organizational context, as a way of sharing knowledge and helping the process of learning.

Structural capital. The component of intellectual capital represented by organizational assets such as processes, databases, systems etc. Other components of intellectual capital are customer capital and human capital.

Tacit knowledge. Knowledge that is not codified but held in people's heads. Intuitive, experiential, judgemental and context-sensitive, it may be difficult to articulate. Contrast with explicit knowledge (q.v.).

Tag. Instruction for an application or formatting tool, such as an Internet browser. Tags are used in markup languages (SGML, HTML and XML) and are enclosed in ⟨ ⟩ brackets.

Taxonomy. A classification system for a body of knowledge. Shows relationships between terms and concepts. Contrast with knowledge mapping (q.v.) and thesaurus (q.v.).

Text mining. Extracting the essential concepts and meaning from large amounts of textual information. Natural language analysis techniques are used. *See also* Text summarizing.

Text summarizing. The result of text mining a single document and producing a summary which includes some of its key sentences. Typically, all the main concepts of a large document can be summarized in less than 20 per cent of its original size.

Thesaurus. A controlled vocabulary of terms for a corpus of information. The relationships between terms are defined, such as related terms and synonyms. *See also* Taxonomy.

Trusted Third Party (TTP). An independent and reliable third party that can be entrusted with holding security keys and validating the authenticity of their owners.

TTP. *See* Trusted Third Party

UMTS (Universal Mobile Telephone System). A set of protocols and standards, developed in Europe, for high-speed communications between wireless devices, using any combination of cellular, satellite or fixed networks. UMTS will be an integral part of many 3G (q.v.) services.

URL (Uniform Resource Locator). The location of a unique Internet resource. It comprises a domain name (q.v.) of the server followed by a directory name and file name. Web pages start with the server type http: e.g. http://www.skyrme.com/resource/kmres.htm. Other common URL prefixes are ftp:// denoting File Transfer Protocol (q.v), and mailto: denoting that an email address follows.

USP (Unique Selling Proposition). Used in sales and marketing to denote a feature or combination of features that is unique, and therefore gives a distinctive advantage over competitors.

Utility value. The value of an asset when put to use, such as knowledge when applied to improving business performance. Contrast with intrinsic value (q.v.).

Value Added Network Services (VANS). Private electronic networks that provide data transmission services and other online applications, such as order processing.

VANS. *See* Value Added Network Services

Vertical portal (Vortal). An online portal that addresses a wide range of needs for a specific group of users, such as a professional or industry group. Contrast with a horizontal portal which offers specific services to a broad range of users.

Videoconferencing. Communications over an electronic network using video. Systems range from desktop units on PCs (see Desktop conferencing) to dedicated systems that use cameras and monitors in a conference room setting.

Viral marketing. Using the Internet to spread a marketing message in a manner similar to the way that a virus spreads. The marketer makes it interesting and easy for each recipient to pass the message onto his or her colleagues.

Virtual organization. An organization whose participants are geographically separated but who work together through online communications. Less commonly, the term refers to a temporary organization or network that is created for a specific purpose, but whose members remain independent.

VoIP (Voice over Internet Protocol). Converting speech that is analogue into digital format, and transmitting it over the Internet. A growing number of telecommunications links use IP (see page 49). VoIP also refers to the use of microphone and PC to interact with a website.

Vortal. Vertical portal (q.v.). Can also refer to voice portal (a portal for mobile telephone access to the Internet).

W3C. The World Wide Web Consortium. An international organization created in 1994 to oversee the development of WWW standards and to develop the Web to its full potential.

WAP (Wireless Access Protocol). A protocol for communications between hand-held wireless devices including palm-top PCs and mobile telephones over a wide range of cellular networks. The information transmitted between WAP devices is formatted in WML (q.v.)

Watermark. See Digital watermark.

Web. Shortened version of World Wide Web (WWW), but also used as an adjective, e.g. Web pages, Web servers etc.

Web conferencing. The use of computer conferencing (q.v.) over the Internet. Users can browse through messages, usually grouped by topic, and can reply to a message or create a new one under a new topic. *See also* Message board, Community.

Web ring. A group of websites addressing similar interests that are linked into a ring. Users of any website in the ring can click on hypertext links to reach adjacent sites.

Web server. One of the many computers on the Internet that hosts and 'serves' Web pages.

WML (Wireless Markup Language). A subset of HTML optimized for wireless devices, where small screen and navigation without a keyboard limit functionality. Used by WAP (q.v.) devices.

World Wide Web (WWW). A service on the Internet for displaying information stored in HTML format. It is provided by a network of distributed Web servers.

Wrapper. *See* Knowledge wrapper

WWW. *See* World Wide Web

XML (eXtensible Markup Language). A Web-based markup language that allows a wide range of user-defined tags. If a community uses a common XML schema, then structured data records can be transferred between computer applications, such as happens with EDI (q.v.). HTML could be considered as a specific subset of XML, since there is a defined set of tags.

Bibliography

Alle, Verna (1997) *The Knowledge Evolution: Expanding Organizational Intelligence*. Butterworth–Heinemann.

August, Vicki (2000) 'Dot.com bubble will burst by June', *Computer Weekly* (3 February): 5.

Borrus, Amy (2000) 'How Marriott never forgets a guest', *Business Week* (21 February): 83.

Branson, Richard (1998) *Losing My Virginity*. Virgin Publishing.

Browning, John (1998) 'A Nasdaq for bandwidth', *Wired* (London) (April).

Cauldwell, Clive (1999) 'Knowledge management', *Management Consultancy* (December): 12.

Conference Board, The (2000) *Beyond Knowledge Management: New Ways to Work and Learn*.

Dalton, Ricky (1999) 'Scots discover global market for learning', *Sunday Times* (11 April): 3.11.

Daniel, Caroline (2000) 'Matchmaker, matchmaker', *The Business, FT Weekend Magazine* (16 September).

Davenport, Thomas H. and Prusak, Laurence (1998) *Working Knowledge: How Organizations Manage What They Know*. Harvard Business School Press.

Davis, Stan and Botkin, Jim (1994) 'The coming of knowledge-based business', *Harvard Business Review* (September/October): 165–170.

Denning, Stephen (2000) *The Springboard: How Storytelling Ignites Action in Knowledge-Era Organizations*. Butterworth–Heinemann.

Despres, Charles and Chauvel, Daniele (eds) (2000) *Knowledge Horizons: The Present and the Promise of Knowledge Management*. Butterworth–Heinemann.

Echikson, William (2000) 'Schmooze Tuesdays', *Business Week e.biz* (15 May): 54–55.

Edvinnson, Leif and Malone, Michael S. (1997) *Intellectual Capital: Realizing Your Company's True Value by Finding Its Hidden Brainpower*. HarperBusiness.

Evans, Philip and Wurster, Thomas S. (1999) *Blown to Bits: How the New Economics of Information Transforms Strategy*. Harvard Business School Press.

Fabris, Tom (1999) 'You think tomaytoes, I think tomahtoes', *CIO* (1 April).

Foresnki, Tom (2000) 'IBM: Awarded record number of US patents', *Financial Times, FT–IT* (12 January).

Gotshcall, Mary G. (1999) 'Streamline leverages customer knowledge', *Knowledge Inc.* (4) 6 (June): 1.

Gotschall, Mary G. (1998) 'Chase Manhattan builds powerful relationships', *Knowledge Inc.* (3) 11 (November): 1–4.

Hamel, Gary (2000) 'Reinvent your company', *Fortune* (12 June).

Hargrave, Sean (1997) 'Clever uniforms help casualties', *Sunday Times, Innovation* (29 June): 13.

Higson, Chris and Briginshaw, John (2000) 'Valuing Internet business', *Business Strategy Review*, 11 (1) (Spring): 10–20.

Hildebrand, Carol (1999) 'Making KM pay off', *CIO* (15 February).

Hill, Steve and Dinnick, Richard (2000) 'The 15 greatest events in Net history', *Internet Magazine* (July): 80–86.

Hof, Robert D. (2000) 'Who will profit from the Internet Agora?', *Business Week e.biz* (5 June).

Hofer-Alfeis, Joseph (1999) 'Developing knowledge management for successful implementation', *Most Admired Knowledge Enterprises 1999* (19 May). London: Business Intelligence Conference.

Jackson, Tim (2000) 'Sweeping costs aside', *Financial Times* (5 September): 15.

Janal, Dan (2000) *Guide to Marketing on the Internet*. John Wiley & Sons.

Jubert, Anne (1998) 'The Internet connection', *Knowledge Management*, 1 (2) (September): 20–23 (Ark Publishing).

Karlenzig, Warren (1999) 'Chrysler's new Know-mobiles', *Knowledge Management* (May) (Freedom Technology Media Group).

Kotler, Philip and Armstrong, Gary (2000) *Principles of Marketing*, 9th Edition. Prentice Hall.

Kotler, Philip, Armstrong, Gary, Saunders, John and Long, Veronica (1998) *Principles of Marketing*, 2nd European edition. Prentice Hall.

Kover, Amy (2000) 'The hot idea of the year', *Fortune* (26 June).

KPMG (2000) *Annual Knowledge Management Survey 1999*.

Lewis, Jane (2000) 'Working together – separately', *Computing* (1 June): 52–53.

Malone, Thomas W. and Laubacher, Robert J. (1998) 'The dawn of the e-lance economy', *Harvard Business Review* (September): 28–36.

Maroney, Tyler (2000) 'The new online marketplace of ideas', *Fortune* (17 April): 229–230.

McGirk, Tim (1998) 'Dealing in DNA', *Time* (30 November): 58–64.

Nash, J. Madelaine (2000) 'Battle pending', *Time* (17 April): 67.

Nielsen, Jakob (1999) 'The top ten mistakes of Web design' and other articles, *Alertbox*. http://www.useit.com/alertbox.

Nonaka, Ikujiro and Takeuchi, Hirotaka (1995) *The Knowledge-Creating Company: How Japanese Companies Create the Dynamics of Innovation*. Oxford University Press.

Nyland, Andrea L. (1999) 'From recipes to theses, it's a knowledge market', *Knowledge Management* (October): 12–13 (Freedom Technology Media Group).

Petch, Geoffrey (1998) 'The cost of lost knowledge', *Knowledge Management* (October) (Freedom Technology Media Group).

Pierer, Heinrich v. (2000) 'Siemens – the e-driven company', Press Conference, Siemens (10 October).

Polyani, Michael (1997) 'Tacit knowledge', chapter 7 in *Knowledge in Organizations* (ed. Laurence Prusak). Butterworth–Heinemann.

Polyani, Michael (1966) *The Tacit Dimension*. Routledge & Kegan Paul.

Porter, Michael E. (1980) *Competitive Strategy*. Free Press.

Poynder, Richard (1999) 'Out of the labs and into profit', *Knowledge Management* (December 1999/January 2000) (Learned Information).

Prusak, Laurence (ed.) (1997) *Knowledge in Organizations*. Butterworth–Heinemann.

Roberts, Paul (1999) 'An inside job', *Exec!* (May): 37–39 (Unisys).

Robin, Michael (1999) 'Cultural evolution', *Knowledge Management* (May): 16–17 (Learned Information).

Sager, Ira (2000) 'Big Blue gets wired', *Business Week e.biz* (3 April).

Schrage, Michael (1996) 'Provices and serducts', *Fast Company* (August).

Schwartz, Nelson D. (2000) 'Greed disease', *Fortune* (29 May): 63–68.

Shande, Dawne (2000) 'Distributing nuggets of knowledge', *Knowledge Management* (April): 98 (Freedom Technology Media Group).

Sharpe, Rochelle (2000) 'Virtual couch', *Business Week e.biz* (18 September): 91–93.

Shillingford, Joia (2000) 'Author's new online route to publishers', *Financial Times, FT–IT* (7 June): XIV.

Singh, Simon (1999) *The Code Book*. Fourth Estate.

Skyrme, David J. (1999) *Knowledge Networking: Creating the Collaborative Enterprise*. Butterworth–Heinemann.

Skyrme, David J. and Amidon, Debra M. (1997) *Creating the Knowledge-based Business*. Business Intelligence.

Snowden, David (1999) 'Three metaphors, two stories and a picture – how to build common understanding in knowledge management programmes', *Knowledge Management Review*, 7 (March/April).

Strassmann, Paul (1996) 'The value of computers, information and knowledge' (January). http://www.strassmann.com.

Sveiby, Karl Erik (1997) *The New Organizational Wealth: Managing and Measuring Knowledge-based Assets*. Berrett–Koehler.

Sveiby, Karl Erik (1992) 'The Know-How Company', *International Review of Strategic Management*, 1(3): 167–186 (John Wiley & Sons).

Sveiby, Karl Erik and Lloyd, Tom (1987) *The Know-How Company*. Bloomsbury.

Trimmers, Paul (1999) *Electronic Commerce: Strategies and Models for Business-to-Business Trading*. John Wiley & Sons.

Vasey, Martin and Pratt, Ken (1999) 'Sweating knowledge assets in BG technology', *Knowledge Summit '99* (November). London: Business Intelligence Conference.

Vickers, Marcia (2000) 'Model from Mars', *Business Week*, p. 58 (4 September).

Voss, Chris (2000) 'Developing an eService strategy', *Business Strategy Review* (Spring): 21–33.

Ward, Victoria (1999) 'Is franchising the business model for KM?', *Knowledge Management Review* (March/April): 5.

Wenger, Etienne (1999) *Communities of Practice*. Cambridge University Press.

Wenger, Etienne (2000) 'Communities of practice: the structure of knowledge stewarding', chapter 10 in Charles Despres and Daniele Chauvel (eds), *Knowledge Horizons: The Present and the Promise of Knowledge Management*. Butterworth–Heinemann.

Wiig, Karl (1993) *Knowledge Management Foundations*. Arlington, TX: Schema Press.

Wilson, Dr Ralph F. (2000) 'The six simple principles of viral marketing', *Web Marketing Today*, 70 (February): http://www.wilsonweb.com.

Yu, Albert (1998) *Creating the Digital Future: The Secrets of Consistent Innovation at Intel*. Free Press.

Index